TIME AND SCHOOL LEARNING

Time and School Learning

THEORY, RESEARCH, and PRACTICE

EDITED BY
LORIN W. ANDERSON

ST. MARTIN'S PRESS
New York

© 1984 Lorin W. Anderson

All rights reserved. For information, write:
St. Martin's Press, Inc., 175 Fifth Avenue, New York, NY 10010
Printed in Great Britain
First published in the United States of America in 1984

Library of Congress Cataloging in Publication Data
Main entry under title:

Time and school learning.

   1. Schedules, School—Addresses, essays, lectures.
2. Students—Time management—Addresses, essays,
lectures. 3. Learning—Addresses, essays, lectures.
I. Anderson, Lorin W.
LB1038.T55   1984   370.15'23   83-11009
ISBN 0-312-80505-5

CONTENTS

To my parents, Willard and Bette

FOREWORD

As observer after observer of curriculum research has noted, the gap between 'theory' and 'practice' is one of the most omnipresent and vexing features of education. While the causes of this gap are many and various, a significant part of the problem must be attributed to the ways in which researchers and theoreticians have defined their concerns. They have typically ignored the social and group-centred nature of the classroom to focus on either subject-matter or individual learning. As a result, images of 'tutors' rather than 'teachers' have tended to capture the attention of educational researchers when they seek to put forward 'practical' consequences that emerge from their work.

As all teachers know, however, they are not tutors assisting personal clients, but rather teachers of classes with little time to devote to individual concerns. Their central tasks are to direct the learning of these classes, to keep their attention, and to cover a syllabus. These tasks are the focus of this book: in the terms used by all the contributors, the teacher's work consists of the management of pupils' *attention* over *time* and over a *curriculum* — with the problem being how this core activity is managed now, and how it could be managed better.

As Professor Anderson notes in his introductory chapter, this sense of teaching was at the heart of 'method' from the beginning of classroom teaching in the middle years of the nineteenth century until the 1920s, but has faded as a concern in recent years. The contributors to this book record the rediscovery in the past decade of the concept of teaching as the management of attention over time. For many American researchers, the stimulus that led to this rediscovery was John B. Carroll's paper 'A Model of School Learning' and, appropriately, the book begins with a discussion by Professor Carroll of how he came to write that paper and how it has influenced other researchers. From that starting point the chapters range over the set of theoretical and practical problems which have emerged as the teacher's task of attention management in the classroom has been investigated. In so far as one major finding that has emerged from such research has been the variability of time-on-task, a need to enhance teachers' understanding of these 'variables' has become an important theme for pre-service and in-service education. The collection of papers which Professor

Anderson has assembled devotes considerable attention to these issues, and shows in rich detail some of the approaches and many of the problems which follow as researchers and schools have tried to bridge the gap between theory and practice.

We are convinced of the interest this book will have for those whose research is linked to the developments that have taken place over the past decade in the notions of attention, time-on-task, the management of time and attention in classrooms, and the like. Nor do we doubt that the book will be of considerable interest to teachers and teacher educators who want to see how classrooms and classroom teaching might be better understood and improved, by way of action research and in-service education. And in so far as the book does not adopt a single-minded, do-this-and-all-of-your-problems-will-disappear approach to its themes, it offers a set of appropriate challenges to all its audiences. We are sure that, as the ideas developed here become more widely understood, they will have important implications for curriculum planning, teaching and teacher education.

Ian Westbury
University of Illinois at Urbana-Champaign

W.A. Reid
University of Birmingham

1 AN INTRODUCTION TO TIME AND SCHOOL LEARNING

Lorin W. Anderson

The role of time in school learning has long been a topic of interest and concern to educators and educationists alike. Issues surrounding the allocation of time to various subject areas, class periods, and compulsory schooling were present at the beginning of formal education throughout the world. One of the earliest educational research studies, conducted by Joseph Rice in 1897, involved time as the major independent variable. Specifically, Rice was interested in whether it made any difference in terms of spelling achievement if students spent an additional 15 minutes a day studying spelling. He found no significant difference! Despite this finding, decisions concerning the certification, promotion and graduation of students traditionally have been based on the *amount of time spent* in courses and schools, not necessarily on *what* or *how much students learned* during that amount of time.

For the entire twentieth century schooling has been defined in terms of time. In the USA, for example, Carnegie units, largely time-based entities, are used to certify high school graduates. Similarly, credit hours are the basic unit of awarding a variety of college degrees in the USA. More pragmatically, class periods have been based on the allocation of *fixed* amounts of time; so many minutes are allocated to reading, mathematics, and other academic and non-academic subjects. Since students enter schools and classrooms differing in the knowledge, skills, or abilities they possess, *under these fixed-time conditions* these differences are transformed into differences in student achievement. By operating under fixed-time conditions, therefore, we are guaranteeing that some students will learn a great deal, some will learn moderately well, and some will not learn at all (Good and Dembo, 1973). And, in fact, these differences in student achievement increase dramatically over the long haul of schooling (Carroll, 1974).

During the past two decades new questions have arisen concerning the role of time in school learning. These questions have been raised by three categories of educators: theoreticians, researchers, and practitioners. From a theoretical perspective John Carroll introduced his now-classic model of school learning in 1963. Carroll quite obviously was aware of the transformation of individual differences (particularly differences in aptitudes and ability to understand instruction) into differences in student achievement under fixed-time conditions. But, he wondered, what would happen to such differences under *fixed-achievement conditions*? That is, what if, instead of specifying a fixed amount of time for students to learn something, we very clearly specified what we wanted or expected students to learn?

Carroll suggested that under such conditions individual differences in aptitudes and abilities would be transformed into individual differences in the amount of time that students would need in order to achieve the specified learning outcome or accomplish the specified task. Thus, under such fixed-achievement conditions, aptitudes and abilities would be predictive not of the amount students could learn in a given time period, but of the amount of time they would need in order to learn well. Furthermore, learning was hypothesized to be a function of the extent to which students actually spent the amount of time they needed to spend in order to learn well. Both time spent and time needed were believed to be determined or influenced by other factors or variables. Time spent was believed to be influenced by the opportunity students had to learn, the motivation students had to persevere for sufficient amounts of time, and the students' aptitude for a specified task. Time needed, on the other hand, was thought to be influenced by students' abilities to understand instruction, the quality of the instruction received by the students, and once again, the students' aptitudes.

Carroll's model provided the impetus to researchers and practitioners alike. Benjamin Bloom (1968) adapted the model so as to be applicable in a variety of school settings. This adaptation, which he called learning for mastery (or more familiarly, mastery learning), relies heavily on the provision of extra *time* (and appropriate instructional help) so that students can overcome errors and misunderstandings identified by frequent, short, and highly valid measures of student learning. Thus, the keys to success of mastery learning programs are: (1) the definition of what constitutes mastery (that is, what students are to learn and how well they are to learn it), (2) the assessment of student learning relative to this definition of mastery, and (3) the provision of sufficient productive learning time (including additional time for students who initially do not attain mastery) so that virtually all students achieve mastery. By defining schooling in terms of what is learned rather than how much time is spent, mastery learning programs have been successful in producing higher levels of student learning and a variety of consequences of these higher levels (including positive attitudes, increased task-orientation, and decreased variation in student achievement) (Burns, 1979). Thus, Bloom's adaptation of the Carroll model is supportive of the possibility of exchanging variation in learning for variation in time needed to learn.

The largest, most extensive study whose roots can be traced to the Carroll model is the Beginning Teacher Evaluation Study (BTES) (Fisher *et al.*, 1980). Three categories of time were identified by the BTES researchers: allocated time, engaged time and academic learning time. Allocated time is identical to Carroll's opportunity to learn. It refers to the amount of time that the student is receiving instruction relating to his or her accomplishment of some academic task. Engaged time is identical to Carroll's time spent in learning. It is the proportion of the allocated time that the student is paying attention, trying to learn, or working on the task. Finally, academic-learning time refers to the proportion of engaged time that the student is experiencing a high degree of success in learning.

Several key findings emerged from the BTES. First, different amounts of time were allocated to different subject matter areas (e.g. reading) by different teachers and by teachers in different schools. Secondly, students learned more in subject areas to which greater amounts of time were allocated. Thirdly, large differences in students' engaged time were observed both within classrooms and across class-rooms. Fourthly, students who were engaged in learning for greater proportions of the allocated time learned more. Fifthly, student learning was maximized when more of the students' time was spent engaged in successful learning experiences. Sixthly, a variety of teaching practices were associated with higher degrees of engaged time and academic-learning time (see Chapter 7).

In addition to academicians and researchers, the American public and their elected government officials have begun to question whether simply spending time in school or on particular subject areas was sufficient for awarding either promotion from grade level to grade level or a high school diploma. A rash of mandated minimum competency programmes were initiated in a large number of states within the USA (Pipho, 1978). The major purpose of these programmes is to ensure that some minimum level of learning has been attained by students prior to grade promotion or high school graduation. In the vast majority of these programmes schools are held responsible for providing additional time (plus additional instruction) to those students whose learning was less than acceptable (as determined by performance standards on so-called minimum competency tests).

In summary, then, a number of theoretical, practical, and empirical developments have occured over the past two decades. Much has been examined, much has been written, much as been said, and much has been done – all having some connection with the meaning and use of time in schools. As in any area in which information is accumulating at a rapid rate, there exists a need for thoughtful consideration, integration, and synthesis of available information. In combination the chapters of this volume provide such a consideration, integration, and synthesis.

This book is organized around the three aforementioned perspectives – theory, research and practice. A balanced treatment of these three perspectives is provided in three separate parts, each containing three chapters. The sequence of the sections – theory, then research, then practice – represents (1) the way in which the concept of time has evolved over the past two decades, and (2) the ultimate concern of the book as a whole; namely, the improvement of educational practice through an understanding of the meaning of time and the proper application of what has been learned about time. The remaining sections of this chapter describe briefly the three major parts of this volume. In order, these sections discuss (1) the meaning of time in the context of classroom instruction and school learning, (2) what we know about time expenditure and use of this time, and how time use is related to teaching and learning, and (3) ways in which what we know can be used to foster improved teaching and learning in classrooms throughout the world.

The Meaning of Time (Part One)

Understanding time in relation to schooling is difficult because time itself has no inherent meaning; rather, time is a metric – a unit of measurement. Carroll (1963) initially selected time as a metric 'in order to capitalize on the advantages of a scale with a meaningful zero point and equal units of measurement' (p. 724). As humans we attribute meaning to time. Hence, when things are slow we *kill* time. And when we are having a good time, time *flies*. Sometimes we try to *save* time. Sometimes time is not even time, as when, for example, time is money. Time is important to us because, as Jackson (1977) writes, 'it marks the expenditure of a previous commodity – human life' (p. 38).

In relation to school learning the meaning of time is determined by many factors. As Carroll (see Chapter 2) nicely put it

> the model [of school learning] does not claim that time is the only variable in learning, or even the most important variable, as critics . . . seem to allege. Although several of the model's variables (e.g. aptitude, perseverance, and opportunity to learn) are expressed in terms of time, *what goes on in that time is more important*. Critics are confusing necessity with sufficiency: time is undoubtedly necessary, but not sufficient. (p. 34) (my italics)

'What goes on in that time' is quite difficult to explain or comprehend. Part of 'what goes on' goes on in the head of the learner; part goes on in the classroom itself. Both the thoughts, feelings and dreams of the learner, and the activities of the classroom influence the meaning of the time that elapses while children are in school.

In the Carroll model, reviewed in the next chapter, aptitude influences the time students need in order to learn well. Perseverance influences the amount of time students are willing to spend in order to learn well. Both of these factors are *internal* to the learner. Opportunity to learn, on the other hand, is *external* to the learner, and is determined by the amount of time made available to the learner by the teacher.

None the less, while aptitude, perseverance, and opportunity to learn influence time use in classrooms, more needs to be known about precisely *how* that time is used by students and by teachers. What is the student doing while persevering? What activities are made available by the teacher while he or she is providing students with an opportunity to learn?

In Chapter 3 I discuss the internal factors that influence the meaning of time for individual learners. What is learned in any given amount of time is believed to depend primarily on the attentional processes of the learner. The teacher's primary task, therefore, is to direct and sustain these attentional processes in such a way that the desired learning will occur. The nature of those attentional processes are described, and what it means for students to spend time 'engaged in learning' or 'on-task' is discussed. Furthermore, what teachers can do in order to direct and sustain attention is outlined.

The historical perspective taken in Chapter 3 permits the comparison of what we currently know about attention and learning with what was hypothesized to be true nearly three-quarters of a century earlier. Although we have become increasingly sophisticated in our methods of study, our knowledge of the nature of attention remains basically what it was near the turn of the century. The result of all of this speculation and study is that attention is one of the key internal factors that gives meaning to time allocated and used in schools and classrooms.

In Chapter 4 Ross is concerned with a major external influence on the meaning of time, namely the activity in which the student is engaged. She uses the concept of activity segment to describe and delineate the nature of classroom operations. Activity segments have three critical features: (1) concerns (that is, aims or purposes), (2) activity patterns (that is, acceptable programmes or action), and (3) physical and temporal boundaries. Seatwork and recitation are two of the most frequently observed activity segments.

Ross suggests that the behaviour of both teachers and students is influenced by the activity patterns of the various activity segments. Thus, for example, certain activity segments (e.g. recitation) are associated with more meaningful, productive use of student time than others (e.g. lectures). Similarly, certain teacher behaviours (e.g. questioning) are more likely to occur and be understood with the context of certain activity segments (e.g. recitation).

The structure of the school day can be defined in terms of activity segments. Specifically, Ross suggests that this structure is determined by (1) the number and duration of activity segments, (2) the sequence of the activity segments, and (3) the presence or absence of simultaneous activity segments (as is the case when multiple groups are present in the same classroom). Each of these features affects the complexity of the structure of the school day. The presence of simultaneous activity segments, for example, is more complex than their absence.

As the structure of the school day increases in complexity, less of the available time is likely to be used productively (at least from an academic-learning perspective). Instead, an increased amount of classroom time will likely be spent managing the activity segments themselves as well as the transitions between or among activity segments. Ross's chapter concludes with a discussion of the importance of teacher planning in the effective, productive use of available school time.

In combination the three chapters in the first part suggest that the meaning of time in schools is determined primarily by the way in which it is allocated and used. Productive learning time depends on the activity segments in place in the classroom and the attentional processes of the students.

What We Know About Time (Part Two)

A large number of research studies on time and school learning have been conducted over the past decade. In addition, studies dating back to the 1920s and 1930s have been uncovered. The body of knowledge gleaned from these studies is summarized in Part Two. This body of knowledge is at the same time enlightening and confusing. The enlightment comes from the apparent consistency of the results of many of the studies. The confusion stems primarily from three sources: (1) the differences in the way time is measured, (2) the differences in the way that the results are summarized and interpreted, and (3) the gaps that still remain in our knowledge about time in the context of classroom instruction and school learning.

In Chapter 5 Burns summarizes what is currently known about the way in which time is spent and used in schools, and he begins with a general discussion of what the school day looks like in terms of time. As might be expected, the vast majority of the time is spent on instructionally related activities; the remainder is spent on non-instructional activities such as lunch and recess. In order to understand how time is used, therefore, we must begin to understand the nature of the instructional activities that take place.

Burns reviews different conceptions of instructional activities that have been offered by a variety of researchers. He then presents an organizing framework to aid in the interpretation of the vast array of data that have been gathered for different reasons and by different researchers. Burns highlights the difficulty of making sense of the large amount of available data *without* a conceptually based organizing framework.

The data are summarized in terms of the key properties of instructional activities: grouping arrangements, instructional delivery systems, control of pacing, expected cognitive level of the assigned tasks, teacher behaviours, and student behaviours. The data present an interesting patchwork quilt of life in classrooms. Burns concludes by suggesting that a major dimension of classroom activities is not necessarily how these activities *fill* school time, but how these activities *flow in time*.

In Chapter 6 Smyth reports on research examining the time-achievement relationship. As expected, the mere allocation of time to the study of subject-matter areas is not as strong a predictor of achievement in those areas as is the *productive* use of that time. Furthermore, the relationship of achievement with allocated time is not as consistent across studies as is that of achievement with engaged time. At best, however, time *in any form* (e.g. allocated, engaged, academic learning) is but a moderately strong predictor of achievement. As a consequence, Smyth advises against using the available research results as fundamental truths about teaching and learning. Rather he suggests that the findings be 'treated as a group of orienting variables teachers might keep in mind when monitoring the effects of their own teaching' (p. 137).

In this vein Smyth advocates a model of teacher-as-researcher. A focus on time presents a unique opportunity for successful application of the teacher-as-researcher model, since time 'is a medium through which [teaching and learning] can be examined simultaneously' (p. 128). Various profiles of time-use can be extremely beneficial to teachers. Ethnographic profiles of attending and non-attending students, for example, can help teachers understand the types of students who will likely not readily engage in learning and may ultimately engage in disruptive behaviour. Similarly, profiles of the ways in which teachers orchestrate their own time can allow them to reflect upon their performance and experiences. Such profiles could include the allocation of time to various topics and content as well as to different students in the classroom.

In Chapter 7 I summarize the available evidence on the relationship between instruction and time, specifically engaged time or time-on-task. Interestingly, time has been included in a number of studies conducted by researchers from a wide variety of perspectives: behavioural psychology, ecological psychology, curriculum design, teacher effectiveness, and programme evaluation. Despite the differences in the purposes, theoretical bases, and philosophical assumptions of these researchers, the results of the studies have been quite consistent. Several key elements of instruction have been found to be associated with high levels of time-on-task. Among the most common elements are (1) the assignment of tasks of appropriate difficulty, (2) the maintenance of the flow of activity in the classroom, (3) the communication of learning expectations to the learners, (4) the monitoring of student behaviour and learning progress, and (5) the provision of knowledge of learning progress to the students coupled with the provision of additional time and help as needed.

Chapter 7 begins with a summary of available evidence from studies within each of the several aforementioned perspectives. A composite summary is then presented followed by a set of implications for educational practice. Specifically, five implications are discussed: (1) the need for curricular sequencing, (2) the need for appropriate curriculum evaluation, (3) the need for instructional planning, (4) the need to consider school and classroom contexts in planning and implementing instruction, and (5) the need to continuously monitor the teaching-learning process.

In combination the three chapters in the second part present an interesting portrait of what we know about time and school learning. Knowledge of how time is used by both teachers and students, how time use is related to student learning, and how instruction influences student time-use can aid in understanding the nature of effective classroom instruction and school learning. Ultimately, such knowledge can be useful in the development of effective and efficient instructional programs and teaching practices.

How to Use What We Know About Time (Part Three)

One of the major problems in attempting to improve schooling lies in the fact that much of what is known is not put into practice. That is, we seem to learn a lot about certain things, but we stop short (for any number of reasons) of applying what is known. The three chapters in the third and final part of the book describe attempts to implement what is currently known about time and school learning.

In Chapter 8 Wang describes the Adaptive Learning Environments Model (ALEM). The model includes features thought to be particularly effective in (1) reducing the amount of time needed to learn, (2) increasing the amount of time allocated to teaching, and (3) increasing the amount of time students spend engaged in learning. Each program component is analyzed in terms of its likely effect on time allocated, time needed or time spent.

Diagnostic testing, prescribing appropriate learning goals, monitoring and diagnosing student learning, record-keeping, creating and maintaining instructional materials, developing student self-responsibility, providing staff development, and encouraging parent involvement are all hypothesized to *reduce the time needed for learning*. The use and management of teacher aides, establishing and communicating rules and procedures, using multi-age grouping, using instructional teaming, and, once again, developing student responsibility, providing staff development, and encouraging parent involvement are believed to result in an *increase in the amount of allocated time*. Finally, diagnostic testing, prescribing appropriate learning goals, monitoring and diagnosing student learning, record-keeping, creating and maintaining instructional materials, arranging space and facilities, establishing and communicating rules and procedures, developing student self-responsibility, providing staff development, and encouraging parent involvement are expected to *increase the amount of time students spend engaged in learning*. Quite obviously there is a relationship between those components believed to increase time spent and those believed to decrease time needed, since one way of reducing time needed is in fact to spend increased amounts of time engaged in learning.

Wang includes in her chapter a brief description of the staff-development programme used to provide teachers with the knowledge and skills necessary to properly implement the programme. In addition, she describes the variety of instruments that are used to monitor the fidelity of the programme as it is implemented. She presents data relating to the extent to which teachers can be taught to implement the programme as designed. Based on these data, she concludes that teachers can be taught to employ the programme in a reasonably short time period with resultant increases in productive use of class time, student achievement and student attitudes.

In Chapter 9 Huitt and Caldwell describe the Achievement Directed Leadership programme, a comprehensive instructional improvement programme that includes time as one of the central variables. Huitt and Caldwell introduce what they term a four-phase instructional improvement cycle as the vehicle for promoting instructional improvement. The cycle begins with the gathering of information on current classroom conditions and processes. This information is then compared with data obtained from a variety of research studies, and opportunities for instructional improvement based on this comparison are identified. Specific changes or modifications in existing classroom conditions and processes are selected and planned. Finally, the modifications are implemented in the classroom and are monitored from time to time.

Huitt and Caldwell display and describe the materials and procedures that are used to implement the time component of the Achievement Directed Leadership programme. They summarize the results of successful programme implementation in terms of teacher affect, teacher behaviour, student behaviour and student achievement. They conclude from their experiences that the basis for designing effective staff development or teacher training programmes 'rests in the proper understanding and use of a research-based, decision-making process to effect changes that improve students' use of a valuable resource, time' (p. 226).

As the title of Chapter 10 implies, Ghory describes a case study of one attempt to implement such a research-based, decision-making process in a large urban school district in the USA. The chapter is a careful study of the successes and failures of this attempt. The successes came largely from the ability of district personnel to successfully implement the Stallings Effective Teaching Practices Training Programme. The failures stemmed primarily from the inability of the school system to sustain the programme, despite its success, for more than two years. In Ghory's words, 'whereas development efforts have become increasingly sophisticated and effective, the longevity of successful innovation is short, and the art of implementing and sustaining successful innovation remains stubbornly problematic' (p. 229).

Ghory contends that the failure came about largely because 'we did not do enough to adapt the setting to the programme by re-defining existing roles and responsibilities' (p. 251). In this regard the major portion of this chapter lists and describes nine criteria that must be met if innovative, research-based instructional programmes are to be successfully implemented and sustained. Five of these criteria must be met at the school district level; four must be met at the local school level. Ghory also includes suggestions of approaches that can be used to satisfy the criteria. These approaches, which he labels the full-cost approach, the shoe-string approach, and the middle-path approach, differ in the amount of time, effort, and financial support they require.

In many ways a book such as this one is dated before it is published. New understandings derived from theoretical developments and empirical evidence occur almost daily. Similarly, new approaches and strategies for putting into practice what we already know continue to be developed. None the less, the ideas and information contained in this volume represent some of the best of what we know about and are able to do with a single critical aspect of school learning — time. Hopefully, the ideas and information presented here form a cogent body of knowledge that can be built upon as educators throughout the world attempt to improve the quality of education for an increasing number of youngsters.

References

Bloom, B.S. (1965) 'Learning for Mastery', *Evaluation Comment, 1*(2)

Burns, R.B. (1979) 'Mastery Learning: Does it Work?' *Educational Leadership, 37,* 110-13

Carroll, J.B. (1963) 'A Model of School Learning', *Teachers College Record, 64,* 723-33

———— (1974) 'Fitting a Model of School Learning to Aptitude and Achievement Data over Grade Levels' in D.R. Green (ed), *The Aptitude-Achievement Distinction,* Monterey, California: CTB/McGraw-Hill

Fisher, C., Berliner, D., Filby, N., Marliave, R., Cahen, L. and Dishaw, M. (1980),
'Teaching Behaviors, Academic Learning Time, and Student Achievement: an
Overview' in C. Denham and A. Lieberman (eds), *Time to Learn*, Washington,
DC: National Institute of Education

Good, T.L. and Dembo, M. (1973) 'Teacher Expectations: Self-report Data',
School Review, 81, 247-53

Jackson, P.W. (1977) 'Looking into Education's Crystal Ball', *Instructor, 87*, 38

Pipho, C. (1978) 'Minimum Competency Testing in 1978: A look at State
Standards', *Phi Delta Kappan, 59*, 585-8

PART ONE

THE MEANING OF TIME

2 THE MODEL OF SCHOOL LEARNING: PROGRESS OF AN IDEA*

John B. Carroll

'A Model of School Learning' was published in the *Teachers College Record* in 1963. The article (Carroll, 1963a) represented an attempt to give a unified perspective on the types of basic variables, and their interrelationships, that were proposed as affecting a student's degree of achievement in school subjects like reading, mathematics, and others that involve the cumulative acquisition of skills and knowledges. It seems to have been one of my more influential writings, even though I classify it as a 'think piece' rather than a solid report of research. I count 168 citations of it listed in the volumes of the *Social Sciences Citation Index* over the years 1969-80, but many other references to it are to be found. Further, the article has been reprinted and translated a number of times.[1] It has been a matter of some curiosity and interest to me to work through the various citations and subsequent research to see how the ideas set forth in the original article have been used, interpreted, emphasized, supported, not supported, questioned, or criticized over the years since its first publication. In this chapter I take the opportunity to comment on these uses and reactions, and to discuss the climate of educational theory and practice over the past several decades that nurtured the continuing interest in the model of school learning (MSL).

Over the years my research interests had centred on various problems connected with the teaching and learning of foreign languages (Carroll, 1966), in particular, the prediction of success in learning foreign languages through measurements of 'foreign-language aptitude' (see Carroll, 1981). Chiefly with the support of the Carnegie Corporation of New York, I had developed a battery of tests (Carroll and Sapon, 1959) that seemed under many circumstances to have high effectiveness in predicting the degree of such success. But they did not always have high validity; in fact, sometimes the validity coefficients were essentially zero. In preparation for a presentation that I had been invited to give at a symposium to be held at the University of Pittsburgh in February

*From C. Fisher and D. Berliner (forthcoming) (eds), *Perspectives on Instructional Time*, reprinted with permission, Longman Inc., New York.

1960 on Training Research and Education (Glaser, 1962), I resolved to survey all my results to try to see what factors, in the light of the varying settings in which my studies had been conducted, seemed to affect the predictiveness of the tests. It seemed that there were many varieties and conditions of foreign-language instruction.

One variable was the amount of intensiveness — from the highly intensive courses in which individuals were put under considerable pressure to keep up with a fast moving course in which they had as much as 5 to 8 hours of instruction per day, to the much less intensive, 3-hours-per-week courses in liberal arts colleges and universities. Generally, aptitude measures were much more predictive in intensive courses than in non-intensive courses. But there were other variables: students might be uniformly highly motivated, or there might be wide individual differences in motivation. Instruction could be conducted in a rather 'intellectual', formalistic way with much discussion of grammar and language features, or it could be conducted with much active practice, drill and feedback. Thinking about the way in which all these variables might interact with one another and affect the predictiveness of aptitude measurements, I somehow got the idea of developing a general learning model that could explain my results. I remember that it was one Sunday morning in the summer of 1959 that in just a couple of hours, I made a rough draft of my model, listing classes of variables and postulating their relationship.

It all seemed so simple and obvious, once one thought about it. A critical variable was time: people took different amounts of time to achieve a given level of proficiency. There were several reasons why they might take different amounts of time: it was certainly conceivable, and much evidence supported the idea, that there were inherent differences among people in their learning rates, and that these inherent differences were reflected in performance on my aptitude battery. But also, people might take different amounts of time because some were well motivated and attended to their learning with much effort, while others gave less attention and effort to their learning during periods when they were nominally engaged in study. Further, some might take more time because they had difficulty understanding what they were to do, or the content of their lessons. When the instruction was relatively formal and 'intellectual', this would affect students of relatively lower intellectual ability more than those of high intelligence, who would be able to figure out the instructional content on their own. Finally, when instruction was paced at a higher rate than a student could take it, a student would fall behind.

From all this, I derived a 'model for studying the prediction of success in complex learning tasks' (Carroll, 1962) that specified three basic variables in terms of time: (a) 'aptitude', as reflected in the amount of time that a student would need to learn something to a specified criterion, assuming high motivation (perseverance), ample opportunity to learn and an optimal quality of instruction; (b) 'perseverance', as reflected in the amount of time that a student would be willing to engage in active learning; and (c) 'opportunity to learn', as reflected in the amount of time that the organization of a course, or other circumstances, would allow for learning. Two other variables were not specified in terms of time, but would interact with the first three in such a way that they might possibly be measured: (d) ability to understand instruction – a variable that might become more critical as the quality of instruction decreased, and (e) quality of instruction – seen as a variable that could affect the amount of time that a student would need to master a task, and thus affect the importance of the student's aptitude, particularly when quality of instruction was low. I did not try at the time to specify exactly how one might evaluate quality of instruction, but I could have reeled off a whole host of variables that might index instructional quality.

The basic variables in the model were defined formally and put into a functional equation in which degree of learning was expressed as a function of the ratio of time actively engaged in learning (as a function of aptitude, perseverance, and opportunity to learn) to the time that the student would need in view of his or her aptitude, ability to understand instruction, and the quality of the instruction offered. This equation, with some *ad hoc* assumptions, was used in a computer simulation that looked at how the validity of aptitude measurements might vary as a function of different kinds of instructional conditions, and average student motivation (perseverance). The results seemed to explain, in a general way, the variation in actual results that I was getting. Although I never published the actual computer program, the formal statement of the model and detailed results were presented both in the article prepared for the February 1960 Pittsburgh symposium (Carroll, 1962a) and in an article presented at a Harvard symposium in April 1961 on the uses of computers (Carroll, 1962b).

At the time of the Pittsburgh symposium I looked upon my model as an interesting theoretical exercise. While I felt it might be useful in my further studies of foreign-language aptitude, I had no plan to generalize it to types of learning other than foreign-language learning. Somehow my work came to the attention of E. Joseph Shoben, Jr, at that time the editor of the *Teachers College Record*. Apparently impressed with the possibilities of applying my model to other types of learning, he communicated with me and encouraged me to write an article for his journal that would develop my ideas for wider dissemination. I did so, introducing my essay as giving 'a schematic design or conceptual model of factors affecting success in school learning and of the way they interact' (Carroll, 1963a, p. 723), and adding a few comments about its implications for concepts of under-achievement and overachievement. I called the model a model of *school* learning because I desired to distinguish it from models in the general theory of learning, even though, as Garner (1978) notes, 'there is nothing about school in it', and it was certainly not intended to be limited to applications in schools. The article was tucked away as the last formal article published in the May 1963 issue; it was not even featured by having its title listed on the front cover of that issue. Apparently the article drew little attention at the time; at least, I am not aware that it directly stirred up any great interest.

There the matter rested for several years, except that I myself used the model in designing and interpreting some of my further research in foreign-language education, and referred to it in my teaching and in a number of public appearances, seminars, workshops and the like. For example, during the summer of 1964, in serving as a group leader at a six-week advanced workshop for young educational researchers held at Stanford University under the leadership of Lee Cronbach, I featured the MSL and encouraged the participants in my group to think about how it might be further elaborated and studied in educational contexts. At times we thought the model was so general and flexible that it was not really testable as a theory of instruction. Nevertheless, I gave an evening public lecture on it that was eventually published under the title 'School Learning over the Long Haul' (Carroll, 1965). Subse-quently, I was also able to promote the model in educational research workshops that took place in Europe – in Sweden in 1968, in France in 1970, and in West Germany in 1971 (Edelstein and Hopf, 1973). As a result, the model was given considerable discussion in the European literature (e.g. Achtenhagen, 1978; Bönsch, 1977; Flammer, 1975; Lundgren, 1972).

Examples of use of the MSL in my research on foreign languages and related topics are my studies of the parameters of foreign-language learning in programmed instruction in Mandarin Chinese (Carroll, 1963c), in intensive foreign-language instruction in the Peace Corps (Carroll, 1966), in the interpretation of survey results on language proficiency among seniors majoring in a foreign language in US colleges and universities (Carroll, 1967), and among students of French at elementary and secondary school levels in eight countries (Carroll, 1975). The model has consistently been found useful in guiding foreign-language instruction, and has often been cited by theorists of foreign-language instruction (Bockman, 1972; Carroll, 1974c; Jakobvits, 1970). In an article prepared for a conference on the aptitude/achievement distinction (Carroll, 1974b), I pointed out that foreign-language-aptitude research offers many examples where a clear distinction between aptitude and achievement can be made, and I offered a special set of criteria for distinguishing these concepts not only in foreign-language research but also in other areas of school-success prediction.

Prompted by an associate, I helped design and conduct a small experimental study of the MSL (Carroll and Spearritt, 1967). Using a programmed instruction technique involving the learning of an artificial foreign language, the experiment sought to determine the effect of manipulating quality of instruction, opportunity for learning, and perseverance, in interaction with measures of IQ taken from school records. The results suggested that poor-quality instruction depressed performance of children at all intelligence levels, and that it led to reduced perseverance on the part of children of high intelligence. Learning was also shown to be highly inefficient when students had insufficient opportunity for learning. The empirical data thus generally confirmed the trends hypothesized in the model, though not in every detail.

One other paper prepared and presented at the conference on the aptitude/achievement distinction seemed of particular interest and significance (Carroll, 1974a). Through mathematical elaboration of the MSL, it showed that it could be applied to large-scale cross-sectional data on aptitude and achievement measures to indicate that students are *consistently* and very systematically spread out in achievement according to measured aptitude, at least in school systems using conventional procedures of instruction, and that the degree of dispersion increases systematically from grade 1 to grade 12. The results led me to think that there is no necessary connection between aptitude and achievement, but that the connection arises because of customary modes of placing, teaching and promoting students. Presumably, if those modes were altered in some way, the connection between aptitude and achievement might not be as strong as it is usually observed to be.

Genesis of the Model: Some More Indirect Influences

It would seem that the feature of the MSL that has attracted most attention is its assertion that aptitude is a matter of individual differences in the amount of time that people need to master a task, and the implication that nearly anyone can learn any task if given enough time to do so. (In framing this part of the model, I assumed that some students might need an infinity of time to master a task, and thus in practice could not be expected to do so.) Certainly this is not a new idea. Cronbach (1972) traced it back to John Locke, and it has been pointed out (Bloom, 1974a) that the idea is implicit in writings of educational philosophers such as Comenius and Herbart. I cannot claim to have been directly influenced by these writers, for I have paid relatively little attention to the philosophy of education. I had been dimly aware that educational experiments in the 1920s had tried manipulating time and opportunity to learn (Morrison, 1926; Washburne, 1922; Washburne, Vogel and Gray, 1926), but again, I would not claim intellectual ancestry from those sources. Rather, my notions developed more directly from observations of individual differences in time requirements in foreign-language learning, programmed instruction, and related settings. Such observations were also the source of my notions about opportunity to learn, perseverance, ability to understand instruction and quality of instruction. I had also become fascinated with time as a variable from reading research studies on human learning. Time (or its exchange equivalent, number of trials) has always been recognized as a critical variable in designing and analyzing experiments on various kinds of human learning. Around the time that I constructed my model, verbal-learning theorists were excited by findings of Bugelski (1962) to the effect that total presentation time − however it was divided into separate trials − seemed to be the critical variable in a variety of learning experiments. Also, I had been stimulated by what I regarded as the elegance of Thurstone's (1930) theoretical derivation of a function relating learning time to list length, and I and a student conducted an experiment to verify certain aspects of Thurstone's formulation (Carroll and Burke, 1965). In the back of my mind was the notion that all task and skill learning might ultimately be described more precisely in terms of parameters for task characteristics and individual differences.

Extension of the MSL

Around 1967 or 1968, in personal contacts with Benjamin Bloom and some of his students, I became aware that Bloom himself had become very much interested in the MSL, and was attempting to apply it to promote better and more efficient learning. I understood, in fact, that he was conducting an extensive series of experiments in what he was calling 'mastery learning' in Chicago schools and in his own graduate courses. Naturally, I was gratified that someone with the brilliance, creativity and energy of Bloom was taking an interest in the MSL and putting it to use. I myself was too much occupied with other matters to try to mount practical experiments with it, even in foreign-language instruction. For the most part, I preferred to take the role of theorist with respect to the MSL, rather than active experimenter.

Bloom's first publication on mastery learning appears to have been an essay published in a newsletter of the Center for the Study of Evaluation of Instructional Programs at the University of California at Los Angeles (UCLA) (Bloom, 1968). The essay presented the model pretty much as I had originally formulated it, and pointed out how 'mastery' of learning tasks might be attained by manipulating variables of time, opportunity and quality of instruction. Bloom emphasized the possible role of 'formative evaluation' (a term that had been promoted by Michael Scriven). He also suggested that various 'alternative' learning resources such as small-group tutorial sessions, and feedback and correction would promote learning. One of his doctoral students (Kim, 1968) mounted an extensive programme of mastery learning in his native country, South Korea, apparently with spanking success.

Over the subsequent years Bloom's ideas on mastery learning developed and flourished. Principles of mastery learning were an important focus of a *Handbook on Formative and Summative Evaluation of Student Learning* (Bloom, Hastings and Madaus, 1971). Some of Bloom's students were particularly energetic in bringing these principles to the attention of the educational community (Block, 1973, 1974a; Block and Anderson, 1975; Torshen, 1977), and by 1976 enough research evidence had accumulated for Block and Burns (1976) to write an extensive review of this work, pointing out that most of this evidence suggested that mastery-learning programmes could be highly successful. As research progressed, Bloom and his colleagues came to feel that the original form of the MSL had to be modified to allow for the fact that in the course of continuing programmes of mastery learning, the time that students needed to master learning tasks seemed to decrease both in central tendency and variance (Bloom, 1974a). In a major work Bloom (1976) presented a new formulation of mastery-learning principles, and summarized the research evidence that supported it.

Together with Bloom's work, the MSL inspired still other major lines of development. David Wiley and Annegret Harnischfeger (1974) saw the relevance of the MSL model, with certain revisions and refinements that they developed (Harnischfeger and Wiley, 1976, 1978) to the evaluation of total school programmes, particularly when attention was paid to total 'quantity of schooling'. Similarly, at the Learning Research and Development Center at the University of Pittsburgh, research on its programmes of Individually Prescribed Instruction (IPI) developed under the leadership of Robert Glaser made use of the MSL in formulating research evaluations (Wang and Lindvall, 1970; Wang and Yeager, 1971; Yeager and Lindvall, 1967). Wang (1970) confirmed that learning rate was not necessarily a general trait, but could be highly task specific. Cooley and Lohnes (1976) urged use of the MSL in categorizing the variables to be studied in educational evaluation, and these ideas were realized in a number of evaluative studies (Cooley and Emrick, 1974; Cooley and Leinhardt, 1975; Leinhardt, 1977a, 1977b, 1978, 1980). Still other interesting extensions of the MSL have been proposed by Bennett (1978) and Centra and Potter (1980).

Certainly the most extensive and systematic use of the MSL in research on school learning occurred in the Beginning Teacher Evaluation Study in California (Denham and Lieberman, 1980; Fisher, Marliave and Filby, 1979). The concept of student time-on-task was further reformulated to focus on what has been called Academic Learning Time (ALT) (Rosenshine and Berliner, 1978), that is, time during which the student is actively engaged in learning tasks that are somewhat challenging, but on which a high success rate can be attained. The project discovered that there could be wide variation among classes and among students in the proportions of ALT even with similar amounts of allocated time, and that these proportions were correlated significantly with student achievement. In its dissemination phases the project directors encouraged teachers to organize their work so as to optimize ALT proportions for all students.

In the meantime, frequent mention and use of the MSL was made in numerous reports of mastery-learning programmes in a variety of subjects at various levels of schooling. Mastery learning, as based on the MLS, became a guide to the formulation and evaluation of new reading programmes (e.g. Fredrick, 1977; Guthrie and Tyler, 1978; Kiesling,

1978; Paradis and Peterson, 1973; Smith and Katims, 1977; Trogdon, 1980). Similar developments occurred in school mathematics (e.g. Burrows and Okey, 1975; Hymel, 1974; Kretschmann and Malburg, 1976), science (Latta, Dolphin and Grabe, 1978), foreign languages (Bockman, 1972; Nieman and Smith, 1978), educational psychology (Denton and Seymour, 1978; Lee and McLean, 1979; Terrill, Berger and Mulgrave, 1973), statistics and test theory (Airasian, 1972; Pfaff and Schmidt, 1974), nursing education (Geissler, 1974; Huckabay, 1978; Huckabay and Arndt, 1976; Mentzer and Scuglia, 1975; Wolf and Quiring, 1971), pharmaceutical training (Manasse and Lasker, 1976) and dentistry (Brundo, 1976). Dorsel (1978) suggested applying the model to the learning of athletic skills — golf, football, bowling. The model has also served as a basis for a number of mathematical models of the learning process, the allocation of instructional time, or causal effects in education (Besel, 1972; Bulcock, Lee and Luk, 1979; Chant and Luenberger, 1974; Cotton, 1975; Hicklin, 1976; Munck, 1979; Sagiv, 1979).

New concepts and inventions are often arrived at independently at approximately the same time or period in history. Keller's (1968) Personalized System of Instruction (PSI) bears much similarity to Bloom's mastery learning, and is founded on many of the same ideas that are formulated in the MSL, but contrary to what is suggested by some writers (e.g. Rupley and Longnion, 1978), Keller was not influenced by the MSL, as I have confirmed through personal communication with him. Nevertheless, it seems legitimate to consider research on PSI as relevant also to the MSL, as Block and Burns (1976) have done. Also, one need not regard PSI and mastery learning as competing models; they have the same general aims, and entail generally similar procedures and problems. The MSL does, however, lay more stress on aptitude and time variables.

The model of school learning has had, then, a consistent and perhaps increasing influence in many areas of education, not only in the USA but also in a number of both developed and developing countries abroad. It has come to the attention of the public in such prestigious media as the *New York Times* (Fiske, 1980), and has been featured in a number of textbooks and readings in educational psychology (e.g. De Cecco, 1968; Willerman and Turner, 1979). It seems to have been an idea whose time has come and that is here to stay.

The Appeal of the Model

Why, I have mused, during this period in the history of education has the model of school learning and its derivatives so captured the attention of educators that it has had the influence it seems to have had (Guskey, 1980; Husén, 1979; Ladas, 1980)? Its ideas were oversimplified and in most respects not really new. The idea that learning takes time is so obvious as to be almost trivial: in commenting on the BTES project an editorial writer in a recent issue of *Basic Education* (1980) wondered why 'so much research is necessary to validate the obvious'. (But then, much scientific attention has been devoted to the effects of gravity, also an 'obvious' variable.) Of only slightly more novelty is the proposition that variations in aptitude can be correlated with variations in the amount of time a student needs to master a task: teachers have always recognized differences between 'fast' and 'slow' learners. Yet the implication of this proposition, that students should be allowed to proceed at their own rate in order to take the amount of time they need, has been the linchpin for all sorts of applications and interpretations of the model. Perhaps the model's appeal to educators in general lies in its suggestion that a radical revision of customary school practices in this regard was needed. Bloom's mastery-learning concept added the suggestion that if all the elements of the model were properly orchestrated, all or nearly all students could master almost any task demanded in the school curriculum.

Of course the model did not rely solely on learning time as such. It suggested that only time that the student was actively engaged in learning really counted toward achievement. It recommended also that instructional quality should be adjusted to meet the needs of students of lesser aptitude, particularly when a student might have difficulty understanding what was to be learned and what had to be done to accomplish this learning.

The practical application of these ideas took some years to evolve to its present state (Hyman and Cohen, 1979). Bloom (1976) concentrated on insuring that students had adequate 'cognitive entry characteristics' and providing students with necessary 'feedback and correction'. The BTES project recognized that it was not solely the amount of time devoted to a learning task that counted, but that it was the *kind* of time utilization, or more specifically, the kinds of learning events that took place during this time, that were critical. As has been mentioned, Academic Learning Time was defined in the BTES project as time during which students were mastering new tasks in which they could have a high success rate. Berliner (1979, p. 121) contrasts this 'academic focus' of time with situations in which 'large amounts of time were spent in telling stories or in art, music, and play activities'. (One hopes that this does not mean that telling stories, or art, music and play activities were to be totally excluded from school programmes.)

All this suggests that while it is 'obvious' that time is a variable in learning, it is *not* obvious how available learning time can best be used. The history of educational research on teaching demonstrates that, with rare exceptions, this was a critical point that was too often neglected. Rosenshine (1979) assigns the MSL and its extensions to a 'third cycle' of research on teaching. In a first cycle, beginning in the 1930s, interest focused on finding out whether measurable 'teacher characteristics' were related to student achievement; in general the findings were negative or highly unclear. Perhaps these research efforts might have been more productive if they had been concerned with any teacher characteristics that might relate to teachers' use of available learning time. A second cycle of research, occurring in the 1950s and 1960s, focused on classroom interactions; again, despite small victories, no major theory or model of school practice emerged. It may be suggested that classroom interaction research should attend to interactions that result in higher amounts of Academic Learning Time. The third cycle, then, turned attention on 'direct' instructional variables, that is, variables that could be demonstrated both logically and empirically to affect learning outcomes. The virtue of the MSL was that it suggested what these direct instructional variables might be, and how they might be related. In this sense the MSL became, it seems, a much needed guide to educational research and educational evaluation (Cooley and Lohnes, 1976; Hambleton, 1974; White and Duker, 1973). Obviously, the model could not have spelled out all the details, but those details are gradually being filled in by the many educational researchers who have been guided by it.

Components of the Model: Research Questions

What are these details? It is impossible to survey here all the research that has some bearing on the MSL and its extensions; for reviews and general treatments, see for example Block and Burns (1976) and Peterson and Walberg (1979). Attention will be focused on certain highlights of this research and certain problems arising in connection with the components suggested by the model.

A general comment is in order on whether the model 'works' and is scientifically valid. Block and Burns (1976) summarizing research on whether the model 'works' came to a generally affirmative conclusion. They continued:

> The approaches have not had as large effects on student learning as their advocates propose are possible, but they have had consistently positive effects. In quantitative terms, mastery approaches have usually produced greater student learning than nonmastery approaches, and they have usually produced relatively less variability in this learning. In qualitative terms, mastery approaches have typically helped students acquire higher-order learning, though there is some question as to whether this higher-order learning has been retained. (p. 25)

The reader may be reminded that in some early discussions of the MSL at the 1964 summer seminar mentioned earlier, some of the participants and I tended to feel that the MSL may not be a truly testable model, in the sense that any failures in its working might be attributed to failures to implement the model adequately, either in the design of educational programmes, the measurement of relevant variables or the analysis of data. Certainly there seem to be a number of instances in which apparent failures of mastery learning can be characterized in this way. For example, Smith (1979) obtained results that suggested that 'the usefulness of allocated time as a potent variable in planning or evaluations of instruction seemed questionable' (p. 231). In evaluating such a finding, one would have to ask whether 'allocated' time was defined in such a way as to limit it to what the BTES project called Academic Learning Time. (Other problems in Smith's study included the relevance of the instruction to the criterion measure chosen.) Similarly, Kibby's (1979) finding that time was not a significant variable in certain phases of an experiment on teaching 'initial word learning' to beginning readers, would have to be appraised in terms of the particular instructional conditions used in the study (see also Frederick and Walberg, 1980).

On the other hand, the model is testable in the sense that it makes predictions concerning the effects of its variables, and if the variables are appropriately manipulated and measured, sound tests can be conducted. Among experiments illustrating this point are those by Anderson (1975), Arlin (1974), Carroll and Spearritt (1967), Carver (1970), Block (1974b, 1975), James (1975), and Lewis (1970). In general, predictions made by the model were confirmed in these experiments; where they were not, possible refinements or modifications of the model could be considered.

Time, Time-on-Task

Comments made above have already suggested that sheer quantity of time allocated to learning is not necessarily the critical variable. This has been pointed out by many observers (e.g. Buss and Poley, 1976; Eigler, Macke, Nenniger, Poelchau and Straka, 1976; Harnischfeger and Wiley, 1978). The quality of learning that goes on in the allocated time, possibly captured by the BTES project's concept of 'academic engaged time' (Denham and Lieberman, 1980; see also Grannis, 1978) is what is crucial. This principle has suggested to some investigators that time-on-task, interpreted as time accompanied by student involvement, should itself be a modifiable, 'alterable' variable (Anderson, 1980; Bloom, 1980; Stuck, 1980). But how can student involvement time be manipulated? Programmed instruction has been proposed as one method, and while programmed instruction generally produces greater student learning on the average, it has not been particularly effective in reducing individual differences in learning (Carroll, 1963d; Flammer, 1973). Increasing the intensiveness of instruction has been considered by other workers (Hefferlin, 1972; Meyen and Lehr, 1980, with particular reference to 'mildly handicapped children'). Giving students data on estimated completion time was tried and found wanting (Colton, 1974).

There has been considerable research on the effects of self-pacing versus teacher-pacing of mastery-learning instruction. While no significant differences were found between these two procedures by Morris, Surber and Bijou (1978), significant interactions with remediation strategies (Denton and Seymour, 1978) or with student ability levels (Arlin and Westbury, 1976; Latta, Dolphin and Grabe, 1978) have been found. Nevertheless, the types of interactions with ability found by Arlin and Westbury were quite different from those observed by Latta *et al*. Sanderson (1976) learned from student interviews that some students disliked mastery-learning procedures, and thus spent less time than they needed — less time than under traditional techniques where teachers provided pacing. Apparently the effect of self-pacing under mastery-learning procedures depends on many additional variables.

Perseverance

The MSL postulated that time-on-task would be a function of the amount of time the student is 'willing' to spend on learning, and that the amount learned would depend on the amount of time actually spent, regardless of whether the student 'liked' this learning. Research has not given adequate attention to verifying these predictions, although some of the research on increasing student involvement would have a bearing. Perhaps the original statement of the MSL was unclear on what would be meant by student 'willingness' to spend time. Actually, it was intended that anything that might motivate students to spend active or engaged learning time would produce 'perseverance', but use of the term 'motivation' was avoided because of difficulty in its definition.

An obvious case in which students in 'alternative schools' showed reduced perseverance in learning as compared to students in more conventional schools was cited by Skager and Morehouse (1973). Clifford (1973) investigated conditions under which liking and learning are positively correlated, finding that such a correlation is a multiplicative function of task commitment on the part of the student, and the extent to which the student feels personally accountable for performance outcomes. Possibly mastery-learning research should pay more attention to developments in motivational psychology (Atkinson, Lens and O'Malley, 1976; Atkinson and Raynor, 1974; Weiner, 1974), which indeed are very much conerned with learning time variables.

Aptitude

In view of the fact that the MSL was developed in the context of research on aptitude (in foreign-language learning), it is rather surprising that mastery-learning research has paid relatively little attention to this variable, which was postulated to be measurable separately from learning time needed and yet to be a predictor of it. Some mastery-learning studies have included measures of general intelligence or general scholastic aptitude in their study designs and analyses (e.g. Carver, 1970; Latta *et al.* 1978; Sjogren, 1967), but there have been few attempts to link specific variables of individual differences in aptitude (e.g. those identified by factor analysis) with learning rates or performance outcomes. Bloom (1976, 1980) has continued to take the 'arch-environmentalist stance' (Cronbach and Snow, 1977, p. 109) that any initial differences in aptitude are to be identified with relatively modifiable 'cognitive entry' characteristics such as possession of specific skills and knowledges that are relevant for a new learning task. This stance seems to be reflected in the Cooley-Lohnes (1976) model for educational evaluation, which converts 'aptitude' into a variable of 'initial performance' that can be measured at least in part by general ability tests. Studies employing this model do indeed find a major percentage of predictor variance in general ability tests. For example, Leinhardt (1977a) found 46.6 per cent of outcome variance in a major evaluation study of follow-up classrooms predicted uniquely from an 'input' variable consisting of scores on the Lorge-Thorndike Intelligence Test combined with scores on a 'mathematics placement' test. The report on the BTES project (Denham and Lieberman, 1980, particularly W.R. Borg's chapter therein) similarly found high predictiveness for an input variable ('preachievement'); it does not state exactly how this input variable was measured, but one may assume that it was composed of measures of, or at least reflected, general scholastic ability.

In mastery-learning research, therefore, there seems to have been a tendency to suppress attention to strictly aptitude variables in favour of vaguely defined 'input' or 'prior learning' variables, and further to suppress or de-emphasize the importance of even these input variables. To be sure, the MSL acknowledges the operation of prior learning variables as accounting for lessened 'time needed' among students who have to some extent profited from prior learning, but it was not intended that such prior learning variables would account for all the variance in active learning time needed. Even Bloom's (1976) demonstrations of reduced variance in learning time needed in successive phases of mastery-learning programmes cannot be interpreted as entirely eliminating the effect of aptitude variables, i.e. relatively permanent characteristics of individuals that affect learning rates. Flammer (1975, pp. 230-48) has reviewed some of the evidence for the persistent effects of such aptitude variables; indeed, Flammer claims that individual differences tend to increase under programmed instruction. Carroll (1974a) analyzed cross-sectional data from nationally administered aptitude and achievement tests to show that the variance of aptitude-dependent achievement increases markedly and systematically over grades 1-12, although one might suppose (perhaps unrealistically) that such results might not have been obtained if mastery-learning procedures had been applied nation-wide over the corresponding time period.

Of particular interest in this connection are results reported by Gettinger and White (1979), who found that work-sample tests of 'time to learn' (TTL) were superior to ordinary IQ tests as predictors of school-learning outcomes. The generally strong predictiveness of the Modern Language Aptitude Test (Carroll, 1962a, 1963c, 1966, 1974b) may possibly be explainable in part as due to the fact that many subtests of this battery are in effect work-sample learning tests. Of course, the mere fact that an aptitude test is a work-sample test does not exclude the possibility that it is in part a measure of prior-learned skills and knowledges, but it also leaves open the possibility that basic, relatively permanent individual differences in aptitude are reflected in work-sample tests. This possibility is strengthened by the observation that many aptitude and work-sample measurements are relatively resistant to improvement in scores through practice and training.

In short, the question of aptitude as a determinant of learning time needed remains relatively unexplored in the literature on mastery-learning approaches. Because this question must be left open, one must avoid taking the 'arch-environmentalist' position taken by many mastery-learning advocates. Environment and nurture are important, manipulable variables, but it is difficult to believe they are the whole story, much as one might like to believe this.

Opportunity to Learn

Strictly speaking, opportunity to learn was defined in the original MSL as the amount of time allowed for learning a task. The implication was that if this time was less than the time a student needed, learning would be less than complete, and that opportunity to learn in conventional teaching programmes would be less than desirable for many students. Research in mastery learning and direct instruction has explicitly considered opportunity to learn in this definition when conventional teaching programmes, with limited time allowances, are contrasted with mastery-learning programmes in which ample time is allowed — perhaps through required homework assignments, tutorial sessions for selected students and the like. Pratzner (1972) has considered the problem of estimating the amount of time needed, setting boundaries around the 'most likely time' as 'optimistic time' and 'pessimistic time'; he did not, however, propose using aptitude measures to make these estimates, as the MSL would suggest. In the BTES project (Denham and Lieberman, 1980) opportunity to learn seems to correspond to 'allocated time', and the concern was to use this allocated time with maximal efficiency by making a maximal proportion of it 'academic engaged time'.

In many writings about mastery learning and direct instructional procedures, however, 'opportunity to learn' has been equated to 'content covered'. As Walker and Schafferzick (1974, p. 101) remark, at a minimum a curricular element must be *presented* in order to be learned. That is, at least *some* time must be devoted to presenting it. Rosenshine (1979, p. 32) takes opportunity to learn in this sense, and after citing a number of studies concludes that 'in all studies but one, significant relations were found between content covered and gains in student achievement'. A further study supporting the importance of covering content is by Arehart (1979), who also manipulated amount of emphasis given to different curricular objectives. Such studies and the ideas on which they are based represent a valid and highly useful extension of the MSL, particularly since it seems unfortunately to be the case that school programmes do not always give adequate coverage to all instructional objectives.

Quality of Instruction

In this term, the original MSL attempted to summarize aspects of instruction and instructional material that conveyed a clear presentation of the learning task — its nature, objectives, content, hierarchical structure (if any). A host of other factors might contribute to quality of instruction — motivating and inspiring students, teaching in an interesting and vivid manner, giving praise, feedback and correction, and so forth — could have been mentioned. Indeed, the notion of quality of instruction covers a very broad region of educational psychology. Feldhusen, Hynes and Ames (1976, p. 14) interpret the MSL as defining quality of instruction 'in a circular manner as follows: Instructional quality is adequate if a student learns successfully from it.' Such a circular definition was not intended, although it might provide a basis for testing elements of instructional quality. In studies of the MSL, there seem to have been few attempts, other than in a study by Carroll and Spearritt (1967), to manipulate quality of instruction, e.g. by deliberately degrading certain elements of it. The assumption seems to be that in all studies of mastery learning, quality of instruction should be maintained at as high a level as possible, while other elements are manipulated. Thus, we have little if any evidence to confirm the MSL's proposal that quality of instruction interacts with aptitude and ability to understand instruction in such a way as to increase needed learning time for low-aptitude students.

Ability to Understand Instruction

It was the intent of the original MSL to make a clear distinction between those student characteristics that were directly relevant to learning time needed for the task *per se*, and those that would interact with quality of instruction. As in the case of research on true-aptitude variables, as discussed above, there has been little research on ability to understand instruction and its possible interaction with instructional quality. A case where such interaction might be expected would be one where the vocabulary and readability level of instructional material is pitched above a student's ability to comprehend it, but such cases appear not to have been explicitly investigated in the context of the MSL and its extensions. It is possible, however, that studies that have used general ability measures as input variables (e.g. Carver, 1970; Thompson, 1980) illustrate an effect of the ability to understand instruction. Thompson, for example, found that most outcome variance in a calculus course was accounted for by 'aptitude' (as measured by high school GPA and scholastic-aptitude tests), and there was no significant interaction of aptitude with treatment (individualized mastery learning versus traditional instruction systems). In practice it may be difficult to distinguish comprehension ability from task-specific aptitudes. Anderson (1979) points out that when one is predicting performance in a diversity of courses and subject matters, general ability measures are probably of greater use than specific aptitude measures.

Degree of Learning

The MSL suggested that the degree of learning at any time during the course of learning would be a function of the ratio between the time taken (in active learning) and the time needed; it avoided specifying whether this function would be linear, because the function might depend on the type of learning task. For example, some simple tasks might have all-or-none achievement, in which case the learning curve would be a step function. For incremental learning of complex skills as in foreign-language learning, the function can be approximately linear (Carroll, 1963c); such a function was also found by Sjogren (1967) with programmed instruction in several different subjects.

Learning Rate

Learning rate is a concept that is difference from degree of learning; it pertains to the relative speed with which students complete learning, and would be computed as the ratio between a measure of progress or gain over a certain period (whether or not mastery is attained during that period) and the length of the period. The model assumes that there are individual differences in learning rate, but that these might be specific to a given task. It also assumes that learning rates could be predicted by appropriate measures of aptitude.

Individual differences in learning rates predicted from aptitude measures can be clearly discerned in studies of foreign-language learning in adults, whether under programmed instruction (Carroll, 1963c) or in intensive group instruction (Carroll, 1966). It appears to have been more difficult to obtain consistent and reliable measures of learning rate in elementary school subjects like reading and mathematics. Perhaps this is because children's learning behaviour is not as well organized as is that of adults. Working within the framework of Individually Prescribed Instruction, Yeager and Lindvall (1967) found that several measures of rate showed little consistency over separate units of instruction, even in the same subject matter, and generally negligible correlations with IQ. Number of units completed per year did, however, correlate with initial levels of placement. In the same context Wang (1970) concluded that learning rates are task specific; while some rate measures could be fairly well predicted from measures of IQ and previous achievement, the patterns of predictor correlations were too heterogeneous to support any clear explanations for the relationships. It is possible that these early results in the IPI setting were cloudy because IPI's management system was still under development; also, the concept of academic engaged time had not been evolved. In a later report Wang (1979) found that task-completion rates could be significantly well predicted from measures of aptitude and quality of instruction. Some of the results from the BTES project (Denham and Lieberman, 1980) are also of relevance. Apparently much further work is needed to clarify the measurement and prediction of learning rates. Although several proposals have been made about this topic (e.g. Packard, 1972) a thorough review and critique of the available evidence is needed before useful investigations can be initiated.

Criticisms of the Model of School Learning

In the educational literature one can find sporadic critical comments, either of the Carroll MSL specifically, or of some of its extensions such as Bloom's mastery-learning concept. The comments do not always specify which model or concept they refer to. Whatever their targets, these critical comments merit consideration, and in many cases response.

Criticisms can be roughly classified into those of (a) the philosophical basis of the model, (b) its underlying theory, and (c) its efficacy or practicality as applied in the conduct of educational programmes.

Philosophical Basis

Those who criticize the philosophical basis of these concepts (e.g. Kepler, 1980; Szilak, 1976) are disturbed with the narrow, rigid and mechanistic view of the educational process that seems to be assumed by the MSL or its extensions; that is, the view that education can be specified as a series of tasks to be learned, each with clearly defined behavioural objectives and characteristics, and each capable of being taught in the light of a series of learning parameters. As the originator of the MSL, I would disavow any such narrow view of education. I carefully limited the application of the MSL to those aspects of education that *can* be specified as learning tasks of a certain kind, and I do not believe it can be denied, even by critics, that at least *some* aspects of the school curriculum can and must be specified in this way. Children have to learn to read before they can appreciate literature; musicians have to learn theory and technical skills before they can work with the subtler varieties of style that make for good music, and so forth. The MSL and mastery learning would apply to learning skills in reading or music, not to appreciating literature or fine music. Mueller (1976) claims that use of the MSL and mastery learning does not promote independent learning. But the model is not intended to apply to promoting independent learning; there are other ways of doing this.

Far from criticizing the model for an unduly narrow view of the learning process, Chadwick (1979) is concerned that though the model is a 'systematic approach', its adherents fail to adopt a 'systems approach', that is, that its potential impact is lessened by failure to perceive how specific learning programmes must be implemented within the broader context of the total educational process. This criticism is quite probably fair and deserves serious consideration.

Underlying Theory

Those who criticize the theory underlying the model are, I fear, often guilty of misunderstanding it. The model does not claim that time is the only variable in learning, or even the most important variable, as critics as widely separated as Cronbach and Snow (1977, p. 109) and Szilak (1976) seem to allege. Although several of the model's variables are expressed in terms of time, what goes on in that time is more important. Critics are confusing necessity and sufficiency: time is undoubtedly necessary, but not sufficient. The model does not by any means claim, as Satterly and Telfer (1979, p. 169) allege, that 'teaching behaviour does not directly influence a child's achievement'. Quality of instruction is an important variable in the model, and teachers' decisions also affect other variables, such as the opportunity to learn and student perseverance.

The complaint of Eigler *et al.* (1976) that the MSL and mastery learning deal with 'one-dimensional' objectives is unfounded; these models can apply to multiple goals simultaneously, each with its own characteristics and implications for how learning should proceed. Buss and Poley (1976) reiterate that 'time explains little by itself' and state they they favour an objective of 'maximizing potential' rather than the attainment of specific objectives. But the MSL, at least, is not in conflict with the goal of maximizing potential; in fact, it should further the attainment of such a goal. According to the MSL, aptitude is relevant to potential in the sense that it predicts how long a student needs to learn a task; if that time is not so long as to be unreasonable in the light of other circumstances, the other variables in the model can guide efficient attainment of potential.

There has been much discussion (e.g. Buss, 1976; Flammer, 1973, 1975) about Bloom's proposal that individual differences will 'vanish' under mastery learning. In my opinion (Carroll, 1976) this hypothesis was more in the nature of a slogan or rallying cry. Under specially contrived conditions, individual differences could be made to 'vanish', that is, by prohibiting further learning after a subject has met a certain criterion of performance. This would not be the normal case, however; students are usually allowed to continue learning after reaching a criterion. Bloom apparently meant only to suggest that through mastery-learning procedures low-aptitude subjects could be brought to attain objectives that they would not normally attain under traditional procedures. Furthermore, normally objectives are set that are within the reach of all, or nearly all, students, given appropriate instruction.

The criticism just discussed relates to the 'arch-environmentalist stance' that has been attributed to Bloom and his followers (Cronbach and Snow, 1977), that is, the position that seems to propose that all or nearly all students can be brought to attain nearly any objective, no matter how difficult or advanced. Such a stance is obviously unrealistic, and is not necessarily implied by the MSL. In fact, the model explicitly assumes that needed learning time for some tasks would be of infinite length for some students, and thus that in practice such students would not be expected to master such tasks. The MSL makes no attempt to assert that all individual differences are of purely environmental origin. On the other hand, the model focuses on those environmental and temporal variables that can be manipulated to maximize students' learning (and thus their potential).

A fundamental criticism often voiced is that mastery-learning procedures guided by the MSL are not universally effective, or that they are not effective for all students (Mueller, 1976). Probably no instructional theory could be devised that would universally and uniformly produce maximal results for all students. Nevertheless, Block's and Burns's (1976) conclusion that mastery-learning procedures *generally* yield more favourable results than non-mastery procedures suggests that mastery learning, and the MSL on which it is based, have represented an important forward step in the development of more effective instructional procedures. Indeed, I have occasionally been made aware of complaints that mastery-learning procedures are *too* effective, because when most students attain all the goals of a course, it becomes problematic to utilize the 'grading on the curve' philosophy that underlies much instruction, particularly at secondary and collegial levels.

Mastery learning does, of course, entail problems (Horton, 1979), and many of these remain to be resolved or worked out. For example, Nance (1976) points out that students may be held back unnecessarily when they fail to meet a high performance standard. Block's (1972, 1974b, 1975) experiments in manipulating performance standards suggest, in fact, that such standards need not be set at excessively high levels; requiring 75 per cent performance may be generally better than insisting on 95 per cent. In the context of PSI with student teachers of reading, Miller and Ellsworth (1979) found that a modified mastery approach (MMA) in which students were given only two trials on each unit was superior to a mastery approach (MA) in which students were given unlimited trials. In the time constraints of an academic semester, the MMA students were able to attempt more units and achieved higher scores on a final examination than MA students, probably because through partial learning of more material they were able to cover more of the course objectives.

Other problems with mastery learning relate to the amount of extra learning time needed by low-aptitude students, how best to utilize this extra learning time through 'remedial' or 'corrective' work (see, for example, O'Connor, Stuck and Wyne, 1979), and how much such extra study time may interfere with the student's other activities, both curricular and extracurricular. Block and Burns (1976) identify research that suggests, tentatively, that these problems are not as serious as might be thought, and that they can be solved. This is a prime area for further research, however.

Overall Evaluation of the Model

It is hoped that this chapter does not exude the 'feigned optimism' about the MSL and mastery learning that disturbed Myers (1974). The

MSL was never offered as an educational panacea; it was intended chiefly as a guide to research on direct instruction and to the interpretation of variations in student achievement. For these purposes it seems to have served well, as the many research investigations cited here testify. Its extensions and refinements have enabled educational researchers to perceive and formulate their research problems about instruction more clearly and penetratingly. Still, it is obvious that much work remains to be done to utilize the model and its extensions to the fullest. Many aspects of the MSL have never been adequately investigated – for example, relations between aptitudes and learning rates, and those phases of quality of instruction that relate to assisting low-aptitude students to make their learning more effective.

It is gratifying, nevertheless, to have seen the MSL serve as the basis for planning and evaluating new types of educational programmes. Programmes based on Bloom's mastery-learning concept, the University of Pittsburgh's Individually Prescribed Instruction, and the Beginning Teacher Evaluation Study are cases in point, and all appear to have proved themselves to be superior to traditional or conventional programmes beyond a mere Hawthorne effect. None of these programmes can be expected really to reduce individual differences in learning and achievement to 'a vanishing point', but if they are applied 'over the long haul' (Carroll, 1965) they hold promise of raising levels of educational achievement to new highs – if, indeed, the many worrisome countervailing trends in contemporary society do not throw sand in the wheels of progress.

Note

1. Reprintings and translations of which I am aware are the following: in P.E. Johnson (1971) (ed.), *Learning: Theory and Practice*, New York: Crowell, pp. 326-39; in H.V. Perkins (1972) (ed.), *Readings in Human Development*, Belmont, CA: Wadsworth, pp. 66; in M. Mohan and R.E. Hull (1974) (eds), *Individualized Instruction and Learning*, Chicago: Nelson-Hall, pp. 33-50; in L. Willerman and R.G. Turner (1979) (eds), *Readings about Individual and Group Differences*, San Francisco: Freeman, pp. 106-19; (German) in W. Edelstein and D. Hopf (1973) (eds), *Bedingungen des Bildungsprozesses*. Stuttgart: Klett, pp. 234-50.

References

Achtenhagen, F. (1978) *Beanspruchung von Schülern: Methodisch-didaktische Aspekte*. Bonn: Bundesminister für Bildung und Wissenschaft

Airasian, P.W. (1972) 'An Application of a Mastery-learning Strategy', *Psychology in the Schools, 9*, 130-4

Anderson, L.W. (1975) 'Student Involvement in Learning and School Achievement', *California Journal of Education, 26*, 53-62

—— (1979) 'Considerations for Setting Performance Standards on Entrance Examinations', *Educational Technology, 19*(7), 22-5

—— (1980) 'New Directions for Research on Instruction and Time-on-task', Paper presented at the annual meeting of the American Educational Research Association, Boston

Arehart, J.E. (1979) 'Student Opportunity to Learn Related to Student Achievement of Objectives in a Probability Unit', *Journal of Educational Research, 72*, 253-9

Arlin, M.N., Jr. (1974) 'The Effects of Formative Evaluation on Student Performance' in H.F. Crombag and D.N. DeGruijter (eds), *Contemporary Issues in Educational Testing*, The Hague: Mouton, pp. 203-17

—— and Westbury, I. (1976) 'The Leveling Effect of Teacher Pacing on Science Content Mastery', *Journal of Research in Science Teaching, 13*, 213-19

Atkinson, J.W., Lens, W. and O'Malley, P.M. (1976) 'Motivation and Ability: Interactive Psychological Determinants of Intellective Performance, Educational Achievement, and Each Other' in W.H. Sewell, R.M. Hauser and D.L. Featherman (eds), *Schooling and Achievement in American Society*, New York: Academic Press, pp. 29-60

—— and Raynor, J.O. (eds) (1974) *Motivation and Achievement*, Washington, DC: V.H. Winston

Basic Education (1980) 'Time on task, and off', *Basic Education, 24*(10), 13-14

Bennett, S.N. (1978) 'Recent Research on Teaching: A Dream, a Belief, and a Model', *British Journal of Educational Psychology, 48*, 127-47

Berliner, D.C. (1979) 'Tempus Educare' in P.L. Peterson and H.J. Walberg (eds), *Research on Teaching: Concepts, Findings and Implications*, Berkeley, CA: McCutchan, pp. 120-35

Besel, R. (1972) 'A Linear Model for the Allocation of Instructional Resources', *Socio-Economic Planning Sciences, 6*, 501-6

Block, J.H. (1972) 'Student Learning and the Setting of Mastery Performance Standards', *Educational Horizons, 50*, 183-91

—— (1973) 'Teachers, Teaching and Mastery Learning', *Today's Education, 62*(7), 30-6

—— (ed.) (1974a) *Schools, Society and Mastery Learning*, New York: Holt, Rinehart & Winston

—— (1974b) 'Student Learning and the Setting of Mastery Performance Standards' in E.P. Torrance and W.F. White (eds), *Issues and Advances in Educational Psychology* (revised edition), Itasca, Ill.: F.E. Peacock

—— (1975) 'Mastery Performance Standards and Student Learning: A Replication', Santa Barbara, CA: University of California

—— and Anderson, L.W. (1975) *Mastery Learning in Classroom Instruction*, New York: Macmillan

—— and Burns, R.B. (1976) 'Mastery Learning', *Review of Research in Education, 4*, 3-49

Bloom, B.S. (1968) 'Learning for Mastery', *Evaluation Comment, 1*(2) [Unpaginated]

—— (1974a) 'A Introduction to Mastery-learning Theory' in J.H. Block (ed.), *Schools, Society and Mastery Learning*, New York: Holt, Rinehart & Winston, pp. 3-14

—— (1974b) 'Time and Learning', *American Psychologist, 29*, 682-8

—— (1976) *Human Characteristics and School Learning*, New York: McGraw-Hill

—— (1980) (ed.), *The State of Research on Selected Alterable Variables in Education*, Chicago: Department of Education, University of Chicago

——, Hastings, J.T. and Madaus, G.F. (eds) (1971) *Handbook of Formative and Summative Evaluation of Student Learning*, New York: McGraw-Hill

Bockman, J.F. (1972) 'An Analysis of the Learning Process: A Rationale for the Individualization of Foreign-Language Instruction' in H.B. Altman (ed.), *Individualizing the Foreign Language Classroom: Perspectives for Teachers*, Rowley, Mass.: Newbury House, pp. 33-52

Bönsch, M. (1977) 'Zym gegenwärtigen Stand der Begabungsforschung und seiner Berücksichtigung in der Unterrichtspraxis', *Unterrichtswissenschaft, 5*, 66-76

Brundo, G.C. (1976) 'In-service Teacher Training in Removable Prosthodontics', *Journal of Prosthetic Dentistry, 35*, 674-9

Bugelski, B.R. (1962) 'Presentation Time, Total Time, and Mediation in Paired-associate Learning', *Journal of Experimental Psychology, 63*, 409-12

Bulcock, J.W., Lee, W.F. and Luk, W.S. (1979) 'The Variance Normalization Method of Ridge Regression Analysis'. Paper presented at the meeting of the American Educational Research Association, San Francisco

Burrows, C.K. and Okey, J.R. (1975) 'The Effects of a Mastery-learning Strategy on Achievement'. Paper presented at the meeting of the American Educational Research Association, Washington DC [ERIC Doc. ED 109 240]

Buss, A.R. (1976) 'The Myth of Vanishing Individual Differences in Bloom's Mastery Learning', *Journal of Instructional Psychology, 3* (special edition, Summer), 4-14

—— and Poley, W. (1976) *Individual Differences: Traits and Factors*, New York: Gardner

Carroll, J.B. (1962a) 'The Prediction of Success in Intensive Foreign-language Training' in R. Glaser (ed.), *Training Research and Education*, Pittsburgh: University of Pittsburgh Press [New York: Wiley-Interscience, 1965], pp. 87-136

—— (1962b) 'Computer Applications in the Investigation of Models in Educational Research' in A.G. Oettinger (ed.), Proceedings of a Harvard Symposium on Digital Computers and their Applications, *Annals of the Computation Laboratory of Harvard University, 31*, 48-58

—— (1963a) 'A Model of School Learning', *Teachers College Record, 64*, 723-33

—— (1963b) 'Research on Teaching Foreign Languages' in N.L. Gage (ed.), *Handbook of Research on Teaching*, Chicago: Rand McNally, pp. 1060-100

—— (1963c) *Programmed Self-instruction in Mandarin Chinese: Observations of Student Progress with an Automated Audiovisual Instructional Device*, Wellesley, Mass.: Language Testing Fund [ERIC Doc. ED 002 374]

—— (1963d) 'Programmed Instruction and Student Ability', *Journal of Programmed Instruction, 2*(4), 7-12

—— (1965) 'School Learning over the Long Haul' in J.D. Krumboltz (ed.), *Learning and the Educational Process*, Chicago: Rand McNally, pp. 249-69

—— (1966) *A Parametric Study of Language Training in the Peace Corps*, Cambridge, Mass.: Laboratory for Research in Instruction, Harvard Graduate School of Education [ERIC Doc. ED 010 877]

—— (1967) 'Foreign-language Proficiency Levels Attained by Language Majors Near Graduation from College', *Foreign Language Annals, 1*, 131-51

—— (1974a) 'Fitting a Model of School Learning to Aptitude and Achievement Data Over Grade Levels' in D.R. Green (ed.), *The Aptitude-achievement Distinction*, Monterey, CA: CTB/McGraw-Hill, pp. 53-78

—— (1974b) 'The Aptitude-achievement Distinction: The case of Foreign-language Aptitude and Proficiency' in D.R. Green (ed.), *The Aptitude-achievement Distinction*, Monterey, CA: CTB/McGraw-Hill, pp. 289-303

—— (1974c) 'Learning Theory for the Classroom Teacher' in G.A. Jarvis (ed.), *The Challenge of Communication*, Skokie, IL: National Textbook Co., pp. 113-49

—— (1975) *The Teaching of French as a Foreign Language in Eight Countries*, Stockholm: Almqvist & Wiksell; New York: Wiley (Halsted)

—— (1976) 'Comment on Buss's Article', *Journal of Instructional Psychology, 3* (special edition, Summer), 20

—— (1981) 'Twenty-five Years of Research on Foreign-language Aptitude' in K.C. Diller (ed.), *Individual Differences and Universals in Language-learning Aptitude*, Rowley, MA: Newbury House, pp. 83-118

—— and Burke, M.L. (1965) 'Parameters of Paired-associate Verbal Learning: Length of List, Meaningfulness, Rate of Presentation, and Ability', *Journal of Experimental Psychology, 69*, 543-53

—— and Sapon, S.M. (1959) *Modern Language Aptitude Test*, New York: The Psychological Corporation

—— and Spearritt, D.A. (1967) *A Study of a Model of School Learning*, Cambridge, Mass.: Harvard University Center for Research and Development of Educational Differences

Carver, R.P. (1970) 'A Test of an Hypothesized Relationship Between Learning Time and Amount Learned in School Learning', *Journal of Educational Research, 64*, 57-8

Centra, J.A. and Potter, D.A. (1980) 'School and Teacher Effects: An Inter-relational Model', *Review of Educational Research, 50*, 273-91

Chadwick, C.N. (1979) 'Why Educational Technology is Failing (and What Should Be Done to Create Success)', *Educational Technology, 19*(1), 7-19

Chant, V.G. and Luenberger, D.G. (1974) 'A Mathematical Theory of Instruction: Instructor/learner Interaction and Instruction Pacing', *Journal of Mathematical Psychology, 11*, 132-58

Clifford, M.M. (1973) 'How Learning and Liking are Related – A Clue', *Journal of Educational Psychology, 64*, 183-6

Colton, F.V. (1974) 'Effects of Giving Students Data on Task Completion Time in a College Media Course', *Audio-Visual Communication Review, 22*, 279-94

Cooley, W.W. and Emrick, J.A. (1974) 'A Model of Classroom Differences Which Explains Variation in Classroom Achievement'. Paper presented at the meeting of the American Educational Research Association, Chicago

—— and Leinhardt, G. *The Application of a Model for Investigating Classroom Processes*, Pittsburgh: Learning Research and Development Center, University of Pittsburgh

—— and Lohnes, P.R. (1976) *Evaluation Research in Education*, New York: Irvington (Halsted)

Cotton, J.W. (1975) 'Theoretical Perspectives for Research on College Teaching: A Cognitive Viewpoint', *Instructional Science, 4*, 59-98

Cronbach, L.J. (1972) 'Book Review of Block, J.H.' (ed.), *Mastery Learning: Theory and Practice, International Review of Education, 18*, 250-2

—— and Snow, R.E. (1977) *Aptitudes and Instructional Methods: A Handbook for Research on Interactions*, New York: Irvington

De Cecco, J.P. (1968) *The Psychology of Learning and Instruction: Educational Psychology*, Englewood Cliffs, NJ: Prentice-Hall

Denham, C and Lieberman, A. (1980) (eds), *Time to Learn: A Review of the Beginning Teacher Evaluation Study*, Washington, DC: National Institute of Education

Denton, J.J. and Seymour, J.A.G. (1978) 'The Influence of Unit Pacing and Mastery-learning Strategies on the Acquisition of Higher-order Intellectual Skills', *Journal of Educational Research, 71*, 267-71

Dorsel, T.N. (1978) 'Mastery-learning Approach to Practicing Athletic Skills', *Perceptual & Motor Skills, 46*, 1243-6

Edelstein, W. and Hopf, D. (eds) (1973) *Bedingungen des Bildungsprozesses*, Stuttgart: Ernst Klett

Eigler, G., Macke, G., Nenniger, P., Poelchau, H-W. and Straka, G.A. (1976) 'Mehrdimensionale Zielerreichung in Lehr-Lern-Prozessen', *Zeitschrift für Pädagogik, 22*, 181-97

Feldhusen, J.F., Hynes, K. and Ames, C.A. (1976) 'Is a Lack of Instructional Validity Contributing to the Decline of Achievement-test Scores?', *Educational Technology, 16*(7), 13-16

Fisher, C.W., Marliave, R.S. and Filby, N.N. (1979) 'Improving Teaching by Increasing "academic learning time" ', *Educational Leadership, 37*, 52-4

Fiske, E.B. (1980) 'New Teaching Method Raises Hopes in Inner City', *New York Times*, 30 March

Flammer, A. (1973) 'Individuelle Differenzen in Lernen nach der "Mastery-learning"-Strategie', *Zeitschrift für Experimentelle und Angewandte Psychologie, 20*, 529-46

—— (1975) *Individuelle Unterschiede im Lernen*, Weinheim: Beltz

Frederick, W.C. (1977) 'The Use of Classroom Time in High Schools Above or Below the Median Reading Score', *Urban Education, 11*, 459-64

—— and Walberg, H.J. (1980) 'Learning as a Function of Time', *Journal of Educational Research, 73*, 183-94

Garner, W.T. (1978) 'The Public Economics of Mastery Learning', *Educational Technology, 18*(12), 12-17

Geissler, E.M. (1974) 'A New Way of Looking at Old Ideas', *International Nursing Review, 21*, 169-71

Gettinger, M. and White, M.A. (1979) 'Which is the Stronger Correlate of School Learning? Time to Learn or Measured Intelligence?', *Journal of Educational Psychology, 71*, 405-12

Glaser, R. (1962) (ed.), *Training Research and Education*, Pittsburgh: University of Pittsburgh Press

Grannis, J.C. (1978) 'Task Engagement and the Consistency of Pedagogical Controls: An Ecological Study of Differently Structured Classroom Settings', *Curriculum Inquiry, 8*, 3-36

Guskey, T.R. (1980) 'Mastery Learning: Applying the Theory', *Theory into Practice, 19*, 104-11

Guthrie, J.T. and Tyler, S.J. (1978) 'Cognition and Instruction of Poor Readers', *Journal of Reading Behavior, 10*, 57-78

Hambleton, R.K. (1974) 'Testing and Decision-making Procedures for Selected Individualized Instructional Programs', *Review of Educational Research, 44*, 371-400

Harnischfeger, A. and Wiley, D.E. (1976) 'The Teaching-learning Process in Elementary Schools: A Synoptic view', *Curriculum Inquiry, 6*, 5-43

—— and Wiley, D.E. (1978) 'Conceptual Issues in Models of School Learning', *Curriculum Studies, 10*, 214-31

Hefferlin, J.B.L. (1972) 'Intensive Courses: An Old Idea Whose Time for Testing has Come', *Journal of Research and Development in Education, 6*(1) 83-98

Hicklin, W.J. (1976) 'A Model for Mastery Learning Based on Dynamic Equilibrium Theory', *Journal of Mathematical Psychology, 13*, 79-88

Horton, L. (1979) 'Mastery Learning: Sound in Theory, but . . .', *Educational Leadership, 37*, 154-6

Huckabay, L.M. (1978) 'Cognitive and Affective Consequences of Formative Evaluation in Graduate Nursing Students', *Nursing Research, 27*, 190-4

—— and Arndt, C. (1976) 'Effect of Acquisition of Knowledge on Self-evaluation and the Relationship of Self-evaluation to Perception of Real and Ideal Self-concept', *Nursing Research, 25*, 244-51

Husén, T. (1979) 'General Theories in Education: A Twenty-five Year Perspective', *International Review of Education, 25*, 325-45

Hyman, J.S. and Cohen, S.A. (1979) 'Learning for Mastery: Ten Conclusions After 15 Years and 3,000 Schools', *Educational Leadership, 37*, 104-9

Hymel, G.M. (1974) *An Investigation of John B. Carroll's Model of School Learning as a Theoretical Basis for the Organizational Structuring of Schools*, (Final Rep., NIE Project No. 3-1359), U. of New Orleans, New Orleans, Louisiana

Jakobovits, L.A. (1970) *Foreign-language Learning: A Psycholinguistic Analysis of the Issues*, Rowley, Mass.: Newbury House

James, A. (1975) 'A Experimental Comparison of Conditions Related to Concept Learning from Written Instruction', *Bulletin of the British Psychological Society, 28*, 238

Keller, F.S. (1968) 'Goodbye, Teacher . . .', *Journal of Applied Behavior Analysis, 1*, 79-89

Kepler, K.B. (1980) 'BTES: Implications for Preservice Education of Teachers' in C. Denham and A. Lieberman (eds), *Time to Learn*, Washington, DC: National Institute of Education, pp. 139-57

Kibby, M.W. (1979) 'The Effects of Certain Instructional Conditions and Response Modes on Initial Word Learning', *Reading Research Quarterly, 15*, 147-71

Kiesling, H. (1978) 'Productivity of Instructional Time by Mode of Instruction for Students at Varying Levels of Reading Skill', *Reading Research Quarterly, 13*, 554-82

Kim, H. (1968) 'Learning Rates, Aptitudes and Achievements'. Unpublished doctoral dissertation, University of Chicago

Kretschmann, R. and Malburg, H. (1976) 'Generelle und differentielle Effekte dreier verschiedener Formen adaptiven Unterrichts', *Zeitschrift für Pädagogik, 22*, 889-900

Ladas, H.S. (1980) 'A Handbook of Irreducible Facts for Teaching and Learning', *Phi Delta Kappan, 61*, 606-7

Latta, R.M., Dolphin, W.D. and Grabe, M. (1978) 'Individual Differences Model Applied to Instruction and Evaluation of Large College Classes', *Journal of Educational Psychology, 70*, 960-70

Lee, M.M. and McLean, J.E. (1979) 'A Comparison of Achievement and Attitudes Among Three Methods of Teaching Educational Psychology', *Journal of Educational Research, 72*, 86-90

Leinhardt, G. (1977a) 'Evaluating an Adaptive Education Program: Implementation to Replication', *Instructional Science, 6*, 223-57

—— (1977b) 'Program Evaluation: An Empirical Study of Individualized Instruction', *American Educational Research Journal, 14*, 277-93

—— (1978) 'Applying a Classroom Process Model to Instructional Evaluation', *Curriculum Inquiry, 8*, 155-76

—— (1980) 'Modelling and Measuring Educational Treatment in Evaluation', *Review of Educational Research, 50*, 393-420

Lewis, L.A. (1970) 'A Test of Carroll's Model of School Learning'. Unpublished doctoral dissertation, Florida State University

Lundgren, U.P. (1972) *Frame Factors and the Teaching Process*, Stockholm: Almqvist and Wiksell

Manasse, H.R., Jr. and Lasker, P.A. (1976) 'Some Considerations Regarding Norm-referenced and Criterion-referenced Testing in Pharmaceutical Education', *American Journal of Pharmaceutical Education, 40*, 275-8

Mentzer, D.S. and Scuglia, R.C. (1975) 'Teaching Life Science to Student Nurses: A Modular Approach', *American Biology Teacher, 37*, 358-60

Meyen, E.L. and Lehr, D.H. (1980) 'Least Restrictive Environment: Instructional Implications', *Focus on Exceptional Children, 12*(7), 1-8

Miller, J.W. and Ellsworth, R. (1979) 'Mastery Learning: The Effects of Time Constraints and Unit Mastery Requirements', *Educational Research Quarterly, 4*(4), 40-8

Morris, E.K., Surber, C.F. and Bijou, S.M. (1978) 'Self-pacing, Versus Instructor-pacing: Achievement, Evaluations and Retention', *Journal of Educational Psychology, 70*, 224-30

Morrison, H.C. (1926) *The Practice of Teaching in the Secondary School*, Chicago: University of Chicago Press

Mueller, D.J. (1976) 'Mastery Learning: Partly Boon, Partly Boondoggle', Teachers College Record, 78, 41-52

Munck, I.M.E. (1979) *Model Building in Comparative Education: Applications of the LISREL Method to Cross-national Survey Data*, Stockholm: Almqvist & Wiksell, (*IEA Monograph Series*, No. 10)

Myers, D.A. (1974) 'Why Open Education Died', *Journal of Research and Development in Education, 8*(1), 60-7

Nance, D.W. (1976) 'Bloom's "Mastery Learning" in College Math Limits Critical and Essential Coverage', *Journal of Instructional Psychology, 3* (special edition, Summer), 23-7

Nieman, L.L. and Smith, W.F. (1978) 'Individualized Instruction: Its Effects Upon Achievement and Interest in Beginning College Spanish', *Modern Language Journal, 62*, 157-67

O'Connor, P.D., Stuck, G.B. and Wyne, M.D. (1979) 'Effects of a Short-term Intervention Resource-room Program on Task Orientation and Achievement', *Journal of Special Education, 13*, 375-85

Packard, R.G. (1972) 'Models of Instructional Instruction: The Search for a Measure', *Educational Technology, 12*(8), 11-14

Paradis, E. and Peterson, J. (1973) 'Concept of Mastery Learning Applied to Reading', *Journal of Research and Development in Education, 6*, monograph, 166-73

Peterson, P.L. and Walberg, H.J. (eds), (1979) *Research on Teaching: Concepts, Findings and Implications*, Berkeley, CA: McCutchan

Pfaff, J.K. and Schmidt, W.H. (1974) 'Mastery-learning Strategies: Application to the Teaching of Statistics'. Paper presented at the meeting of the American Educational Research Association, Chicago [ERIC Doc. ED 097 357]

Powell, B.S. (1976) *Intensive Education: The Impact of Time on Learning*, Newton, Mass.: Education Development Center

Pratzner, F.C. (1972) 'Estimates of Teaching-learning Time', *Educational Technology, 12*(8), 58-62

Rosenshine, B.V. (1979) 'Content, Time and Direct Instruction' in Peterson P.L. and Walberg H.J. (eds), *Research on Teaching: Concepts, Findings and Implications*, Berkeley, CA: McCutchan, pp. 28-56

—— and Berliner, D.C. (1978) 'Academic Engaged Time', *British Journal of Teacher Education, 4*, 3-16

Rupley, W.H. and Longnion, B.L. (1978) 'Mastery Learning: A Viable Alternative?' *Reading Teacher, 32*, 380-3

Sagiv, A. (1979) 'General Growth Model for Evaluation of an Individual's Progress in Learning', *Journal of Educational Psychology, 71*, 866-81

Sanderson, H.W. (1976) 'Student Attitudes and Willingness to Spend Time in Unit Mastery Learning', *Research in the Teaching of English, 10*, 191-8

Satterly, D.J. and Telfer, I.G. (1979) 'Cognitive Style and Advance Organizers in Learning and Retention', *British Journal of Educational Psychology, 49*, 169-78

Sjogren, D.D. (1967) 'Achievement as a Function of Study Time', *American Educational Research Journal, 4*, 337-43

Skager, R., Morehouse, K., Russock, R. and Schumacher, E. (1973) *Evaluation of the Los Angeles Alternative School: A Report to the Board of Education of the Los Angeles Unified School District*, Los Angeles, CA: Center for the Study of Evaluation, University of California

Smith, J.K. and Katims, M. (1977) 'Reading in the City: The Chicago Mastery Learning Reading Program', *Phi Delta Kappan, 59*, 199-202

Smith, N.M. (1979) 'Allocation of Time and Achievement in Elementary Social Studies', *Journal of Educational Research, 72*, 231-6

Stuck, G.B. (1980) 'Time-on-task and School Achievement: Classroom Intervention Research'. Paper presented at the meeting of the American Educational Research Association, Boston

Szilak, D. (1976) 'Strings: A Critique of Systematic Education', *Harvard Educational Review, 46*, 54-75

Terrill, A.F., Berger, V. and Mulgrave, N.W. (1973) 'The Application of a Modified Mastery Approach to the Teaching of Graduate Educational Psychology', *Psychology in the Schools, 10*, 253-8

Thompson, S.B. (1980) 'Do Individualized Mastery and Traditional Instructional Systems Yield Different Course Effects in College Calculus? *American Educational Research Journal, 17*, 361-75

Thurstone, L.L. (1930) 'The Relation Between Learning Time and Length of Task', *Psychological Review, 37*, 44-58

Torshen, K.P. (1977) *The Mastery Approach to Competency-based Education*, New York: Academic Press

Trogdon, E.W. (1980) 'An Exercise in Mastery Learning', *Phi Delta Kappan, 61*, 389-91

Walker, D.F. and Schaffarzick, J. (1974) 'Comparing Curricula', *Review of Educational Research, 44*, 83-111

Wang, M.C. (1970) 'The Use of the Canonical Correlation Analysis in an Investigation of Pupil's Rate of Learning in School', *Journal of Educational Research, 64*(1), 35-45

—— (1979) 'Maximizing the Effective Use of School Time by Teachers and Students', *Contemporary Educational Psychology, 4*, 187-201

—— and Lindvall, C.M. (1970) *An Exploratory Investigation of the Carroll Model and the Bloom Strategy for Mastery Learning*, Pittsburgh, PA: Learning Research and Development Center, University of Pittsburgh [ERIC Doc. ED 054 983]

—— and Yeager, J.L. (1971) 'Evaluation under Individualized Instruction', *Elementary School Journal, 71*, 448-52

Washburne, C.W. (1922) 'Educational Measurements as a Key to Individualizing Instruction and Promotions', *Journal of Educational Research, 5*, 195-206

——, Vogel, M. and Gray, W.S. (1926) 'Results of Practical Experiments in Fitting Schools to Individuals', supplementary educational monograph, *Journal of Educational Research*, Bloomington, Ill.: Public School Publishing Co.

Weiner, B. (1974) 'Motivational Psychology and Educational Research', *Educational Psychologist, 11*, 96-101

White, M.A. and Duker, J. (1973) 'Models of Schooling and Models of Evaluation', *Teachers College Record, 74*, 293-307

Wiley, D.E. and Harnischfeger, A. (1974) 'Explosion of a Myth: Quantity of Schooling and Exposure to Instruction, Major Educational Vehicles', *Educational Researcher, 3*(4), 7-12

Willerman, L. and Turner, R.G. (eds), (1979) *Readings About Individual and Group Differences*, San Francisco: W.H. Freeman

Wolf, V.C. and Quiring, J. (1971) 'Carroll's Model Applied to Nursing Education', *Nursing Outlook, 19*, 176-9

Yeager, J.L. and Lindvall, C.M. (1967) 'An Exploratory Investigation of Selected Measures of Rate of Learning', *Journal of Experimental Education, 36*(2), 78-81

3 ATTENTION, TASKS AND TIME

Lorin W. Anderson

> Every one knows what attention is. It is the taking possession of the mind, in clear and vivid form, of one out of what seem several simultaneously possible objects or trains of thought. Focalization, concentration, of consciousness are of its essence. It implies withdrawal of some things in order to deal effectively with others. (James, 1890, 403-4)

While everyone 'knows what attention is', the importance of attention in classroom instruction and school learning is overlooked from time to time. With the current interest in academically engaged time, or time-on-task, the flame of student attention has been rekindled. Unfortunately, in this rekindling many educators have focused exclusively on *time* without a complementary focusing on what it means for students to be *engaged* or *on-task*. The purpose of this chapter is to refocus attention on attention.

This chapter is divided into five sections. In the first section a perspective on the importance of attention in understanding the complexities of classroom instruction and school learning is described. The second section presents an historical view of attention, learning and teaching. The third section discusses the modern view of attention, learning and teaching. The fourth section presents information relating to the current controversy over engaged time and time-on-task. In this section the relationship between time and attention is discussed. In the fifth and final section speculations on the future of attention, tasks and time are offered.

Classrooms, Tasks and Attention: A Perspective

'Trying to observe instruction in an active first-grade classroom can be a humbling experience. So much is going on and the distractions are so many, the wonder is that teacher and student make any sense of the situation' (Piontkowski and Calfee, 1979, p. 297). The complexity of life in classrooms has been brilliantly documented by Jackson (1968).

This complexity stems from two sources: the social psychological aspects of the classroom, and the nature of the learning tasks. Let us consider each in turn.

In 1953 Cherry conducted a study of attention within the framework of what he referred to as the 'cocktail party problem'.

> The cocktail party serves as a fine example of selective attention. We stand in a crowded room with sounds and conversations all about us. Often the conversation to which we are trying to listen is not the one in which we are supposedly taking part. (Norman,1969, p. 13)

In many ways life in classrooms resembles a cocktail party. In the words of Piontkowski and Calfee, 'so much is going on and the distractions are so many'. A number of stimuli — both external (e.g. sounds, sights) and internal (e.g. thoughts, feelings) — all compete for the attention of teachers as well as students. But somehow the majority of teachers and students do make a certain amount of 'sense of the situation'. Attention is postulated as the mechanism by which order is made out of the apparent chaos.

Students 'tune in' to certain classroom events, and then either 'tune in' to other events or literally 'tune in(ward)' to spend some time 'daydreaming'. A student may listen to a teacher for a period of time, pay attention to a note received from a friend, and then think about the party to which the note invites him or her. Similarly, a student working with one group of students in the classroom may become interested in the discussions taking place in another group of students.

From a social psychological perspective, then, classrooms are extremely complex entities. The number of students, the number of groups, the climate of the classroom, and the variety of remembrances and future plans of the students all combine to produce this complexity. Incredibly, in the midst of all of this social psychological complexity, students are expected to learn something. In more technical terms students are expected to accomplish a set or series of *learning tasks*. The second source of complexity of life in classrooms stems from the complexity of the assigned learning tasks.

Doyle (1979a, 1979b) defines a task as a goal to be accomplished and a set of operations related to the attainment of that goal. Similarly, Carroll (1963) defines a learning task as 'the learner's task of going from ignorance of some specified fact or concept to knowledge of it, or of proceeding from incapability of performing some specified act to capability of performing it' (p. 723). A learning task, then, has two parts: (1) a goal, objective, or desired outcome (not already attained or achieved), and (2) a set of mental and/or physical operations which must be performed in order to achieve the goal, objective, or desired outcome.

Several characteristics of a learning task effect its complexity. First, the goal can be complex. Learning to memorize pairs of objects (e.g. states-capitals, poems-poets), make appropriate inferences about information contained in prose passages, solve mathematical word problems and write coherent essays are difficult goals for many students to achieve. Secondly, the operations may be difficult to perform. Solving mathematical word problems, for example, becomes even more difficult for students who cannot perform the mental operations necessary to read and understand the material in which the problem is embedded, or have not mastered the required algorithms. Similarly, writing coherent paragraphs becomes increasingly difficult for students who have not mastered the psychomotor activity of cursive writing. Thirdly, the nature of the task itself may not be clear. The student may not understand either what the goal actually is, or how the goal is to be accomplished (that is, the operations that should be performed in order to accomplish the goal).

Finally, the complexity of life in classrooms would appear to be geometrically increased when both sources of complexity (that is, the social psychological aspects of the classroom and the difficulty of the learning task) are in operation at the same time. In an *unruly classroom*, for example, students working at a *difficult learning task* must feel overwhelmed and frustrated. It can come as no surprise that attention is removed from the learning task and shifted to external events (e.g. the causes of the unruliness or internal thoughts and dreams).

In summary, then, classroom life is complex socially, psychologically and mentally. The environment containing a large number of people and objects, to which a person brings a variety of knowledge and attitudes, and which places a variety of behavioural and intellectual demands on the person, is not easy to navigate. One of the primary vehicles of navigation is the person's attentional processes. In order to help students better to navigate these complex environments we need to understand better the nature of those attentional processes. The promotion of such understanding is the goal of the next two sections.

An Historical Perspective on Attention and Learning

That attention is a necessary condition for learning has been accepted by a variety of educators and psychologists for centuries.

> The early practitioner of the art of memory realized that attention is a prerequisite of memory. In 400 BC the written rules of memory contained statements such as, 'This is the first thing: if you pay attention the judgement will better perceive the things going through it'. (Norman, 1969, p. 1)

The importance of attention for learning was highlighted in the latter part of the nineteenth century and the early part of the twentieth century. In what is commonly accepted as the first psychology text-book, William James (1890) devoted fully fifty-seven pages to the concept of attention. Concerning the attention-learning relationship James wrote 'my experience is what I agree to attend to. Only those items which I notice shape my mind' (p. 402). Educator Harry Wheat (1931) actually defined learning in terms of attention: 'Learning is the activity of giving attention effectively to the essential phases of a situation' (p. 1). He continued, 'it may be said that, other things being equal, the amount or the quality of learning is in direct proportion to the effectiveness of the attention which the learner is induced to give' (p. 12). Henry Morrison (1926) stated the converse of Wheat's proposition when he wrote: 'perhaps the commonest cause of non-learning is poor attention' (p. 82).

Two general types of attention were differentiated by these early writers: selective attention and sustained attention. Both types are alluded to in the James's quote which began this chapter. In simplest terms, *selective attention involved focalization; sustained attention involved concentration*. In essence, selective attention referred to the focusing of the mind on one object, event, or idea at the expense or exclusion of others. Once a particular object, event, or idea was selected for attention, that attention had to be sustained on the object, event, or idea for sufficient periods of time if adequate learning was to occur. In Morrison's (1926) words, sustained attention extends over a fairly lengthy period of time 'with only occasional and momentary intermissions' (p. 104).

The nature of sustained attention was discussed by both Morrison, an educator, and James, a psychologist. The difference in the discussion parallels in many ways the differences in the perspectives of their fields of expertise. Morrison (1926) suggested that attention could be sustained over long periods of time provided the learner was *absorbed* in the object, event or idea. James, on the other hand, contended 'there is no such thing as . . . attention sustained for more than a few seconds at a time. What is called sustained . . . attention is a repetition of successive efforts which bring back the topic to mind' (p. 240). For James, then, sustained attention was 'multiple selection attention' and required what may be called 'mental effort'. In any case, both selective and sustained attention were hypothesized to be necessary for learning to occur.

To these early writers attention was associated with a variety of concepts in addition to learning. Absorption, interest, motivation and genius all were considered to be linked with attention. Morrison's belief that absorption is necessary for sustained attention has already been mentioned. James linked absorption, attention, and 'absent-mindedness'. 'When absorbed in intellectual attention we may be so inattentive to outer things as to be "absent-minded" ' (p. 419). The linkage of absorption and attention implies the existence of different degrees or intensity of attention. One may be minimally attentive to an object, event or idea, or be totally immersed in the object, event or idea. Thus, there were believed to be *degrees* of attention.

Attention also was linked with interest, although the nature of the linkage is quite different. Concerning interest, James wrote: 'The things to which we attend are said to *interest* us. Our interest in them is supposed to be the *cause* of our attending' (p. 420). In this regard Wheat differentiated what he termed 'forced attention' from 'spontaneous attention'.

> Forced attention is from without the individual. It is imposed on him, or he imposes it on himself. Because it comes from without it is aways divided — divided between that which provokes it and its intended object. Spontaneous attention comes from within the individual. It is not a divided attention, because the cause of the attention and the object of the attention are one and the same. (p. 12)

Wheat suggested that interest is intricately linked with spontaneous attention. Thus, while absorption was a *type* of attention, interest was a *cause* of attention.

Morrison (1926) suggested a relationship between motivation and attention.

The major elements in the learning situation are *motivation* and *attention*. The two elements seem to be mutually related. There is not likely to arise a sustained attention, apart from the establishment of motivation, and conversely no real motivation is possible without the development of capacity for voluntary attention to the subject matter of teaching and study (p. 103).

Morrison went on to interrelate all of the aforementioned concepts: attention, absorption, interest and motivation.

As applied to the mastery of the objectives of any given course . . . the doctrine of *interest* requires the establishment of what is called in current pedagogical terminology '*motivation*,' that is, a desire to learn. It further requires that such motivation shall not only be sustained but shall increase in intensity as the learning process goes on. A pupil studying under the influence of powerful *motivation* exhibits a characteristic type of *attention* to which we shall apply the term *absorption*. (p. 104) (my italics)

Finally, James suggested an integral relationship between attention and genius.

Geniuses are commonly believed to excel other men in their power of sustained attention . . . But it is their genius making them attentive, not their attention making geniuses of them. And when we come down to the root of the matter, we see they differ from ordinary men less in the character of their attention than in the nature of the objects upon which it is successively bestowed. (p. 423)

Thus, genius permitted an individual to attend to appropriate objects, events, and ideas (selective attention) and to concentrate for whatever period of time is necessary (sustained attention) to 'master' the object, event or idea. One is reminded of Thomas Edison's oft quoted homily that genius is one per cent inspiration (selective attention) and ninety-nine per cent perspiration (sustained attention). James's point, however, was that without the inspiration no amount of perspiration is sufficient.

Given the strength of the hypothesized attention-learning relationship, it is not surprising that implications for pedagogy were frequently discussed by writers of this era. In fact, Wheat (1931) defined teaching as 'the activity of *directing* attention effectively to the *essential* phases of a situation' (p. 1) (my italics). Some sixty years earlier Currie (1869) suggested that the

> art of teaching . . . comprehends all of the means by which the
> teacher *sustains* the attention of his class. By attention, we do not
> mean the mere absence of noise and trifling . . . The only satisfactory
> attention is that which is given voluntarily and steadily . . . during
> instruction'. (p. 264) (my italics)

In the context of the previous discussion Wheat emphasized *selective
attention* (e.g. 'the essential phases of a situation'), while Currie emphasized *sustained attention.* Effective teachers, then, were those who
directed and sustained the attention of their students.

What are some of the means by which teachers could direct and
sustain the attention of their students? Currie (1869) suggested that
'attention requires clear and unwavering exposition of the points to be
attended to' (p. 92). Wheat (1931) elaborated on Currie's suggestion.
'It makes little difference how effectively the teacher may direct
attention or how effectively the pupil may give his attention; if the
attention is fixed upon non-essentials, the intended learning will not
take place' (p. 8). As a consequence, 'if the teacher is to understand
the task of directing the attention of his pupils to the essentials in a
subject, he must first determine what the essentials are' (p. 8). For
example, 'in early number work the attention of the pupil must be
given, not to the objects used, but to the way they are grouped. The
grouping, not the objects, is the essential thing in this case' (p. 10).
Thus, focusing attention on relevant aspects of the learning situation,
instructional materials and learner activities was viewed as one principle
of effective pedagogy.

James (1890) suggested a second pedagogical principle:

> The only general pedagogic maxim bearing on attention is that the
> more interest the child has in advance in the subject, the better he
> will attend. Induct him therefore in such a way to knit each new
> thing on to some acquisition already there; and if possible awaken
> curiosity, so that the new thing shall seem to come as an answer, or
> part of an answer, to a question pre-existing in his mind. (p. 424)

Thus, effective teachers were to have (1) selected learning tasks that
were interesting; (2) related the new learning tasks to previously
acquired tasks, and (3) awakened the curiosity of the student.

In addition to the above two principles, Currie (1869) proposed a set of 'motives' for securing attention.

> We can not secure attention by mere compulsion . . . We must gain
> consent to the effort by suitable motives, and work with the law of
> habit to strengthen the power. The motives on which we must rely
> are mainly these: curiosity, love of activity, and sympathy. (p. 90)

Currie enumerated some specific ways by which curiosity, love of
activity and sympathy can be established. With respect to curiosity, for
example, 'the teacher who speaks to the intelligence of his pupils, and
interests their feelings, has no difficulty in fixing their attention' (p. 91).
Thus, teachers were to be attentive to both the intellectual and emotional qualities of their students.

'Love of activity is another motive which will sustain the child in the
act of attention . . . The teacher should, therefore, not condemn [the
child] to be a passive listener under instruction, but exercise his mind
on its subject' (p. 91). Thus, the assigned activities were to have been
enjoyable, and students needed to be engaged in learning if the students
were to learn.

Finally,

> sympathy is another guarantee for attention; which will exist in the
> pupil in proportion to the kind and degree of personal ascendency
> which the teacher has obtained. If this be well established, the child
> will make great efforts to enter into the work of the teacher, both
> from his instinct of imitation, and the happiness he derives from
> sympathy. (p. 91)

In summary, then, teachers who aroused curiosity, provided activities
that will actively engage students in the learning process, and presented
themselves as appropriate role models to be emulated and imitated by
students were likely to sustain the attention of their students.

Finally, Morrison (1926) suggested there were, in fact, pedagogical
techniques (in addition to pedagogical principles and motives) that
were appropriate for securing and holding students' attention. Such
pedagogical techniques, which Morrison referred to as 'control techniques', were believed to be necessary because not all learning had its
'own initial appeal' (p. 104). In Morrison's words,

> many of the essential elements of learning are not initially appealing
> to all pupils, and perhaps some elements lack this quality entirely. It

is conceivable that the program of study might be so skillfully arranged and teaching so aptly applied that all normal pupils would grow from interest to interest and spend their school days in a delightful career of self-motivated studies. Such an ideal school would, however, be useless unless it were the introduction to a self-motivated world. Quite the contrary, the world in which we have to live and find our happiness is full of duties and opportunities which are far from initially interesting, and the individual who has learned to react only to that which is self-motivated becomes a flabby incompetent in the world of realities. (p. 104)

Thus, sustained attention 'requires not only a willing and attentive pupil but an intelligible and forceful teacher conscious of the necessity of keeping every member of the class group with the reach of a compelling personality' (p. 107).

According to Morrison, a proper control technique would begin with the establishment of 'definite objectives of teaching in the form of mastery of definite learning units' (p. 109). Next, the teacher must be aware of the attention of their students. In this vein Judd (1918) advocated that teachers watch their students and, based on these obser-vations, address the following questions.

Attention during recitation
1. How long does a child keep his attention focused on one thing?
2. What distractions does a school room present?
3. What concession does the teacher make when pupils do not keep up concentration? For example, does he repeat questions?
4. What positive devices are adopted to keep up attention?
5. What are the physical symptoms of attention and its absence?
6. What individual differences are to be noted?
7. Do you note differences in attention at different times in the day or at different periods of the recitation?

Attention during periods of study
1. Note the way in which the student goes about his work. Is he ready to begin at once, or does he have to get matters together deliberately after he sits down?
2. Note whether he reads continuously from the book which he is studying.
3. Pay attention to the sort of thing that the student does when he looks away from the book. Does he turn his attention to other

objects, or is he trying to think about the book itself? In general, what are the distractions that seem to take his attention from his work?

4. Is his rate of work evidently slow or rapid? This can be judged by watching him long enough to see how much time he spends reading a given page.

5. Note, if you can, the different ways students study different subjects. For example, is their work in history different from their work in mathematics? If so which one seems to you to secure the highest degree of attention? (p. 324)

Based on the answers to these questions teachers were to plan specific strategies for securing and holding students' attention. Among the more common aspects of the approaches, according to Morrison, were the 'reduction of the mechanical detail of class conduct to the minimum' (p. 112), and 'control of the physical conditions under which learning goes on' (p. 113).

Despite his emphasis on control techniques, Morrison was quick to point out the limits of exclusive reliance on good control techniques in order to produce good learning.

> While poor control techniques always mean poor learning, good control technique does not necessarily mean good teaching. The material itself may be unsuitable and even false. It may be wrongly placed in the pupil's program of study . . . Control technique is of primary importance but not necessarily of chief or ultimate importance. (p. 111)

In the terminology of this chapter, if the learning tasks were inappropriate for the students, then any means of gaining attention would be to no avail. Appropriate tasks were thought to be necessary for any attempt to direct or maintain attention to be useful.

Historically, then, attention has been seen as a necessary condition for learning. More specifically, if learning was to occur learners must first have focused their attention on what they wished (or were expected) to learn. Secondly, that attention must have been sustained for sufficient periods of time. Furthermore, the teacher's role was defined in terms of the learner's role. Put simply, teachers were expected to *direct* and *maintain* the attention of their students.

The Modern Perspective on Attention and Learning

Psychologists and psycholinguists have conducted a number of empirical investigations of attention and learning over the past quarter century. Interestingly, the assumptions underlying these studies are similar to the major propositions concerning attention and learning advanced by the early educators and psychologists. What these studies have done is to provide empirical support for the validity of many of these early propositions while at the same time expanding our understanding of the nature of attention and learning as independent constructs in the context of classroom teaching and learning. This section begins with a discussion of the similarity of the assumptions underlying the present empirical examinations of attention and learning to the propositions made by the early educators and psychologists. The remainder of this section discusses additional insights that have been gained from the conduct of empirical studies over the past 25 years.

As recently as 1979 Piontkowski and Calfee found it necessary to assert that 'attention is critical to learning. If the student isn't paying attention to instruction, he won't profit from it' (p. 317). Similarly, Underwood (1976) suggested that 'unless we attend to a stimulus we are unable to remember and respond to it' (p. 169). Finally, Rothkopf (1970) contended that 'in most instructional situations, what is learned depends largely on the activities of the student' (p. 325). Rothkopf coined the phrase 'mathemagenic behaviours' to refer to such activities, a phrase which emphasizes that these activities or behaviours of the student give 'birth to learning'. In 1976 Rothkopf went a step further in relating attention to learning from written materials.

> The most carefully written and edited text will not produce the desired instructional results unless the student acts in a suitable way. The student has complete veto power over the success of written instruction. The student also has the opportunity to extend its scope substantially. (p. 94)

It is somewhat comforting to note that the attention-learning relationship is still strong and essential after all these years.

The concern of teachers for student attention also remains virtually the same as it was in the early 1900s. Consider Jackson's (1968) perspective on what teachers are trying to accomplish in their classrooms.

> Certainly no educational goals are more immediate than those that

concern the *establishment* and *maintenance* of the students' absorption in the task at hand. Almost all other objectives are dependent
for their accomplishment upon the attainment of this basic condition (p. 85) (my italics)

Then Jackson adds, almost ruefully, 'this fact seems to have been more
appreciated in the past than it is today' (p. 85).

In choosing activities and materials for use by students Jackson
suggests that teachers seem to be

> making some kind of educated guess about what would be a bene-
> ficial activity for a student or group of students and then doing
> whatever is necessary to see that participants remained involved in
> that activity. The teacher's goal, in other words, is student involve-
> ment rather than student learning. It is true, of course, that the
> teacher hopes the involvement will result in certain beneficial
> changes in the students, but learning is in this sense a by-product
> rather than the things about which the teacher is most directly con-
> cerned (p. 162).

Based on her research Merritt (1982) makes several points similar to
and supportive of Jackson's. 'The teacher wants and needs to have
access to every child's attention, with minimum effort, more or less
whenever the teacher demands it' (p. 226). Furthermore, 'teachers are
aware that for children to become sufficiently involved in their work
or to be really on-task they (the students) must tune out a great deal of
what is perceptually available to them' (p. 226). Finally, Merritt asserts
that 'teachers . . . have an important role in distributing equitably their
own attention, and also in directing each child's attention to what he or
she is expected to be involved in' (p. 233).

> The issues of distribution [of teachers' attention] may be construed
> as one of educational equity; the issue of direction (of students'
> attention) as one of educational efficacy. In these terms, it is hard to
> imagine any two aspects of classroom communication that have
> greater salience for educational practice. (p. 240)

Thus, from a pedagogical perspective, teachers remain concerned
with directing and sustaining the attention of their students. Because
of the number of students in their classrooms they also are concerned
with distributing their own attention according to the needs, interests,

and demands of their students. Also because of the number of students in their classrooms teachers are concerned with 'keeping things moving' or 'maintaining the flow of classroom activity'. This concern has been documented by a number of ecological psychologists and is described in the excellent chapter by Ross in this volume.

As can be seen the basic assumptions concerning the attention-learning and the teaching-attention relationships have changed little over the past 75 years. None the less, the modern emphasis on empiricism has lent support to these more philosophically based contentions while at the same time broadening our understanding of the nature of the complex interrelationships among the teaching, attention and learning that occurs in schools. Let us examine in somewhat greater detail the modern view of the nature of attention, and the means by which it can be gained, directed and sustained.

While early psychologists and educators had identified *two* phases of attention – selective and sustained – modern theorists and researchers have agreed that there are, in fact, *three* phases of attention. Rothkopf (1970), for example, describes what he terms three forms or classes of mathemagenic activities or behaviours. The first class is *orientation*, which refers to students being in the 'vicinity of instructional objects' (p. 328) and remaining there for suitable periods of time. The second class is *object acquisition*, which refers to 'selecting and procuring appropriate instructional objects' (p. 328). The final class is labelled *translating and processing*, which refers to 'scanning and systematic eye fixations on the instruction objects', 'translation into internal speech or internal representation', and 'discrimination, segmentation, processing, etc.' (p. 328).

Calfee (1981), attempting to synthesize the research of physiological and behavioural psychologists, also identified three phases:

1. Alertness – the general level of awareness and sensitivity to the environment;
2. Selectivity – the scanning of the environment in search of salient and goal-appropriate features;
3. Concentration – the focal act of attention, where selected elements are analyzed in detail. (p. 13)

Depending on the perspective of the particular research or theorist various synonyms exist for each of Calfee's labels. Orientation (Rothkopf, 1970) and arousal (Pribram and McGuiness, 1975) are similar in meaning to alertness. Activation (Pribram and McGuiness,

1975) is used by the physiological psychologists in place of selectivity. Finally, effort (Pribram and McGuiness, 1975; Kahneman, 1973) and central processing (Posner and Boies, 1971) are virtually identical with concentration. And, of course, *selectivity* is similar to the older concept of *selective attention*, while *concentration* is similar to the older concept of *sustained attention*.

We also have begun to understand more about the nature of these three attentional phases, particularly selectivity or selective attention. We have learned, for example, that 'the human information-processing system can concentrate on only a small number of elements at one point in time. The mind must choose continuously what to think about and how deeply to think about it' (Calfee, 1981, p. 11).

We have learned there are two cognitive processes involved in selective attention: filtering and pigeonholing (Broadbent, 1977). 'Filtering is the selection of a stimulus feature on the basis of possible interpretations. Pigeonholing is a subsequent process that matches the filtered input with information stored in the "pigeonholes" of long-term memory' (Piontkowski and Calfee, 1979, p. 308). This matching of the new material with already learned material gives meaning to the new material. If no such match is possible, no meaning can be derived.

We also have learned that concentration may or may not be necessary. Cognitive psychologists such as Neisser (1967) and physiological psychologists such as Pribram and McGuiness (1975) have proposed two levels of human information processing. While Neisser refers to these levels as preattentive and focal, Pribram and McGuiness refer to them as automatic processing and mental effort. The difference between these two levels has been stated succinctly by Piontkowski and Calfee (1981).

Preattentive or automatic processing occurs when properties of the stimulus are familiar and readily linked to experience, when they are noticed quickly and *without noticeable concentration* . . . On the other hand, focal attention takes time and intellectual effort, and often intrudes on consciousness. Only one or two tasks that require focal attention can be handled simultaneously, and anything else going on at the same time is disregarded. (p. 315) (my italics)

Thus automaticity greatly reduces, or may eliminate entirely, the need for concentration. In fact, LaBerge (1975) defines automaticity in terms of the 'gradual elimination of attention in the processing of information' (p. 58). In addition, Norman (1976) suggests that automaticity results from extensive practice. 'A general rule appears to be that when a skill is highly learned – perhaps because it has been practiced for years and years – then it becomes automated, requiring little conscious awareness, little allocation of mental effort' (p. 65).

In summary, attention appears to consist of three phases: alertness, selectivity and concentration. Quite clearly, these phases are sequential in nature. Furthermore, selectivity is composed of two subphases: filtering and pigeonholing. Finally, while alertness and selectivity are always important phases of attention, the importance of concentration depends on (1) the familiarity of the stimulus or instructional object, and (2) the degree to which practice has produced a level of automaticity of response.

In many ways the implications for teaching that can be derived from this conceptualization of attention are simple and straightforward. Teachers need to, first, generate a general level of alertness or arousal on the part of their students. Secondly, teachers need to direct students' attention to the relevant features or elements of the instructional task, material and learning experiences so as to ensure that students are on-target or on-task. Thirdly, teachers must help or encourage students to put forth the mental effort, when necessary, so that desired learning outcome or product can be acquired by the students.

Fortunately, some ideas on how teachers can perform these teaching tasks have been generated from fairly recent research studies. Introducing variety into the learning tasks keeps students alert.

> Livening a lecture with humor, posing a cut-and-dried problem in a new way, confronting students with unexpected questions, changing the art work on the walls, introducing variety into the schedule – all these make the classroom situation more interesting, novel, and stimulating. (Piontowski and Calfee, 1981, p. 303)

Similarly, providing feedback about task performance maintains student attention. Students pay attention when they are informed periodically of their progress.

Furthermore, as has been indicated earlier, focusing student attention selectively requires that the teacher point out the significant features of instructionally relevant tasks, materials, objects and situations. The teacher can do this in several ways. The teacher can, for example:

1. Emphasize critical features of a stimulus. The different parts of a

chart on blood circulation becomes distinct when each is given its own bright color.

2. Eliminate irrelevant features. In Britten's *Young Person's Guide to the Orchestra* each musical instrument has its solo moment in the concerto, when its unique sound is emphasized and all other instruments are muted.

3. Put an old stimulus in a new context. The rubbish in a local stream goes unnoticed normally, but collected and piled at the front of the classroom it becomes impressive. (Piontkowski and Calfee, 1979, p. 307)

Concentration or mental effort appears to be related to the difficulty of the task and the enjoyment in performing the task (Laffey, 1982). As a consequence, tasks should be assigned to students that they (the students) feel able to deal with comfortably and effectively. Similarly, students should enjoy engaging in the assigned tasks. Maintaining student effort or concentration also requires effective monitoring on the part of the teacher. Given the number of internal and external distractions of students in classrooms, teachers should periodically check student attention (via classroom questions and informal observation) and learning (via exercises, homework and formal tests), and redirect student attention back to the relevant features of the task as necessary. Supervising seatwork and effectively managing classrooms are two additional examples of monitoring.

If we examine the recommendations offered by our present educators, researchers and psychologists, and compare them with those offered by the early educators and psychologists, the similarities are striking (see Table 3.1). The necessity of focusing attention on appropriate tasks and directing attention to the critical features of those tasks is viewed as essential by both early and modern educators. Similarly, the need to make the new learning relevant, yet challenging, is supported by both early and modern educators. Finally, both early and modern educators realize the need to minimize the interference of external factors on the internal state of the learner(s).

The differences between the two groups of educators reside in two general areas. Early educators emphasized the need for the teachers to 'establish personal relationships with students'. Modern educators, on the other hand, realize the need to 'provide feedback (to the students) about task performance'. Thus, early educators advocated more *emotional* linkages between teacher and student; modern educators suggest the use of more *objective* means of enhancing student attention.

Table 3.1: A Comparison of Recommendations Concerning the Gaining, Directing and Sustaining of Attention

Early view	Modern view
1. Assign tasks that are appropriate to the learner	Assign tasks that students feel able to deal with comfortably and effectively
2. Assign interesting tasks	Introduce variety into learning tasks; assign enjoyable tasks
3. Focus attention on relevant aspects of situation, material, and activities	Point out significant features of instructionally relevant materials, objects, and situations
4. Relate new learning to prior learning	Match new material with already learned material ('pigeonholing')
5. Arouse curiosity	Introduce the ambiguous, unexpected; introduce variety into the schedule
6. Establish personal relationships with students	——
7. Control physical conditions under which learning goes on	——
8. Reduce mechanical detail of class conduct to a minimum	Monitor student behaviour and learning
9. ——	Provide feedback about task performance

Much of what is displayed in Table 3.1 can be summarized in a single statement. Teachers must *select* and *assign* appropriate tasks, *engage* students in the process of achieving the assigned tasks, and keep students on-task.

Time-on-task and Student Engaged Time

During the decade of the 1970s the importance of instructional and learning time was increasingly emphasized. Beginning with the publication of Carroll's (1963) 'A Model of School Learning', continuing with Bloom's (1974) treatise on 'Time and Learning', and culminating conceptually in Harnischfeger's and Wiley's (1976) expansion of the Carroll model, and empirically with the results of the Beginning Teacher Evaluation Study (Fisher, Filby, Marliave, Cahen, Dishaw, Moore and Berliner, 1978; Denham and Lieberman, 1980), the crucial role of time in learning has come to be accepted by theoreticians, researchers and practitioners alike.

Fortunately, this increased awareness and acceptance has not been without its critics. Gage (1978), for example, referred to academic learning time as a 'psychologically empty quantitative concept' (p. 75). Stallings (1980) indicated the need to move 'beyond time on task' (p. 11). Frymier (1981) suggested in the title of his essay that 'learning takes more than time-on-task' (p. 634). Finally, McNamara (1981) contended that advocacy of time-on-task was more ideologically based than research based.

In several respects, most of which were addressed in the earlier sections of this chapter, these critics are correct. Without a concern for, and an understanding of, the attentional processes which occur while students are engaged in learning, student engaged time *is* a 'psychologically empty quantitative concept'. Put simply, the concept of attention gives meaning to the term 'engaged'. It is *engaged time*, not simply *time* that is essential to student learning. This fact, however, was clearly pointed out by Carroll (1963) in his original paper.

> First, it should be understood that 'spending time' means *actually spending time on the act of learning*. 'Time' is therefore not 'elapsed time' but the time which the person is oriented to the learning task and actively engaged in learning. In common parlance, it is the time during which he is 'paying attention' and 'trying to learn' (p. 725) (my italics).

Thus, according to Carroll, the processes of orientation, selectivity, and concentration are critical features of 'spending time'.

Similarly, there must be an academic task to which students are expected to attend, become engaged, and ultimately accomplish if time-on-task is to be meaningful. One of Frymier's (1981) major criticisms of time-on-task is that the materials on which students spend their time are largely unrelated to any meaningful learning outcome.

> What is the task on which the student spends time? Almost always it involves some type of curriculum material: textbook, workbook, filmstrip, ditto sheet, or experiences with materials of various kinds. Almost never are students expected (or even allowed) simply to think, reflect, create, contemplate, or conjure up ideas on their own. One explanation for the generalization that time on task is directly related to achievement may be a function of the fact that, when the task itself requires the learner to make sense out of meaningless curriculum materials, more time results in more learning (p. 634).

Frymier continues: 'most of us like to believe that teachers specify objectives, select curriculum materials, and then contrive educational experiences for their students, in that order. Nothing could be further from the truth. Most teachers *start* with the curriculum materials' (p. 634). What Frymier stops short of saying is that many teachers who begin with the curriculum materials fail to align the materials and educational experiences with *any* learning objective or with any *specific* learning objective. Without such an alignment, learning tasks as defined by both Carroll (1963) and Doyle (1979a, 1979b) simply *do not exist*. And, if learning tasks do not exist, *students cannot be on-task*.

Doyle (1979a) highlights the need for such an alignment of materials and learning experiences (or activities) with learning goals or objectives when he differentiates time-on-task from time-on-activity. Doyle (1979a) defines activities as 'bounded segments of classroom time, for example, seatwork, tests, small-group discussion, lecture, recitation, reading' (p. 45). Quite clearly the various types of curricular materials identified by Frymier are embedded within these various activities. Doyle makes explicit the relationship between activities and tasks when he states that 'a task gives meaning to an activity by connecting elements within that activity to a purpose' (p. 45). Thus, without proper alignment of goals with activities (and, by association, with curriculum materials), the activities and materials are in fact meaningless, as Frymier suggests. Doyle (1979a) alludes to the importance of the alignment of goals, activities, and curriculum materials in a footnote. 'Most studies of teaching focus on activities rather than tasks . . . As the terms are being used here, it is more appropriate, for example, to speak of "time on activity" than "time on task" ' (p. 46).

Frymier and another critic, McNamara (1981), also maintain that the tasks must be both appropriate for, and comprehensible to, the students. Frymier suggests that

> trying to comprehend the curriculum materials available in many schools today is like trying to read a dictionary, item by item, page by page. The information is technically correct and factually accurate, in the main, but it is basically meaningless because the possibilities for relating what is there to a learner's past experience are incidental or nonexistent (p. 634).

Similarly, McNamara (1981) contends that

> the result of this sort of research [namely, the Beginning Teacher

Evaluation Study] is an enervating, *artificial curriculum* in which highly structured, mechanical learning is geared to rigid, formal testing . . . It is important that children learn basic skills and that teachers foster their learning but their education must be more than the narrow, mechanistic, *dull* curriculum implicit and explicit in the time-on-task investigations. (p. 295) (my italics)

Just as the criticism of Gage addresses the need to analyze 'what learning processes go on during academic learning time' (p. 75) (that is, the need to be concerned with the term *engaged* in the phrase 'student-engaged time'), the criticisms of Frymier and McNamara focus on the term *task* in the phrase time-on-task. For time-on-task to make sense there must be clearly defined tasks (that is, alignments of goals, curriculum materials and learning experiences) which must be appropriate for and meaningful to the students. Until there is a task, until the students attention is given or directed to the key features of the task, and until that attention is sustained through the use of the appropriate curriculum materials and learning experiences, both student engaged time and time-on-task are, in fact, psychological and pedagogically 'empty'. In light of this discussion the consistent finding that there *is* a substantial positive relationship between time-on-task and student achievement should be *surprising*, not *expected*.

This fact is not admitted by the various critics of the time-on-task research. Furthermore, the failure of many researchers to attend to (no pun intended) variables such as the nature of the learning task; the alignment of goals, materials and experiences; and the attentional or thought processes of students while they are trying to learn (see, for example, Hecht, 1978; Hudgins, 1967; Laffey, 1982), can explain many of the differing results obtained from the spate of time-on-task studies. In summary, then, an understanding of both *attention* and *task* is critical if one is to (1) design appropriate research studies, (2) correctly interpret the results of the increasing number of studies, and (3) make appropriate recommendations concerning teaching practices and techniques which follow from the results of such studies.

The Future of Attention, Task and Time

The assignment (or selection) of appropriate tasks and the provision of sufficient time in which to accomplish those tasks are two key features of effective classroom instruction. Appropriate attentional processes serve to help learners use time efficiently and enhance the likelihood of task accomplishment. Thus, it behoves teachers to assign appropriate tasks, provide sufficient time for students to learn, and find ways of activating the attentional processes.

Increased understanding of the concept of attention, both from a psychological and pedagogical perspective, is quite likely in the near future. More sophisticated instruments for examining attention and more tightly designed research studies for discovering the nature of attention will very likely emerge in the next two decades to lead to this increased understanding.

In contrast however, the likelihood that *appropriate tasks will be assigned* and that *sufficient time for acquiring the tasks will be allocated* appears small. With regard to the concept of tasks, for example, Carroll (1963) wrote that:

> in actual school practice, the various tasks to be learned are not necessarily *treated as* separate and distinct, and the process of teaching is often organized (*whether rightly so or not*) so that learning will take place 'incidentally' and in the course of other activities. (p. 724) (my italics)

Quite simply, teachers do not think in terms of tasks.

The research on teacher planning (e.g. Clark and Yinger, 1979; Shavelson and Stern, 1981) suggests that the subject-matter content and related instructional activities, *not* instructional objectives, are the basic unit of teacher planning. Frymier's (1981) comment that teachers begin with curriculum materials, not with instructional objectives, coincides with the results of this research. Students will very likely continue to engage in learning experiences and use a variety of curricular materials but precisely *what they are to learn from the experiences and materials will very likely remain unclear to both students and teachers*. Until teachers come to view learning tasks as their primary unit of instructional planning and delivery, little will change.

Furthermore, the provision of sufficient time to ensure excellence in learning also is unlikely. Two reasons can be given for this speculation. First, we know very little about the amount of time that is needed for even the brightest or fastest student to accomplish the goals contained in fairly complex learning tasks (e.g. inferring a main idea of a passage containing several paragraphs). Until we gather information about the amount of time needed to learn (which, by the way, is the denominator of Carroll's (1963) algebraic representation of his model), attempts to provide sufficient time to learn will be arbitrary and futile.

Secondly, the vast majority of schools and teachers appear to be far more concerned with *coverage* of material than *mastery* of specific learning tasks. In view of the fact that the amount of time allocated to schooling has changed very little over the past century (e.g. 180 days per year, 6 hours per day) while the amount of knowledge and number of skills available to be taught to students has increased dramatically, there simply is more to cover than there used to be. Until some order is brought out of the chaos of coverage by establishing priorities among the possible learning tasks, time will continue to be allocated to an increasing number of objectives or content areas, with insufficient time being allocated to any given objective or content area.

Despite this negative view of the future, the concept of time-on-task or student engaged time remains central to the learning of a large number of students in a variety of classrooms. Increased understanding of the concept, wise application of it to classroom practice, and constructive criticism of both the concept and its application should result in the continued inclusion of attention, time, and task in any comprehensive model of school learning.

References

Bloom, B.S. (1974) 'Time and Learning', *American Psychologist, 29*, 682-8

Broadbent, D.E. (1977) 'The Hidden Preattentive Processes', *American Psychologist, 32*, 109-18

Calfee, R.C. (1981) 'Cognitive Psychology and Educational Practice' in D.C. Berliner (ed.), *Review of Research in Education, Volume 9*, Washington: American Educational Research Association

Carroll, J.B. (1963) 'A Model of School Learning', *Teachers College Record, 64*, 723-33

Cherry, E.C. (1953) 'Some Experiments on the Recognition of Speech, with One and with Two Ears', *Journal of the Acoustical Society of America, 25*, 975-9

Clark, C. and Yinger, R. (1979) 'Teachers' Thinking' in P. Peterson and H. Walberg (eds), *Research on Teaching*, Berkeley: McCutchan Publishing

Currie, J. (1869) *The Principles and Practice of Common-school Education*, Edinburgh: Thomas Laurie

Denham, C. and Lieberman, A. (1980) *Time to Learn*, Washington: National Institute of Education

Doyle, W. (1979a) 'Making Managerial Decisions in Classrooms' in D. Duke (ed.), *Classroom Management*, Chicago: University of Chicago Press

—— (1979b) 'Classroom Tasks and Students' Abilities' in P. Peterson and H. Walberg (eds), *Research on Teaching*, Berkeley: McCutchan Publishing

Fisher, C.W., Filby, N., Marliave, R., Cahen, L., Dishaw, M., Moore, J. and Berliner, D. (1978) *Teaching and Learning in the Elementary School: A Summary of the Beginning Teacher Evaluation Study, Report VII-1*. San Francisco: Far West Laboratory for Educational Research and Development

Frymier, J. (1981) 'Learning Takes More Than Time on Task', *Educational Leadership, 38*, 634, 649

Gage, N.L. (1978) *The Scientific Basis of the Art of Teaching*, New York: Teachers College Press

Harnischfeger, A. and Wiley, D.E. (1976) 'The Teaching-Learning Process in Elementary Schools: a Synoptic View', *Curriculum Enquiry, 6*, 5-43

Hecht, L. (1978) 'Measuring Student Behavior During Group Instruction', *Journal of Educational Research, 71*, 283-90

Hudgins, B.B. (1967) 'Attending and Thinking in the Classroom', *Psychology in the Schools, 4*, 211-16

Jackson, P.W. (1968) *Life in Classrooms*, New York: Holt, Rinehart & Winston

James, W. (1890) *The Principles of Psychology, Volume 1*, New York: Henry Holt & Co.

Judd, C.H. (1918) *Introduction to the Scientific Study of Education*, Boston: Ginn & Co.

Kahneman, D. (1973) *Attention and Effort*, Englewood Cliffs, NY: Prentice-Hall

LaBerge, D. (1975) 'Acquisition of Automatic Processing in Perceptual and Associative Learning' in P.M.A. Rabbit and S. Dornic (eds), *Attention and Performance*, London: Academic Press

Laffey, J.M. (1982) 'The Assessment of Involvement with School Work among Urban High School Students', *Journal of Educational Psychology, 74*, 62-71

McNamara, D.R. (1981) 'Attention, Time-on-Task and Children's Learning: Research or Ideology? *Journal of Education for Teaching, 7*, 284-97

Merritt, M. (1982) 'Distributing and Directing Attention in Primary Classrooms' in L.C. Wilkerson (ed.), *Communicating in the Classroom*, New York: Academic Press

Morrison, H.C. (1926) *The Practice of Teaching in the Secondary School*, Chicago: University of Chicago Press

Neisser, U. (1967) *Cognitive Psychology*, New York: Appleton-Century-Crofts

Norman, D.A. (1969) *Memory and Attention: An Introduction to Human Information Processing*, New York: John Wiley & Sons

Piontkowski, D. and Calfee, R.C. (1979) 'Attention in the Classroom' in G. Hale and M. Lewis (eds), *Attention and Cognitive Development*, New York: Plenum Publishing

Posner, M.I. and Boies, S.J. (1971) 'Components of Attention', *Psychological Review, 78*, 391-408

Pribram, K.H. and McGuiness, D. (1975) 'Arousal, Activation, and Effort in the Control of Attention', *Psychological Review, 82*, 116-49

Rothkopf, E.Z. (1970) 'The Concept of Mathemagenic Activities', *Review of Educational Research, 40*, 325-36

—— (1976) 'Writing to Teach and Reading to Learn: A Perspective on the Psychology of Written Instruction', *The Psychology of Teaching Methods*, Chicago: University of Chicago

Shavelson, R. and Stern, P. (1981) 'Research on Teachers' Pedagogical Thoughts, Judgements, Decisions and Behavior', *Review of Educational Research, 51*, 455-98

Stallings, J. (1980) 'Allocated Academic Learning Time Revisited, or Beyond Time on task', *Educational Researcher, 9*(11), 11-16

Underwood, G. (1976) *Attention and Memory*, Oxford, UK: Pergamon Press

Wheat, H.G. (1931) *The Psychology of the Elementary School*, New York: Silver, Burdette & Co.

4 CLASSROOM SEGMENTS: THE STRUCTURING OF SCHOOL TIME*

Rhonda P. Ross

At the beginning of each school year teachers are assigned a group of students and given various resources to use to teach them. One of the most important resources provided is time: the teacher has to decide how much time to allocate to various topics and activities. Since the total amount of time is fixed, time allocated for one activity necessarily limits the amount of time given to other activities. A major part of teacher decision-making is deciding how best to use the limited amount of available time.

Descriptive accounts of how teachers use their school time have been approached from a variety of perspectives. The most common approach has been to report the amount of time devoted to various curricular areas. Teachers are in fact often required to account for their time usage in this manner in order to verify that they have met minimum standards set by administrators.

While reports of the amount of time devoted to various *content areas* provide useful information, such reports do not inform us about the many different kinds of *activities* that teachers arrange for students. In this chapter the kinds of activities most common in elementary schools will be examined; and studies testing the relationship between characteristics of an activity and teacher and student behaviour will also be discussed. Finally, several aspects of the *structure* of the school day will be inspected. Structural characteristics of school activities to be considered include: the number of activities occurring throughout the day, the duration of each activity, the sequencing of activities within the daily schedule, and the extent and implications of having more than one activity operate simultaneously within a classroom. It will be argued that decisions regarding the structure of the school day can affect both the amount of time that children have available for learning, and the amount of time that children are manifestly engaged while an activity is in progress. The questions and answers generated by research

*This chapter was written while the author was supported by NICHHD training grant 5T32HD07173-04.

69

on these issues are much conditioned by the research stance and method-ologies employed. Therefore, some discussion of the methodological tools developed by classroom researchers is in order.

The Use of Ecological Methods to Study Classroom Operations

Educators and psychologists are adept at observing the behaviour of individuals, and for the researcher interested in conducting such obser-vations, a myriad of observational tools are readily available. Indeed, Simon and Boyer (1970) compiled a list of 67 observational systems for studying students and/or teachers; yet such instruments are of little value when the focus of one's interest is redirected from the behaviour of a particular individual to the activities operating within an entire classroom. For such research, ecological methods have proved to be useful.

Using Classroom Chronicles to Record Classroom Operations

Building on the methods developed by Barker (1968) and Wright (1967), Gump (1967, 1969, 1974) developed a methodology which he termed 'classroom chronicles'. Based on specimen record methodology, the classroom chronicle strives to be a permanent, narrative description of everyday behaviour in school settings. Basically, to make a classroom chronicle an observer enters a classroom situation and records in every-day language all events that occur in the classroom. To aid in the recording of the many events and messages common in the typical classroom, various mechanial devices (e.g. time-lapse photography, tape recorders, Stenomasks) have been utilized. Gump (1967) has com-pletely described the procedures to be used in making a classroom chronicle.

When an observer makes a traditional specimen record, an individual child is selected for study, and that child is followed by the observer wherever he or she goes throughout the observation period. Similarly, in classroom-chronicle recording, an individual is selected to focus on while making the record. However, unlike a specimen record which records only the environments entered by the individual and the behaviours emitted by the individual, in chronicle recording, the 'target' individual is used only as a means of focusing the observer's attention in the complex classroom environment. In chronicle record-ing the observer must also record activities that occur in the classroom simultaneously to those activities involved in by the target individual.

The purpose of chronicle recording is to obtain as complete a record as possible of the activities operating in a classroom. Classroom chronicles are *not* meant to be a complete record of a particular individual's behaviour. When making a classroom chronicle, it is less important to record every single behaviour and nuance of the target person's behaviour than it is to be complete in the description of the activities operating in the classroom.

Using Activity Segments as a Natural Unit of Classroom Operations

One important feature common to all ecological research methods is that instead of imposing arbitrary units of time when recording and analyzing events (e.g. 5-minute intervals), events are continuously recorded, and the natural boundaries of the events are identified and used in data analyses. The natural unit of classroom activity identified and used by Gump (1969) has been termed an *activity segment*.

Segments are a unit of activity similar to what teachers ordinarily call 'lessons'. However, activities that occur during the day that teachers would consider procedural activities instead of lessons (e.g. attendance and lunch counts, recess, snack time) would also be included as segments. In addition, some lessons that consist of two or more distinct activity patterns would be identified as being composed of more than one segment (e.g. the teacher introducing a new maths concept to a group of children followed by an assignment in which the children complete a worksheet in order to test their understanding of the new maths concept).

There are certain characteristics shared by all activity segments. First, each segment has a *concern*. Concerns may describe various academic fields (e.g. arithmetic, reading, science); artistic matters (e.g. art, music, cooking); or classroom activity maintenance (e.g. attendance, milk-money collection, dismissal routines). The concern of a segment is the segment's 'business' or 'what it is all about'.

Besides having a concern, each activity segment has what Gump (1969) has termed an *activity pattern*. The activity pattern of a segment is the 'programme of action' for a segment and defines how the segment operates. There are many dimensions that could be used to describe the activity pattern of a segment. Gump identified the following five dimensions as descriptors of segment activity: (1) the nature of teacher participation in the activity, (2) the grouping of pupils, (3) the prescribed action relationship between pupils, (4) the kinds of actions taken by pupils, and (5) the way in which pupil action is paced. For each of these dimensions codes have been developed and utilized to describe classroom operations in second-grade classes (Grannis, 1978), third-grade classes (Gump, 1969), in third, fourth and fifth-grade classes (Silverstein, 1979), in fifth-grade classes (Stodolsky, 1979, 1981; Stodolsky, Ferguson and Wimpelberg, 1981), and in schools of open and traditional architecture (Gump, 1974).

In addition to a concern and an activity pattern, activity segments also have physical and temporal boundaries. They occur in a particular location, contain specific behaviour objects, and operate across a particular time span.

A final important characteristic of activity segments is that the behaviours expected or demanded of the participants are congruent with the physical aspects of the setting. This congruence of compatibility of participants' behaviours and physical setting has been termed *synomorphy* (Barker, 1968). In a discussion segment, for example, participants are expected to engage in a verbal interchange of ideas. If the classroom is set up in long rows of desks, all facing toward the front of the room and bolted to the floor, a discrepancy between the behavioural demands and expectations of the segment and the physical arrangement of the classroom exists, and a lack of synomorphy is evident. In such situations modifications must occur in the physical milieu and/or in the nature of the appropriate activities and behaviours until a higher degree of synomorphy is achieved (Gump and Ross, 1977, 1979; Ross, 1980, 1982).

The use of segments makes it possible to describe classrooms in a manner that respects their structure and internal differentiation. When activity segments are identified, coded and analyzed they provide a quantified picture of the classroom day. In the first study utilizing classroom chronicles, Gump (1967), catalogued the activities entered by third-grade students throughout the school day. Not only has this methodology been found to be useful in describing classroom operations, but the activity codes he developed have been found to be useful in predicting student and teacher behaviour in segments of contrasting activity patterns.

Gump's research, as well as the research of other investigators who have adopted his methods, clearly demonstrates that the behaviour of students and teachers is affected by characteristics of the activity. In the next section we will examine the kinds of activity segments in which students and teachers are more frequently involved. We will also examine the relationship between segments with contrasting activity patterns and the behaviour of segment inhabitants.

Activity Segments and their Effects on Behaviour

As already mentioned, most researchers who have examined how time is used in school have catalogued the use of time in terms of the proportion of time spent in different curricular areas. There is substantially less information available regarding the various kinds of activities in which children participate throughout the school day. Further, researchers who have examined the kinds of activities that operate in elementary school classrooms have typically limited their observations to particular curriculum areas, or to comparisons of preselected, contrasting activities. Thus, it is difficult to make generalizations regarding the kinds of activities that typically operate throughout an entire school day.

While the current state of the research literature makes it difficult to make definitive statements regarding the average amount of time spent in different kinds of activities, a few conclusions regarding activity segments can be offered. First, apparently relatively few different kinds of activity formats are used by elementary school teachers. Gump (1967) coded the activity patterns that operated in traditional third-grade classrooms. His code allowed for the logical possibility of 2,535 different kinds of activities, based on the various combinations of the five facets of activity patterns included in his code. Despite this large number of different kinds of activities that were logically possible, seven activity patterns accounted for over half of the 374 segments that he coded and almost two-thirds of the students' time. Furthermore, Gump's data indicated that recitations and seatwork were the two activities that clearly dominated how time was spent in these classrooms. (Recitation refers to a series of teacher questions and student responses, with the teacher commenting on the adequacy of the responses and/or using the responses to provide additional instructionally-relevant information to the students. Seatwork refers to a variety of activities that children do when working at their seats, e.g. reading a book, working computation problems, reading paragraphs or longer passages, and answering assigned questions, practising material taught earlier by the teacher).

The work of other researchers similarly indicates that the formats most frequently used in elementary schools are variations of what could be considered seatwork and recitation activities. Rosenshine (1978) reported that overall, elementary school students spend over two-thirds of their academic time in seatwork and most of their remaining time in recitations. The amount of time students spend in seatwork varies in different curricula areas. Rosenshine (1980) found that during reading, students spend about 66 per cent of their time doing seatwork, while students spend 75 per cent of their time doing seatwork during mathematics.

Of course, not all teachers rely so heavily on seatwork activities. Bossert (1979) conducted a study in which he compared teachers who used predominantly seatwork activities in their classrooms with teachers who relied heavily on recitations. Still, even the teachers in Bossert's study who were characterized as the 'recitation teachers' used seatwork activities for over one-third of the school day. At this time we do not know how much variability exists in the extent to which different teachers use various activities.

A second conclusion that can be made regarding the various activity segments that operate in elementary school classrooms is that the behaviour of teachers and students is significantly related to the activity pattern of segments. A substantial number of studies have found lawful relationships between the format of school activities and the behaviour of activity participants. Three of the earliest studies to examine the relationship between activity formats and student behaviour were conducted by Shure (1963) in a nursery school, by Kowatrakul (1959) in an elementary school, and by Edmiston and Braddock (1941) in a secondary school. More recently, studies have been conducted by Bossert (1977, 1979), Grannis (1978), Gump (1969, 1974), Kounin and his colleagues (Kounin, 1970; Kounin and Doyle, 1975; Kounin and Gump, 1974; Kounin and Sherman, 1979), Silverstein (1979), and Stodolsky and her colleagues (Stodolsky, 1979, 1981; Stodolsky, Ferguson and Wimpleberg, 1981).

While a variety of dependent variables have been used when examining the relationship between the format of an activity and the behaviour of participants, the behaviour most frequently examined has been student involvement. Because of space limitations we will limit our discussion to this one variable. Student involvement has been selected as our focus for discussion not only because there is the most research on this variable, but also because identification of the correlates of student involvement or 'on-task behaviour' is a critical task for educational researchers.

The Importance of Identifying the Correlates of Student Involvement

Teachers apparently have two related concerns regarding the behaviour of students. First, teachers (as well as parents and school administrators) are concerned with the control of misbehaviour (Gallup, 1975).

Secondly, teachers want to gain the attention of their students and to ensure that students become involved, and remain involved, in classroom activities (Doyle, 1979). Not only are teachers evaluated by others by how well they are able to control their students' attention, but teachers often evaluate their own performance in terms of how well children attend to the task (Applegate, 1969; Doyle, 1979; Jackson, 1968; Yinger, 1977). Researchers concerned with the processes involved in teacher planning have collected data which indicate that pupil involvement is the criterion most often used by teachers in judging the adequacy of their plans, both before they are actually implemented and following the completion of the lesson (Yinger, 1977).

Some educators have argued that students can easily learn to look involved, and that using involvement as an objective can foster docility and compliance among students (Winett and Winkler, 1972). However, there exists a large body of research that clearly indicates that the amount of time that students are actively engaged with learning materials is a reliable and significant predictor of student achievement (Block and Burns, 1976; Bloom, 1976; Brophy and Evertson, 1976; Stallings and Kaskowitz, 1974). Clearly, educational researchers need to understand the many factors that influence the amount of time students spend involved with learning materials, and they should be able to suggest ways for teachers to maximize student involvement.

Several different approaches have been taken to identify the correlates of student involvement, including examination of pupil characteristics (e.g. age, SES, ability level) and teacher skills and training (e.g. teaching experience, educational background, clarity of instructions, use of positive reinforcement). Some researchers have also examined characteristics of the educational programme in their search for factors related to student involvement.

Student Involvement in Contrasting Activity Segments

While students spend much of their day in seatwork, research indicates that children often are not engaged in their work for much of the time they are in such activities. Rosenshine (1980) reported that overall, students were engaged or involved in work only 68 per cent of the time during seatwork. In contrast, students were observed as being engaged 84 per cent of the time during recitations. Further, when a large proportion of allocated time was spent in seatwork (e.g. 90 per cent), student engagement was reduced even further, particularly in mathematics. Other researchers who have compared student involvement during recitations and seatwork have similarly found that students are on-task more during recitations than during seatwork activities, and that extended periods of seatwork lower student involvement, particularly among low achievers (Good and Beckerman, 1978; Stallings and Kaskowitz, 1974; Soar, 1973).

It is possible to explain the findings of significantly higher levels of involvement during recitations as compared with seatwork, by examining the activity patterns of these activities. In general, recitations are task oriented, and require continual focus on classroom activities. The teacher generally takes a central role as recitation leader, setting the pace for pupils' performance and directing the lesson. All students are expected to be actively and continually involved in the segment activities, directing their interactions toward the entire group. Physical movement and non-task interaction is actively discouraged by the teacher during such activities. Although seatwork segments are also task oriented, students engaged in seatwork are expected to focus on their own materials and assignments rather than on other students' activities. Typically, the teacher acts only as a supervisor, or sometimes as tutor, during seatwork, and is not available to provide constant feedback to students or answer their questions as they arise. Working alone, seatwork students set their own pace. Students are not required to demonstrate their continuous progress in the activity, although teachers generally do hold students accountable for completing their assignment. Generally, students are not required to interact with one another during seatwork, although they might be allowed to talk or to seek help from their peers.

Gump (1967) found that third-grade students were more involved under the following segment conditions: (1) when student activity was externally paced rather than self-paced, (2) when the students worked with the teacher in small groups rather than with the total class, and (3) when the format of the activity required that students attend to the teacher or to other students for a short contribution from a peer, as opposed to segments that were based on extended peer presentations. The activity patterns that Gump found to be associated with high involvement are characteristics found in most recitations. Conversely, those features which Gump found to be correlated with low involvement are present in many seatwork activities.

Although research clearly indicates that students spend most of their academic time in seatwork activities and that the engagement rate for this format is relatively low, only recently have researchers begun to direct their attention to the study of seatwork activities. Instead, educational researchers have devoted more research effort to the study of recitations than to any other instructional format. (See Hoetker and Ahlbrand (1969) for a review of this literature.)

Future research should concentrate less on the recitation format and instead examine ways to improve student involvement during seatwork. Based on the research discussed in this section, it could be predicted that if teachers modified the kinds of tasks that children were assigned while working individually at their seats, student involvement during seatwork could probably be increased. For instance, teachers could assign seatwork activities in which a source external to the child controlled the pace of the input. The use of audio-visual media, operated by the child, would be one way that this could be accomplished. A second way that teachers could arrange activities for children with an external source of pacing would be by using children as tutors for one another. With one child in the role of the tutor, and another child acting as the tutee, part of the tutor's role becomes control of the pacing of the activity. In such an arrangement the involvement of the tutee should be higher than if the same task was being accomplished independently of a peer. Delquadri, Greenwood and Hall (1979) have indicated how 'opportunity to respond', an aspect of pacing, can be enhanced through peer tutoring.

When researchers select instructional formats to study, one criterion should be to focus on those formats that are utilized most. Another criterion should be to select formats for study that are most difficult for teachers to manage. On the basis of both of these criteria, it appears that the seatwork format is a prime area for future research.

Structure of the School Day

Not only must teachers decide how much time to devote to each content area and what kinds of activities to plan for students, but they must also decide how best to integrate the various activities into the school day. There are few other jobs in our society in which one adult has the responsibility of planning, creating, managing and dissolving a day-long sequence of activities for a group of individuals. Teachers must decide the duration of each activity, how many activities to schedule for a particular day, how to sequence the activities, and whether to schedule activities simultaneously. The results of such decisions all have significant effects upon the *structure* of the school day.

Far more attention has been given to the specific activities teachers use to fill school time than has been given to how teachers structure school time. However, the few researchers who have examined the effects of various activity structures have obtained data that suggest that this is an important aspect of classroom life and a promising area for additional research. In this section we will report the few facts known regarding the structure of the school day, and discuss some of the effects of variations in the structure of segments. Because of the limited amount of information available on this topic, speculations regarding how variations in the structure of segments can affect the amount of time available for instruction will also be included. Some of these speculations might suggest directions for future research in this area.

Number and Duration of Segments

Researchers who have observed classroom operations in elementary schools have reported that at these grade levels, there are typically over 30 segments operating each day (Gump, 1967; Kounin, 1970). Approximately two-thirds of these segments are major changes from the surrounding segments, while the remaining third involve only minor changes in activity, and most often involve subparts of what teachers might consider one lesson (e.g. an entire class viewing a film together, followed by students dividing into groups of five to plan a film-based group project).

In the study of classroom activity segments conducted by Gump (1967) there was little variability in the structure of segments among the teachers or for the same teacher on different days. Gump stated that, 'It may be that the general demands of the prescribed curriculum interacting with the limited time available in one day hold the number of major segments to a relatively constant number.' However, because Gump's sample was restricted to one grade level (third grade), one day of the week (Wednesday), and occurred only in schools with both traditional educational programmes and traditional physical designs, we do not know whether the segment structure would be similar in other kinds of classes. Clearly, more research is needed in which the number and duration of segments that operate throughout the day are observed before generalizations can be made.

Recently, several researchers have used the segment concept to study the number and kinds of segments used within a particular academic curriculum, instead of throughout an entire school day. For instance, Kirley (1981) examined the number of mathematics activity segments fifth-grade students occupied each day. She found that students averaged just over two instructional segments devoted to mathematics per day. Only 13 per cent of class days had more than three mathematics segments.

What are the effects of variations in the number of segments that occur and of variations in the length of segments? Educational folklore would suggest that because children have very short attention spans, a schedule involving many short segments would lead to higher levels of student attention than a schedule with fewer and longer segments. Kirley (1981) recently examined the relationship between the mean number of mathematics segments and student attention. The data indicated that attention was *not* related to the mean number of segments. However, attention was related to the interaction of mean number of segments and length of the mathematics period. Kirley found that when class periods were relatively long, students who experienced more segments attended more than students who experienced fewer segments. In longer periods, three or more segments per period produced a modest increase in attention. However, when class periods were relatively short, an increase in the number of segments experienced was associated with relatively low attention. Kirley concluded that greater variety enhanced attention only if there is sufficient time in the class period to allow for more segments. If there is not sufficient time, having to change one's activities frequently apparently detracts from attention.

Sequencing of Activities

Another structural characteristic of school schedules that teachers must make decisions about is the sequencing of segments. There are no data available that systematically describe the sequences of activities that occur throughout the school day. There are many ways, however, that sequences could be described. For example, it would be possible to describe the sequencing of activities in terms of their length. That is, do teachers alternate relatively long and relatively short segments with one another, or do they tend to have segments of equal duration follow one another?

A second way to describe the sequence of activities that occur throughout the school day would be in terms of the variability in the activity patterns of temporally adjacent segments. Krantz and Risley (1977) found that going from recess directly to story time resulted in 37 per cent off-task behaviour at the beginning of the story. They inserted a short 'rest period' before the story segment, and found that visual attention to the teacher and/or to books throughout the story was much greater when the session was preceded by the rest period than when it was preceded by vigorous activity. Off-task behaviour was reduced to 14 per cent by this manipulation. Further, transition times were longer and more disruptive when the story was preceded by vigorous instead of more passive activities. On the basis of these findings, Krantz and Risley recommended that an activity that prohibits children from being physically mobile should not be immediately preceded by a session that permits or encourages boisterousness or large motor behaviour. Another interpretation of Krantz's and Risley's study would be that long segments should be separated with short segments. Until additional research is conducted regarding the effects of alternate sequencing of activities, we cannot make recommendations to teachers regarding how best to accomplish this task.

Operating Simultaneous Activity Segments

One of the most important characteristics about the structure of school activity segments is that they do not always occur sequentially, but instead two, or sometimes even more, segments completely or partially overlap with one another in time. In an initial study of the structure of the school day, Gump (1967) found that during 35 per cent of the school day traditional third-grade teachers managed overlapping segments. Almost all of the parallel segments involved some students studying in seatwork while the teacher worked directly with another group of students. The maximum number of overlapping segments operating at any time in the six third-grade classes Gump observed was two. However, he reported that one third-grade class observed during a pilot investigation often had three, and sometimes four, segments operating at the same time.

When simultaneous segments operate, the teacher has *created* a relatively complex structure which must then be co-ordinated and supervised. Beginning teachers, who are probably inexperienced with the management of simultaneously operating segments, might prefer to avoid such situations during their first few months of teaching. Unfortunately, this is not a choice they are often permitted. The curriculum guides in areas such as reading and sometimes mathematics are particularly likely to suggest the use of small-group activities. When a sub-sample of the class engages in a small-group activity, the rest of the students obviously must also be given an activity to do during that period of time. If the class is self-contained, and has only one teacher and no aides, it is the responsibility of that one teacher to manage both segments.

When more than one segment operates simultaneously within a

classroom, the situation can be not only difficult for teachers, but also for students. When teachers are actively involved in one segment, students in the other segment(s) are left to 'fend for themselves'. Students generally need to provide their own structure and pacing when they are working without a teacher. Further, most teachers do not allow students to interrupt them when they are involved in a simultaneously operating segment. Thus, students face a dilemma regarding what to do when they need assistance with an assignment, or when they complete an assignment and do not know what to do next (Silverstein, 1979). It is important for teachers to realize when scheduling simultaneous activity segments that if the programme of one segment utilizes the teacher as a continuous source of input for the students, then the programme of the second segment cannot permit children to seek attention from the teacher, but must still ensure that students are able to complete their assignment successfully.

In addition to creating problems for teachers and students, simultaneously operating segments also condition one another. This mutual conditioning becomes an increasingly powerful factor as more and more action centres with different leaders share the same space – as occurs in open-plan schools. The range of activity patterns that can successfully be used when segments operate simultaneously is restricted. When two segments operate simultaneously in a shared space, they must operate without too much intrusion upon one another. Many teachers place small-group-work areas in a corner of the room to diminish intrusions, but even so, the programme of one segment cannot call for loud and exuberant actions if the programme of the second demands silence. Noise stemming from the activity of one segment can become distracting to students in the other segment. Silverstein (1979) reported that in one classroom she observed, a reading group became extremely noisy and excited as pupils enthusiastically acted out parts in a play from their reading text. Many of the students at their seats began to ignore their own work in order to listen to the play.

What are the conditions that lead teachers to create overlapping segments, and how successful are teachers in managing these segments once they are created? Unfortunately, researchers have not yet investigated such questions. Another critical area for future research would be investigations of the kinds of segments that can best operate simultaneously.

Transitions

One of the results of having a sequence of activity segments that operate throughout the day is that each time one segment ends and another is about to begin, some time is spent by the teacher and students dissolving one setting and creating a new one. It is during this transitional time that materials get distributed or put away, pupils and teachers move to new locations, instructions for the upcoming task are given, and behaviour orientations change.

One of the consistent findings of studies on the use of time in elementary schools, is that much time is spent in transitions and other non-instructional activities. Several data sources, both in England (Bennett, Andreae, Hegarty and Wade, 1980) and in the United States (Borg, 1980; Gump, 1974) indicate that approximately 20 per cent of in-class time (approximately 45 minutes) is typically spent in non-instructional activities.

The amount of time spent in transitions and other procedural or non-instructional activities, can be influenced by variables such as grade level, and the 'openness' of the educational building and/or programme of instruction. Bennett *et al.* (1980) found that on the average, more time was spent in non-instructional activities and transitions in infant, as compared to junior schools in England (22.2 per cent and 13 per cent respectively), transitions accounting for most of the non-instructional time. Whether this difference in time usage was due to developmental differences between younger and older children or to differences in their school programmes was not analyzed or discussed.

Gump (1974) documented the amount of time spent in transition in two open and two self-contained schools. Open schools encouraged frequent regrouping of students at new sites. When materials and pupils were in various locations, management of transitions was more complex, and took more time, than when all materials were centrally located and the pupils assigned to the teacher remained the same throughout the day. When a number of teachers and pupils were using a limited number of sites in sequence, rather tight schedules had to be established. An on-going activity in one area had to be promptly terminated at the end of the scheduled time, or the next user group would be kept waiting. In the open-plan schools children were often kept waiting to begin activities because teachers were busy closing out a previous one, or dealing with a special problem. Teachers in self-contained classrooms have more elasticity in their schedules than teachers in open-plan buildings, and have more freedom to control the start of the transition phase. When a teacher and a group stay in one locale, the teacher can handle special problems and still start the next segment.

Reducing the Length of Transitions. While the studies just reviewed indicate that more time is spent in transition among younger, as compared to older students, and in open as compared to traditional buildings, once teachers are assigned to a particular grade level and building they have little control over these factors during the remainder of the school year. However, there are organizational strategies and management techniques that might help teachers reduce the amount of time they spend involved in transitions. This should be a concern of all teachers, since as discussed previously, there is a significant relationship between the amount of time students spend in academic activities and their scholastic achievement. Time spent in transition takes away time that could be used for segments with an academic concern.

Gump and Good (1976) offered two ways that the length of transitions could be reduced in open-design schools. First, they suggested designing 'anchor places' near teaching areas. If needed materials and resources are distant from locations at which teachers begin segment action, increased time to start activities must be expected. Secondly, the location of activities can be manipulated. With fewer major site changes and with longer periods in one place, the length of transitions could be reduced. Unfortunately, neither of these possibilities has been tested experimentally.

Many different kinds of transitions occur in the typical elementary school classroom. Some transitions are much more complex, and thus would probably take longer to complete than others. For example, transitions which involve getting the whole class ready to move to another part of the building (e.g. the gymnasium, music or art room) are quite different from transitions that occur within the classroom (e.g. changing from a reading to a maths lesson). Transitions that involve overlapping activity segments have different managerial demands than have transitions between two sequential activity segments. At this time we do not know how the complexity of a transition and its managerial demands affect its length. The three structural variables discussed in this section (i.e. the number and durations of segments that operate throughout the school day, the way the segments are sequenced, and the extent to which segments operate simultaneously) could all affect the amount of time and effort devoted to transition activities by teachers and students.

While there has not yet been a sufficient number of studies conducted for us to make general statements regarding the structure of the 'average' school day, or to be able to state the degree of variability in the structure within or between classes, it is clear that the school day has a definite structure, and that this structure can be quantitatively described. Such descriptions can be based on features such as the number of segments that operate, the length of segments, the way segments are sequenced, and the extent to which segments operate simultaneously rather than sequentially in time.

We have suggested that the major impact of variations in segment structures is probably on the amount of time available for instruction. As the segment structure increases in complexity, it is likely that more time will be devoted to managing the segments and to the transition phases between segments, thus taking away some of the time that would otherwise be available for academic instruction.

Planning the Use of School Time

Probably one of the most critical periods of the school year is the time when the teacher creates the weekly schedule of activities for his or her class. When planning the activities the teacher can control what will occur in the classroom. Once the teacher has decided which activities will occur and when they will occur, the teacher is left only with the job of implementing the planned activities. Modifications to the schedule can be made throughout the year, and unexpected events will modify the schedule, but generally, what is planned to occur during a particular period of time generally will occur. Once the planned activities begin, the behaviours of the teacher and students are determined to a large degree by the nature of the activities. Teachers generally consider the skill levels of children, their interests and needs, when planning lessons. However, if students behave differently in different kinds of activities regardless of student characteristics, then teachers need to consider also the possible effects of the format of activities when planning lessons for students. As discussed in this chapter, the activity pattern of a lesson can influence the degree to which students maintain their involvement in the activity.

Also discussed in this chapter was the importance of considering carefully the temporal relationship between segments. Unfortunately, there is little research available to help teachers structure the school day. Teachers probably use previous experiences and their intuition regarding how many activities they should plan, and how they can best sequence activities. Do some teachers arrive at better schedules than others? Do some teachers evaluate the success of their schedules and make modifications to their schedule as they obtain feedback regarding the programme of activities that were planned?

For most elementary school teachers the structure of much of the school day is under their control. However, all teachers must work within various constraints when arranging their schedule. Do some teachers, in some schools, have more constraints than others? Are these self-imposed constraints or constraints imposed by other teachers, the principal, or district or state requirements? Most importantly, how do teachers accommodate the many constraints that they might need to consider when arranging their schedules at the beginning of the year? Little is currently known about the constraints that affect the teacher's scheduling of activities, or of differences among teachers in the scheduling of the school day. However, with the capacity to group or to utilize the events of the classroom over time, as is provided in a segment approach to classroom operations, useful research on the structure of the school day should be much facilitated.

References

Applegate, J.R. (1969) 'Why Don't Pupils Talk in Class Discussions?', *The Clearing House, 44*(2), 78-81

Barker, R.G. (1968) *Ecological Psychology: Concepts and Methods for Studying the Environment of Human Behavior*, Stanford, Ca.: Stanford University Press

Bennett, S.N., Andreae, J., Hegarty, P. and Wade, B. (1980) *Open Plan Schools*, Windsor, England: NFER Publishing Co.

Block, J.H. and Burns, R.B. (1976) 'Mastery Learning', in L.S. Shulman (ed.), *Review of Research in Education*, vol. 4, Itasca: F.E. Peacock

Bloom, B.S. (1976) *Human Characteristics and School Learning*, New York: McGraw-Hill

Borg, W.R. (1980) 'Time and School Learning', in C. Denham and A. Lieberman (eds), *Time to Learn*, Washington, DC: National Institute of Education

Bossert, S.T. (1977) 'Tasks, Group Management, and Teacher Control Behavior: A Study of Classroom Organization and Teacher Style', *School Review, 85*, 552-65

—— (1979) *Tasks and Social Relationships in Classrooms: A Study of Instructional Organization and its Consequences*, New York: Cambridge University Press

Brophy, J. and Evertson, C. (1976) *Learning from Teaching: A Developmental Perspective*, Boston: Allyn and Bacon

Delquadri, J., Greenwood, C.R. and Hall, R.V. (1979) 'Opportunity to Respond: an Update' An invited address presented at the fifth annual meeting of the Association for Behavior Analysis, Dearborn, Michigan, June

Doyle, W., (1979) 'Classroom Effects', *Theory into Practice, 18*, 138-44

Edmiston, R.W. and Braddock, R.W. (1941) 'Study of the Effect of Various Teaching Procedures upon Observed Group Attention in the Secondary School', *Journal of Educational Psychology, 32*, 665-72

Gallup, G.H. (1975) 'Seventh Annual Gallup Poll of Public Attitudes Toward Education', *Phi Delta Kappan, 57*, 227-40

Good, T. and Beckerman, T. (1978) 'Time on Task: A Naturalistic Study in Sixth-grade Classrooms', *The Elementary School Journal, 3*, 193-201

86   *Classroom Segments*

Grannis, J.C. (1978) 'Task Engagement and the Consistency of Pedagogical Controls: An Ecological Study of Differently Structured Classroom Settings', *Curriculum Inquiry, 8*(1), 3-36

Gump, P.V. (1969) *The Classroom Behavior Setting: Its Nature and Relation to Student Behavior: U.S. Office of Education Final Report, Project No. 2453. Bureau Report No. 5-0334*, Lawrence: University of Kansas Press

—— (1969) 'Intra-setting Analysis: The Third-grade Classroom as a Special but Instructive Case' in E.P. Willems and H.L. Raush (eds), *Naturalistic Viewpoints in Psychological Research*, New York: Holt, Rinehart & Winston

—— (1974) 'Operating Environments in Schools of Open and Traditional Design', *School Review, 82*, 575-93

—— and Good, L.R. (1976) 'Environments Operating in Open-space and Traditionally Designed Schools', *Journal of Architectural Research, 5*(1), 20-7

—— and Ross, R. (1977) 'The Fit of Milieu and Programme in School Environments' in H. McGurk (ed.), *Ecological Factors in Human Development*, New York: North-Holland Publishing Co.

—— and Ross, R. (1979) 'What's Happened in Schools of Open Design?' (A report to cooperating Staff), *JSAS Catalog of Selected Documents in Psychology, 9*, 12

Hoetker, A.J. and Ahlbrand, W.P. (1969) 'The Persistence of the Recitation', *American Education Research Journal, 6*, 145-69

Jackson, P.W. (1968) *Life in Classrooms*, New York: Holt, Rinehart & Winston

Kirley, J.P. (1981) 'Variety of Procedures and its Effects in Skills-oriented, Fifth-grade Classrooms'. Paper presented at the annual meeting of the American Educational Research Association, Los Angeles, April

Kounin, J.S. (1976) *Discipline and Group Management in Classrooms*, New York: Holt, Rinehart & Winston

—— and Doyle, P.H. (1978) 'Degree of Continuity of a Lesson's Signal System and the Task Involvement of Children', *Journal of Educational Psychology, 67*, 159-64

—— and Gump, P.V. (1974) 'Signal Systems of Lesson Settings and the Task-related Behavior of Preschool Children', *Journal of Educational Psychology, 66*, 554-62

—— and Sherman, L.W. (1979) 'School Environments as Behavior Settings', *Theory into Practice, 18*, 145-51

Kowatrakul, S. (1959) 'Some Behaviors of Elementary School Children Related to Classroom Activities and Subject Areas', *Journal of Educational Psychology, 50*, 121-8

Krantz, P.J. and Risley, T.R. (1977) 'Behavioral Ecology in the Classroom' in K.D. O'Leary and S.G. O'Leary (eds), *Classroom Management: The Successful Use of Behavior Modification*, New York: Pergamon Press Inc.

Rosenshine, B. (1978) 'Academic Engaged Time, Content Covered, and Direct Instruction'. Unpublished manuscript, University of Illinois

—— (1980) 'How Time is Spent in Elementary Classrooms' in C. Denham and A. Lieberman (eds), *Time to Learn*, Washington, DC: National Institute of Education

Ross, R.P. (1980) 'Modification of Space in Open-plan Schools: An Examination of the Press Toward Synomorphy' in R.R. Stough and A. Wandersman (eds), *Optimizing Environments: Research, Practice, and Policy*, Washington, DC: Environmental Design Research Association

—— (1982) 'Variations in School Environments: An Expression of Individual Differences or Evidence of the "Press toward Synomorphy"?' Paper presented at the annual meeting of the American Educational Research Association, March

Shure, M.B. (1963) 'Psychological Ecology of a Nursery School', *Child Development, 34*, 979-92

Silverstein, J.M. (1979) 'Individual and Environmental Correlates of Pupil Problematic and Nonproblematic Classroom Behavior' (Doctoral dissertation, New York University 1979), *Dissertation Abstracts International, 40*, 2567A. (University Microfilms No. 79-25, 292)

Simon, A. and Boyer, E.G. (1970) *Mirrors for Behavior II: An Anthology of Observation Instruments* (vols A and B), Philadelphia, PA.: Classroom Interaction Newsletter

Soar, R. (1973) 'Follow-through Classroom Process Measurement and Pupil Growth. Final report'. Unpublished, Gainesville, Fla: College of Education, University of Florida

Stallings, J.A. and Kaskowitz, D.H. (1974) *Follow Through Classroom Observation Evaluation, 1972-1973*, Menlo Park, California: Stanford Research Institute

Stodolsky, S.S. (1979) 'Ecological Features of Fifth-grade Math and Social Studies Classes and their Relation to Student Involvement'. Paper presented at the annual meeting of the American Educational Research Association, San Francisco

—— (1981) 'Subject-matter Constraints on the Ecology of Classroom Instruction'. Paper presented at the annual meeting of the American Educational Research Association, Los Angeles, April

——, Ferguson, T.L. and Wimpleberg, K. (1981) 'The Recitation Persists, But What Does it Look Like?', *Journal of Curriculum Studies, 13*, 121-30

Winett, R.A. and Winkler, R.C. (1972) 'Current Behavior Modification in the Classroom: Be Still, Be Quiet, Be Docile', *Journal of Applied Behavior Analysis, 5*, 499-504

Wright, H.F. (1967) *Recording and Analyzing Child Behavior*, New York: Harper and Row

Yinger, R.J. (1977) 'A Study of Teaching Planning: Description and Theory Development Using Ethnographic and Information-processing Methods' (Doctoral dissertation, Michigan State University, 1977), *Dissertation Abstracts International, 39*, 207A. (University Microfilms No. 78-10, 138)

PART TWO

RESEARCH ON TIME AND SCHOOL LEARNING

5 HOW TIME IS USED IN ELEMENTARY SCHOOLS: THE ACTIVITY STRUCTURE OF CLASSROOMS

Robert B. Burns

In the past twenty years or so there has been a great deal of renewed interest among educational researchers in the temporal environment that organizes and structures schools, classrooms and student-learning experiences. During this period a large number of 'time variables' have been explored, ranging from years of schooling down to minutes of study time, and there currently exists in the research literature a variety of time constructs such as quantity of schooling, opportunity to learn, time-on-task, and academic learning time.

Much of the current research has focused on how much time teachers supply for learning in various subject matter areas, and how much of that allocated instructional time is consumed by students actively engaged in learning. In general, three major findings have emerged from this research: (1) school and teacher differences in allocated instructional time exist which, when aggregated over the school year, result in large differences between schools and classrooms in exposure time students receive in various topics in the curriculum; (2) student differences in engaged time exist which, when embedded in allocated classroom time and aggregated over the school year, result in even larger differences between students in time involved in learning; and (3) student-engaged time is consistently though modestly related to student achievement or student-achievement gain (see, e.g. Berliner, 1979; Caldwell, Huitt and Graeber, 1982; Denham and Lieberman, 1980; Frederick and Walberg, 1980, Lomax and Cooley, 1979; Rosenshine, 1978, 1981).

While these findings should not be particularly surprising to educational researchers and are certainly not surprising to teachers, they do serve to highlight some manipulable classroom variables which make a difference in student achievement and which are, to a large extent, potentially under the control of teachers (see Stallings, 1980). For teachers however, these findings fall considerably short of their mark prescriptively. The practical implication teachers read in this research is the rather hollow-sounding advice of 'keep your students engaged and involved in learning activities', a piece of advice most teachers not only attempt to follow anyway, but one that appears, as we will see later in this paper, to be a primary guide in teachers' choice of daily lesson activities, and a major cue teachers use to gauge the activity flow of lessons. What is needed is research that goes beyond *how much* time is allocated for or spent on learning, and begins to address *how* that allocated and engaged time is spent by teachers and students. After all, it is the quality of learning time, not the quantity of time *per se*, that will be the primary determinant of student learning.

Accordingly, the purpose of this chapter is to present some descriptive data on what fills the five to six hours students spend each day in elementary classrooms. Based on a number of observational and survey studies, mean time and frequency estimates on different dimensions of classroom activities and tasks will be presented. These data will, hopefully, flesh out in some small way the skeletal outline recently provided by Rosenshine (1981) of *how much* time is allocated in elementary schools, by describing *how* that time is used by teachers and students.

This chapter is organized into four sections. The first section provides a limited amount of data on the broad temporal parameters that organize an elementary school day. The second section discusses the constructs of classroom activities and tasks as a means of conceptualizing how the time in a school day is used. Characteristics of classroom activities and tasks are then used in the third section to loosely organize the descriptive data on what fills the school day in elementary classrooms. In the concluding section it is suggested that a major temporal dimension of classroom activities is not necessarily what activities *fill school time*, but rather how these activities *flow in time*.

The reader is cautioned from the outset about drawing a detailed picture of the 'typical' elementary classroom from the information provided in this chapter. Many of the data reported here are not directly comparable due to differences in coding categories of different observational instruments and differences in time metrics across studies.[1] In addition, there is considerable variability not only between classrooms in how time is spent, but within classrooms across days of the week in the types of activities which occur. This variability is often so great that time-use scores averaged across teachers and days of the week probably do not capture well the true flavour of the temporal organization of life in any given classroom.

What Does the School Day Look Like?

Before examining what fills the time elementary students spend in school, it is informative to get an idea of what the school day looks like. What are the temporal parameters within which classroom and school activities occur?

Surprisingly, there does not appear to be a great deal of research which chronicles and accounts for all the time that is spent at schools each day. Most of the descriptive data on how much time is spent focuses only on selected portions of the school day devoted to the basic curricular areas such as reading, language arts and/or mathematics. Two studies, however, do provide observational and teacher-time-log data which account for each minute of the official school day, excluding before and after-school activities. While these two studies (Fisher, Filby, Marliave, Cahen, Dishaw, Moore and Berliner, 1978; Roehler, Schmidt and Buchmann, 1979) examined time use in a small number of classrooms (25 second-grade and 21 fifth-grade classrooms in the Fisher *et al.* study and 6 elementary classrooms at different grade levels in the Roehler *et al.* study), and should not be considered representative of elementary schools in general, there is remarkable consistency across the two sets of data.

Table 5.1 presents the percentage of the day devoted to three broad and exhaustive categories of school-day time: instructional time, that time devoted to instruction in the major curricular areas of elementary schooling; fixed non-instructional time, that time allocated by school policy to recess and lunch breaks and which is out of the control of teachers; and teacher controlled non-instructional time, that classroom time under the direct control of teachers which is taken up in non-instructional activities such as students waiting for the lesson to begin, transitions between lessons and general class business.

It is important to note that the Roehler *et al.* data in Table 5.1 are mean-percentage scores for individual classes, while the Fisher *et al.* data are mean-percentage scores averaged across classrooms within grade level. Each classroom in the Roehler *et al.* study had a 360-minute school day; in the Fisher *et al.* study, the mean day length was 306 minutes in the second grade and 358.5 minutes in the fifth grade. With this information, reasonably close estimates of time in minutes can be determined from the percentages in Table 5.1. For example, in a 360-minute day each percentage point represents 3.6 minutes.

As mentioned earlier, the data in Table 5.1 are quite similar across the two studies. On the average, approximately 63 per cent of the school day is allocated to instructional time, 22 to 23 per cent is allocated to recess and lunch, and 13 to 14 per cent of the day is lost in teacher-controlled, non-instructional time. For a 360-minute school day these percentages correspond to approximately 227 allocated instructional mintues, 83 minutes of recess and lunch time, and 50 minutes of lost instructional time. Percentages of instructional time devoted to curricular topics are also given in Table 5.1, with the largest percentage of instructional time being allocated to reading and language arts. This is not surprising given that one of the major goals of elementary school ing is the teaching of reading and the development of language skills.

As has become fashionable with time data recently, we can aggregate these daily allocated time estimates over the duration of the typical 180-day school year. For teacher-controlled, non-instructional time, such an aggregation results in approximately 150 hours of lost time, assuming of course that the averages reported in Table 5.1 are consistent for the duration of the school year. Other more striking time estimates could similarly be computed if the between classroom variability from the Roehler *et al.* study is used. For example, in the two self-contained, second-grade classrooms, there is a 10 percentage point difference in teacher-controlled, non-instructional time (i.e. 9 vs 19 per cent). This translates into a 36-minute daily difference, or a 108-hour yearly difference between the two classrooms. Focusing on the 14 percentage point difference in instructional time between these same two classrooms, it can be estimated that students in one classroom would be allocated approximately 151 more hours of instructional time than students in the second classroom. Finally, if time estimates of student engagement rates are considered, even greater differences between students in time use would be found. Three such analyses have recently been done by Caldwell *et al.* (1982), Karweit and Slavin (1981) and Rosenshine (1981), and the reader is encouraged to examine these reports.

In summary, if these data are reasonably typical of elementary classrooms, it appears that about 75 per cent of the school day is spend inside the classroom, and 63 per cent of the school day is allocated to instructional time. This corresponds to about 225 in-class minutes each day for a five-hour school day, and about 270 in-class minutes for a six-hour day. While this information is useful, it is necessary to determine how this time is used in classrooms if we are to begin to get a handle on the quality of time use in elementary schools. It is to this topic which we now turn.

Table 5.1: Per Cent of School Day Spent in Instructional and Non-instructional Time

| | Roehler et al. (1979)[a] | | | | | | | Fisher et al. (1978)[b] | | |
| | Grade level of class[c] | | | | | | | Grade level of class | | |
	2/3	2/3	2	2	5	4/5	Mean %	2	5	Mean %
Instructional time	58	67	73	59	66	58	63.5	61	65	63.0
Language arts	12	19	12	12	10	19	14.0	–	–	–
Reading	19	7	23	11	20	11	15.2	–	–	–
Language arts/reading combined	31	26	35	23	30	30	29.2	28	31	29.5
Music/art/physical education	12	12	15	9	4	9	10.2	18	16	17.0
Social studies	1	11	0	2	9	3	4.3	–	–	–
Science	0	0	3	3	13	4	3.8	–	–	–
Social studies/science combined	1	11	3	5	22	7	8.2	3	6	4.5
Maths	10	9	17	9	8	10	10.5	12	12	12.0
Mixed seatwork	5	9	2	14	2	1	5.5	–	–	–
Fixed non-instructional time	24	24	18	22	25	21	22.3	25	22	23.5
Teacher-controlled non-instructional time	18	9	9	19	9	21	14.2	14	13	13.5
Wait	–	–	–	–	–	–	–	1	1	1.0
Transitions between activities	–	–	–	–	–	–	–	11	9	10.0
General class business	–	–	–	–	–	–	–	2	3	2.5

a. Adapted from Roehler et al. (1979), Figures 1 and 2.
b. Adapted from Fisher et al. (1978), Table 4-1. Percentages are rounded to nearest whole number and based on unweighted means calculated across A–B and B–C periods.
c. 2/3 and 4/5 refer to grade-level combination classrooms.

Activities and Tasks in Classrooms

Describing how time in elementary classrooms is spent is a difficult task if for no other reason than the sheer amount of teacher and student time spent each day in school and the diversity of behavior which obviously fills that time. Considering time in terms of school day duration, there are 225 to 270 minutes of in-class time (see previous section) consumed by teacher and student interaction. Considering time in teacher and student minutes, however, there are 225 to 270 minutes of teacher time, *and* in a class of thirty students, for example, 6,750 to 8,100 student minutes of in-class time that should be taken into account. These two concepts of time, in-class school-day duration and teacher and student minutes of in-class time, are two different but complementary metrics with which to view how time is used (Stodolsky, 1981). Regardless of which view is taken, the sheer quantity is staggering.

Within these hours of teacher and student time there is ample opportunity for behavioural and cognitive activity (and inactivity) to occur. As one small example, consider some data reported by Jackson and Lahaderne (1967) on the hourly rate of teacher and student initiated communications in four sixth-grade classrooms. Averaging across the four classrooms yields a mean hourly rate of 79.3 for teachers and 27.2 for students. Since these data represent only those communications between the teacher and an individual student, not group-directed communications, they underestimate the rate of verbal interaction in the classroom. None the less, they do serve to indicate, however crudely, what Jackson (1968) has so eloquently described, namely, the quantity and complexity of interaction that characterizes the classroom environment.

This sheer quantity of time and behaviour in classrooms poses a difficult problem for researchers attempting to find a useful and meaningful unit of analysis with which to conceptualize classroom environments. One obvious structural unit of the classroom, and the one that will be used in this paper, is that of the instructional activity. Smith and Geoffrey (1968) provide a common-sense description of an activity as the 'work to be done':

In the beginning of school the teacher has many problems. From the organization's perspective the key directive for the teacher concerns the establishment of the activity structure. As we have understood sociologists such as Homans (1950), an important part of the

social structure of a group is the activity of the group, the trans-
actions of the group with the physical facilities and environment. In
the classroom, and Geoffrey's class is no exception, it is the 'work'
to be done. (p. 83)

The importance of activities, at least from the teacher's perspective,
is clearly indicated by the research that has been completed on teacher
planning over the past ten years (for reviews, see Brophy, 1980; Clark
and Yinger, 1979; Shavelson and Stern, 1981). The most consistent
finding of this research is that activities and subject matter content, not
instructional objectives, are the most important components of teacher
planning and organization in the classroom. It is likely that this emphasis on content and activities is related to the continual concern of
teachers of how to fill the classroom time with 'things to do' in the
coming weeks, days, or hours, and which, because of its immediacy,
overrides the concern for what is going to be *accomplished* (MacDonald,
1965). Whatever the reason, content and activities appear to be fore-
most in the minds of teachers during planning.

The apparent simplicity of the concept of activity described by
Smith and Geoffrey is misleading, however, when the use of the construct in the research literature is examined closely. There are a number
of definitions of activity, each with different critical attributes, and a
variety of closely related constructs that are seemingly used in combination with or interchangeably with activity. We appear to have as many
problems defining activities today as was the case in the early 1930s
when an in-depth study of the 'activity movement' was conducted (see
Whipple, 1934). A cursory examination of Table 5.2 should alert the
reader to this conceptual confusion.

A full discussion of the construct of activity is beyond the scope of
this chapter. It is necessary, however, to provide some organization to
the constructs of task, activity, activity structure and activity segment
if the descriptive time-use data presented in this paper are to make any
sense at all. The conceptualization provided in Figure 5.1 is an attempt
to provide this organization. This conceptualization is not meant to be
a model of teacher or student behaviour nor is it meant to be a model
of how lessons progress through time. Rather, it simply attempts to
relate certain structural properties of tasks, activity formats, and
activities and bring these properties within the framework of a classroom lesson.

Table 5.2: *Some Definitions of the Constructs of Activities, Tasks and Segments*

	Construct and definition	Attributes or dimensions
Yinger (1979, p. 111)	*Activities:* 'The equivalent of "controlled" behaviour settings, because not only was the behaviour of the teacher elicited and controlled by the setting (the activities), as the ecological psychologists suggest, but the setting itself was largely created and controlled by the teacher ahead of time.'	(1) location (2) structure and sequence (3) duration (4) participants (5) acceptable student behaviour (6) teacher instructional moves (7) content and materials
Zahorik (1982, pp. 309-10)	*Activities:* 'Learning activities are the means by which teachers bring students into contact with subject matter. Although they contain several dimensions, in terms of the tasks in which they require students to engage, learning activities include reading textbooks, writing reports, taking field trips, watching films, listening to lectures, and other acts.'	
Blumenfeld (1980, p. 1)	*Instructional activity:* no definition, but her analysis 'concentrates on the procedures by which work is accomplished, the steps the learner must take to get the information (both social and cognitive) and the procedures for reproducing it.'	(1) content (2) delivery system; (3) product (4) cognitive complexity (5) procedural complexity (6) general learning skills (7) purpose (8) evaluation
Bossert (1979, pp. 7-12)	*Activity structures:* 'Few studies . . . have examined the consequences of distinctive types of work organizations, or activity structures', (p. 7) 'Every classroom activity, though, can be described in terms of its task characteristics' (p. 10) 'the structure of task activities – a classroom's organization of instruction' (p. 12)	(1) size of work group (2) the number and interdependence of different tasks being completed at same time (3) degree of pupil choice over the task (4) methods used to evaluate pupil performances

Table 5.2 – continued

	Construct and definition	Attributes or dimensions
Doyle (1979, p. 45)	*Activities:* 'In research in classrooms it is necessary to distinguish between two analytical units: activities and tasks. The concept of "activities" . . . designates bounded segments of classroom time . . . [and] refers to distinctive patterns of overt behaviour of teachers and students in classrooms.'	(1) physical space (2) type and number of participants (3) resources or props (4) format for behaviour (5) concern or focal content of the segment
Doyle (1979, pp. 45-6)	*Task:* 'refers to the way in which information-processing demands of an environment are structured and experienced. Such demands are affected not only by the flow of events in an activity but also by the point or end of the activity. A task is defined, therefore, in terms of (a) a goal and (b) a set of operations designed to achieve that goal. In this sense, a task gives meaning to an activity by connecting elements within the activity to a purpose.	(1) risk (2) ambiguity (Doyle, 1980)
Shavelson and Stern (1981, pp. 477-8)	*Task:* 'In order to avoid confusion of the meanings of the term "activity" as it is used in teacher-planning research, we term the basic, structural unit of planning the task (cf. Doyle, 1980). A task is comprised of several elements . . . A third element is *activity* . . . the things the teacher and student will be doing during the lesson. The concept of activity includes sequencing, pacing, and timing the instructional content and materials'	(1) content (2) materials (3) activity (4) goals (5) student (6) social cultural context of instruction

Table 5.2 – continued

	Construct and definition	Attributes or dimensions
Gump (1969, p. 206)	*Segments:* 'Every segment has a *concern:* its business of "what it is about" . . . every segment has an *activity pattern* that may be described in terms of (a) the nature of teacher participation in the activity, (b) the grouping of pupils, (c) the prescribed action relationships between pupils, (d) the kinds of actions taken by pupils, and (e) the way in which pupil action is paced. Finally, linked with the above behavioural aspects are *site* and *object* contributions to the segment's existence.'	(1) concern (2) activity pattern (3) site (4) objects
Gump (1971, pp. 158-9)	*Segments:* 'It is possible to describe particular classrooms in terms of behaviour setting *sub-units* which we designate as *segments* . . . Segments appearing in classrooms include such activity structures as Morning Song and Salute, Red Bird Reading Circle.'	(1) site (2) temporal boundaries (3) behaviour objects (4) participants (5) behaviour or activity format (6) concern
Stodolsky (1981), pp. 4-5)	*Activity structure and activity segments:* 'A description of an activity structure includes noting the salient aspects of the physical environment and a cataloguing of the persons who are present (teachers, teacher aides, boys and girls). An activity structure of a classroom describes the main tasks or types of activities in which the children and teacher are participating . . . The subparts of the activity structure as we have just characterized them are illustrations of activity *segments.* They are parts of the classroom activity structure which have a particular instructional format, participants, materials, behavioural expectations and goals, and space-time boundaries. A segment is defined as a unique time block in a lesson and occurs in a fixed	

Table 5.2 – continued

	Construct and definition	Attributes or dimensions
Ross (see Chapter 4, this text)	*Activity segment:* 'Segments are a unit of activity similar to what teachers ordinarily call "lessons". However, activities that occur during the day that teachers would consider procedural activities instead of lessons . . . would also be included as segments. In addition, some lessons that consist of two or more distinct activity patterns would be identified as being composed of more than one segment . . .'	(1) concern (2) activity patterns (nature of teacher participation, grouping of students, prescribed action relationship between pupils, the kinds of actions taken by pupils, the way in which pupil action is paced) (3) physical boundaries (4) temporal boundaries (5) synomorphy

Note: Also see, e.g. Green (1983); Erikson (1982); Mehan (1979); Philips (1972), all in a sociolinguistic tradition, for other related
   constructs like 'participation structure', 'academic task structure', and 'social participation structure'.

Figure 5.1: Some Structural Properties of a Classroom Lesson

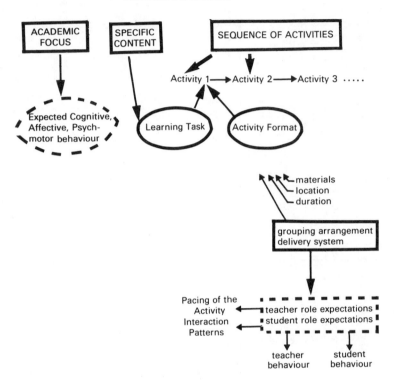

The organization in Figure 5.1 proposes that classroom lessons, within a given curriculum area, consist of three major components: (1) an academic *purpose* or focus, (2) some *specific content* and (3) usually, but not necessarily, a *sequence of activities*. The sequence of activities is chosen or designed by teachers to bring the student in contact with and hopefully involve the student in the content, and thus accomplishing the purpose of the lesson. According to this conceptualization, a possible reason for the prevalence of content and activities in teachers' reports of their planning is that these two components provide the necessary tools to implement a classroom lesson. They provide the temporal and behavioural blueprint, if you will, for what the students as well as the teacher will do during the lesson.

An *activity*, as used here, is what the ecological psychologists have called an activity segment, and is identified primarily by its temporal boundaries (a clear beginning and end) and focal concern. The focal concern may be procedural, as in a transition between one activity and the next, or it may be academic. For example, Evertson (1982) describes the typical sequence of activities in junior high school mathematics classes as follows: (1) an opening activity, primarily procedural, (2) a checking/grading activity, where homework was checked, (3) a lecture/discussion activity, where academic material was presented, (4) a seatwork activity, where students worked on assigned problems, and (5) a closing, procedural activity. The focus of this discussion is on academic activities, although later in this paper we will see that transitional activities have important implications for the successful completion of lessons.

The common names for activities used by Evertson, while useful, provide only a broad characterization of what the activities are about. It is proposed here that a complete description of an academic activity requires information on its two major components, the *learning task*[2] embedded in the activity and the *activity format*. We will hold off discussion of learning tasks for a moment and focus on the activity format.

The activity format structures the activity and provides the organizational means by which learning tasks will be accomplished. The activity format is defined by a number of properties, the most important of which are the *grouping arrangement* of students and the *delivery system*. The delivery system is 'the mode in which knowledge is communicated and in which the learner gains access to information' (Blumenfeld, 1980, p. 2), and is typically referred to as a teaching method (cf. Berliner and Gage, 1976). These two properties of activity formats, grouping arrangement and delivery system, are interrelated in the sense that a decision about one usually limits the choices about the other. A decision to use a lecture delivery system, for example, would typically limit the grouping arrangement to the whole class. Similarly, a decision to use small groups would likely limit the types of delivery systems under consideration.

The grouping arrangement and delivery system strongly influence the teacher and student-role expectations which, in turn, influence the kinds of teacher and student *behaviour* one is likely to see, the type of teacher-student and student-student *interaction patterns* that are likely to occur, and who or what will be responsible for the *pacing* of the activity. An individual seatwork activity format, for example, defines, to a large extent, the role of the teacher and student (e.g. teacher as circulating helper, student as worker), how they will interact (e.g. students will raise their hands when they have difficulty), and who has primary responsibility for pacing (e.g. the student).

The second major component of an activity is the *learning task*. A learning task, as used here. is defined by the specific content of the lesson relevant to the activity and the cognitive, affective, or psycho-motor behaviour expected of the student. Learning tasks are embedded within activities, and the activity format provides the organizational constraints of how the tasks are to be completed. The learning tasks of each activity are organized by the purpose of the lesson. In this sense, it may be appropriate to consider the purpose of the lesson as the super-ordinate task, and the purposes of the activities as the subordinate tasks which make up the lesson. The extent to which there is an explicit link between the learning tasks of each activity and the purpose of the lesson, very likely influences the clarity of the lesson and the extent to which the student understands the lesson requirements (cf. Blumenfeld, Pintrick, Meece and Weesels, 1982).

In summary, during a classroom lesson in some curricular area, teacher and student behaviours and their pattern of interaction occur within a particular grouping arrangement in which content is presented by some type of delivery system. The grouping arrangement and delivery system, along with materials, location and duration, character-ize the activity format and define, in part, the context for teacher and student behaviour. In addition, activities typically focus on some type of learning task which is expected to be accomplished within the organizational structure set up by the activity format. Finally, lessons typically have a purpose which organizes the task components of each activity in the lesson and the particular sequence of activities is likely to influence whether this lesson purpose is accomplished.

If this conceptualization of the classroom lesson is reasonable, then it suggests the nature of the data that are needed to adequately des-cribe how students and teachers spend their time in schools. The data should be contextually rich, with information on the nature of the learning task, the activity format and its properties, and the temporal distribution and duration of activities within the lesson. Without this supporting information it is difficult to assess the significance, for example, of the finding that students listen, read and write about 76, 13 and 2 per cent of the time during social studies lessons (Herman, 1967). This may be appropriate use of classroom time; or it may not.

Unfortunately, there is little time research, to my knowledge, that contains the degree of contextual information suggested here. The recent work of Stodolsky (1983), to be discussed shortly, is an exception. The extensive nature of her data, however, makes it impossible to summarize in one or two tables, and only a portion will be given here. The best that I can offer is to present data on certain properties of activities in a piecemeal manner, and suggest the use of Figure 5.1 as a means of structuring and organizing the information.

How Time Is Used in Elementary Classrooms

In this section, descriptive time use data are presented on seven of the properties of lessons identified in Figure 5.1. These seven properties are: (1) grouping arrangement, (2) delivery system, (3) activity format, (4) teacher behaviour, (5) student behaviour, (6) pacing of an activity, and (7) the cognitive level of tasks.

Grouping Arrangement

Grouping arrangement refers to how students are organized for an activity. Several studies provide relatively good information on grouping arrangements (see Brady, Clinton, Sweeney, Peterson, and Poyner, 1977, tables in Appendix V-A; Good and Beckerman, 1978). The data reported here from an observation study by Lambert and Hartsough (1976) were collected during Phase II of the Beginning Teacher Evaluation Study (McDonald and Elias, 1976). Lambert and Hartsough used a narrative observational system which allowed them to later code the written records according to frequency of particular teacher and target student behaviours and activities. In addition, time data were collected on the duration of several aspects of classroom activities, one being the grouping arrangement of students (what they called instructional context). Second and fifth-grade classrooms (approximately 40 second-grade and 50 fifth-grade classrooms; n's vary somewhat across different analyses) were observed during reading and mathematics lessons on from one to four visits to the classroom, each visit usually consisting of two hours of observation. Data were averaged over visits and teachers within grade level and subject matter.

Table 5.3 presents the mean per cent of total minutes spent in various grouping arrangements defined by their 'instructional-context' category. The definitions of these context categories are given at the bottom of the table. To interpret these codings, it is important to note that only eight target students, chosen to be representative of the class, were observed on a rotating basis and the narrative record described the student behaviour, activity, grouping arrangement and duration, and the teacher's behaviour at the time.

Table 5.3: Mean Per Cent Total Minutes Spent in Grouping Arrangement During Reading and Maths

Grouping arrangement	2nd Grade		5th Grade	
	Reading	Maths	Reading	Maths
Teacher/class	11.28	40.42	10.70	27.33
Adult/class	0.00	0.00	0.00	2.49
Independent/class	4.93	13.53	26.22	31.09
Teacher/group	29.10	15.11	18.84	11.98
Adult/group	8.98	2.66	1.90	0.07
Independent/group	34.40	21.74	34.36	22.13
Teacher/individual	0.50	0.29	0.18	0.02
Adult/individual	0.80	0.45	0.06	0.11
Independent/individual	8.33	3.92	6.04	2.09
Test	0.45	0.79	1.00	2.16

Source: Lambert and Hartsough (1976), Tables 28 and 34.
Notes: Format definitions are:
   Teacher or adult/class: Teacher or adult other than teacher directing activity, and the entire class is participating.
   Independent/class: Entire class working independently; teacher present but not directing.
   Teacher or adult/group: Teacher or adult is directing the activity of one of several small groups.
   Independent/group: A group is working independent of the teacher's direction.
   Teacher or adult/individual: No definition given.
   Independent/individual: A student is working independent of the teacher's direction, and also independently of the rest of the class.

As can be seen in Table 5.3, grouping arrangements vary, as one would expect, according to curricular area. There is more whole-group instruction and less small-group instruction in mathematics than in reading, and this is true at both grade levels. However, there is a consistent trend, in both subject-matter areas, towards fewer small-group arrangements as one moves from second to fifth grade. In reading, whole-class grouping goes from 16 per cent at the second-grade level to 37 per cent at the fifth-grade level; in maths the corresponding percentages are 54 and 61 per cent. Small-group arrangements, on the other hand, occupy 73 per cent of second-grade reading time, but only 55 per cent of fifth-grade reading. In maths these same percentages are 40 and 34.

Whether this trend is substantive or not is unclear from these data or other data I have seen on grouping arrangements. It is clear that this difference is a result of an increase in time spent in the 'independent/ class' grouping arrangement at the fifth-grade level, which I presume is an indication of an increase in seatwork-type activities. The time estimates here are close to those reported by Good and Beckerman (1978) for sixth-grade classrooms across curricular areas. One might speculate that increased management concerns at upper grade levels may force teachers to a whole-class format for increased monitoring purposes. At the same time one would think that small-group arrangements would be more responsive to the increased individual differences which typically occur as one moves up the grade levels. These two apparently conflicting concerns, if they are real, might be worthy of further study.

The category definitions of Lambert and Hartsough combine possible delivery systems with grouping arrangements, and the type of delivery system is not specified. For example, the coding category of 'teacher-class' refers to a whole-class grouping where the teacher is directing the activity, but the delivery system could be lecture, recitation, demonstration, etc. Additional information on these same classrooms concerning delivery systems is provided in a study by Calfee and Calfee (1976). This study was also part of Phase II of the Beginning Teacher Evaluation Study, but a different type of observational instrument was used which provides data on specific delivery systems. It is delivery systems in general, and the Calfee and Calfee study in particular, which we will take up now.

Delivery Systems

Delivery systems refer to how the content of a lesson is to be presented to students. As mentioned earlier, delivery systems are commonly referred to as teaching methods. For example, Berliner and Gage (1976) define teaching methods as:

> . . . recurrent instructional processes, applicable to various subject matters, and usable by more than one teacher. They are *recurrent* in that activities are repeated over intervals measured in minutes or weeks. They are *instructional processes*, such as patterned teacher behavior (for example, lecturing, discussion, and recitation); delivery systems for curriculum (for example, printed matter, film, programmed instruction, and computer-assisted instruction); and organizational structures for promoting learning (for example, tutoring and independent study) (p. 5, authors' italics).

Although this definition of teaching methods is close to the definition of delivery systems as used in this paper, there are two important differences. First, Berliner and Gage include 'organizational structures' as teaching methods; here, an organizational structure would consist of those properties which define an activity format. A second difference is one of perspective. Berliner and Gage discuss teaching methods as if they were relatively well-defined instructional processes which 'exist' on their own. Here, delivery systems are conceptualized as being only one property of the activity format, and which exist only in the context of the larger unit of analysis called an activity. This conceptualization would suggest one possible reason why research results on the comparison of teaching methods have been so ambiguous over the years,[3] and perhaps it would make more sense to compare activities, or more appropriately, sequences of activities, rather than teaching methods.

Delivery systems then, are modes of presenting information to students. In the Calfee and Calfee (1976) study, one of the observational categories that was coded was delivery system (what they called instructional activity). They observed in the same classrooms with the same schedule of visits as in the Lambert and Hartsough study discussed previously. However, their unit of observation was different. Their observational instrument attempted to document how many student minutes were spent in different classroom events. The duration of any particular coding was multiplied by the number of students participating in the event coded. This time metric, which Gump (1967) used and called occupancy time, weights each event coded by the number of students and provides an index of how all student minutes are being spent.

Table 5.4 presents the mean per cent of total student minutes across all classrooms during reading and mathematics lessons within grade level. The numbers in parentheses refer to the percentage of classrooms in which the delivery systems were observed. It should be pointed out that the small number of classroom visits may account, to some extent, for the small percentages of some of the codings. Also, there is a sizeable percentage of student time that is unaccounted for, although the reasons are not specified in the report. Presumably, students were engaged in activities where no delivery system was used, but the nature of these activities is unknown.

The predominance of seatwork in both curricular areas and at both grade levels is clear, taking up roughly 50 per cent of student time. Recitation (question and answer) is also prevalent, accounting for the next highest percentage of student time except in fifth-grade reading. The increase across grade levels in whole-class grouping arrangements seen in the Lambert and Hartsough data is paralleled here by an increase in seatwork delivery systems, and it seems clear that whole-class seat-work activity formats are a major component of elementary classroom activities.

Table 5.4: Mean Per Cent of Total Student Minutes in Reading and Maths Spent in Different Delivery Systems

	2nd Grade			5th Grade		
Delivery system	Reading/language		Maths	Reading/language		Maths
Lecture	1.3	(25)	0.0 (0)	4.0	(23)	3.3 (22)
Discussion	6.2	(55)	11.0 (37)	10.2	(57)	6.2 (31)
Seatwork	42.4	(90)	49.8 (82)	56.6	(96)	62.5 (92)
Recital	9.1	(50)	0.4 (2)	6.1	(47)	0.0 (0)
Question/answer	14.8	(70)	14.7 (45)	9.1	(61)	11.4 (43)
Audio-visual	5.7	(12)	1.5 (5)	0.9	(8)	0.3 (2)
Game	2.6	(25)	8.1 (27)	1.3	(10)	4.3 (20)
Demonstration	1.7	(10)	3.2 (12)	0.2	(4)	1.9 (10)
Student time unaccounted for	16.2		11.3	11.6		10.1

Source: Calfee and Calfee (1976), Table 4.
Note: See text for explanation of data. Numbers in parentheses are percentages of classrooms in which delivery systems were observed.

Activity Formats

Data on the two major properties of activity formats, grouping arrange-ments and delivery systems, were presented above. Here we will present one more set of data that provides a useful summary of these two properties in fifth-grade classrooms. This study by Stodolsky (1983) provides one of the best descriptions of activity formats and activities in the literature today, and it is unfortunate that not all her data could be presented here.

Operating within an ecological psychology framework, and using the activity segment (see Table 5.2) as the unit of analysis, narrative records of classroom activities and observational data on students were obtained by two observers during fifth-grade mathematics and social studies lessons. Twenty maths classes and 19 social studies classes were observed over ten consecutive days, resulting in descriptive data on 535 maths instructional segments (mean duration of 19.5 minutes) and 545 social studies segments (mean duration of 18.4 minutes). Stodolsky used student occupancy time as an index for how time was spent.

Table 5.5 presents, for various activity formats, the percentage of total instructional segments, their mean duration in minutes, and the percentage of student occupancy time. Perhaps the most striking aspect of this segment data is the large amount of time spent in recitation and seatwork during mathematics and social studies lessons, and its similarity to the Calfee and Calfee data for fifth-grade mathematics. Sixty-nine per cent of the maths segments, accounting for 78 per cent of student occupancy time, were carried out in either recitation or seatwork activity formats. The student occupancy time estimates for recitation and seatwork in the Calfee and Calfee study for fifth-grade maths were both 74 per cent. In social studies, 35 per cent of the segments, accounting for 56 per cent of time, were conducted in recitation and seatwork-activity formats. The less time spent in recitation and seatwork during social studies lessons is made up by more time being spent in a greater diversity of segments, most notably in group-work formats.

Table 5.5: Per Cent of Total Segments, Mean Duration of Segments, and Per Cent Student Occupancy Time in Fifth-grade Maths and Social Studies Activity Formats

Format	Per cent of segments		Mean duration of segments (minutes)		Per cent student occupancy time	
	Maths	Social St.	Maths	Social St.	Maths	Social St.
Seatwork	26.8	12.5	21.7	20.4	29.9	21.7
Diverse seatwork	2.6	5.0	30.4	26.0	3.8	6.1
Individualized seatwork	11.0	–	34.8	–	13.7	–
Recitation	29.0	17.6	16.6	17.1	30.9	28.1
Discussion	0.4	3.5	15.0	9.7	0.4	3.1
Lecture	2.2	1.3	10.1	12.0	1.5	1.4
Demonstration	0.6	0.9	7.3	19.6	0.4	1.1
Checking work	7.9	2.2	9.8	11.0	6.0	2.4
Test	3.4	1.8	21.1	24.5	5.1	3.9
Group work	0.2	33.6	39.0	23.1	0.1	10.7
Film/a-visual	–	4.4	–	16.5	–	6.8
Contest	8.2	1.5	21.0	13.8	6.3	1.5
Student reports	–	3.7	–	20.6	–	7.0
Giving instructions	4.1	8.1	3.8	5.8	1.1	3.8
Preparation	2.1	2.6	4.6	8.1	0.7	1.6
Tutorial	1.5	–	21.5	–	0.3	–
Stocks	–	1.5	–	5.0	–	0.8

Source: Stodolsky (1983), Table 1.

It appears then, that whole class recitation and seatwork activity formats have continued to persist on through the 1970s in elementary classrooms (see Hoetcker and Ahlbrand, 1969). These two activity formats provide the major organizational structure and context for student learning and behaviour in the classroom, combining to consume the largest percentage of in-class instructional time. Teacher and student behaviour is influenced, in large part, by the role expectations set up by these activity formats. The next two sets of data describe some of these teacher and student behaviours.

Teacher and Student Behaviour

Table 5.6 presents some additional data from the Lambert and Hartsough study discussed earlier. These data are mean proportional frequencies of different types of teacher behaviours, standardized within classrooms on total number of observational codes per teacher. Most of the behaviour categories are self-explanatory except perhaps 'working with student', which refers to 'general unspecified instructional activity of working with an individual, a group, or the class'. Although these data are not time based, the observational procedures ensure that these frequencies are closely related to duration, and can be considered crude proxy measures of time spent in behaviour.

There does not appear to be any remarkable aspect to this set of data. Teachers are doing a number of different things, most notably behaviours *not* coded in the Lambert and Hartsough observation instrument (i.e. the large frequency of 'working with student'). Given that many of the behavioural categories are what we usually think of teachers doing, the lack of this behaviour may itself be significant. Teachers do appear to spend more time at their tasks in fifth-grade than in second-grade classes. In maths this may be at the expense of circulating around the room, since the proportional frequency of circulating decreases about as much as the frequency of sitting at the desk increases. This is speculation, however, and this trend is not seen for reading lessons. Still, it is interesting that the increase in whole-class seatwork-activity formats from the second to the fifth grade seen in earlier data is accompanied with an increase in teacher desk time.

Turning to student behaviour, Table 5.7 presents data from a study by Good and Beckerman (1978). Observational data were collected in six sixth-grade classrooms for a total of 14 hours each. During the observation each student in the class was observed in turn, and the individual's behaviour was coded as to grouping arrangement, behaviour and curricular topic, and whether or not the student was on-task. The data are reported in frequency of codings and per cent of total codings. Since each student coding presumably took approximately the same amount of time, the percentages of total codes for a given coding category are similar to the teacher behaviour data just reported in that they are crude proxy measures of time spent in different behaviours. These data were, however, collected across curricular areas, and are not comparable to the data presented so far.

Table 5.6· Mean Proportional Frequencies of Teacher Behaviours

	2nd Grade		5th Grade	
Teacher behaviour	Reading	Maths	Reading	Maths
Academic organizing	3.05	2.03	2.49	1.65
Answering	0.66	1.41	3.45	2.83
Asking	6.46	5.39	4.78	4.12
At desk	0.40	0.45	5.65	5.93
At board	1.58	4.86	0.89	1.62
Checking	2.62	6.69	4.85	6.98
Circulating	5.12	12.28	7.21	8.23
Discussion	1.73	2.40	4.07	0.71
Explaining	0.48	2.10	1.42	4.54
Helping	3.64	5.13	3.68	7.38
Instruction giving	2.30	2.93	3.38	3.25
Listening	2.50	0.16	1.70	0.15
Question and answer	1.42	1.51	4.16	1.68
Supervising	1.50	2.69	2.83	2.52
Working with student	46.58	29.37	31.75	22.79

Source: Lambert and Hartsough (1976), Tables 22 and 23.
Note: Due to the different number of activities and observational periods for teachers, raw frequencies could not be used. Within each class each type of activity frequency was converted to a percentage frequency of total number of codes for the teacher. These percentage frequencies were then averaged across teachers.

Table 5.7: Per Cent of Total Behaviours Observed

Student Behaviour	Per Cent
Writing	22.0
Reading	12.1
Listening	16.0
Interacting teacher/adult	7.0
Interacting group	5.0
Drawing	4.0
Examining	3.0
Memory	1.0
Manipulating material	0.9
Academic talking/pupil	4.0
Non-academic talking/pupil	6.0
Sitting	9.0
Walking	5.0
Waiting	2.8

Source: Adapted from Good and Beckerman (1978), Table 4.

In these classrooms writing, reading, and listening account for approximately 22, 12 and 16 per cent of the in-class time. Interacting with the teacher or a teacher's aide accounts for only 7 per cent of the classroom time. We will see similar data in the next section on pacing. This is surely a function of the large amount of time spent in individual seatwork-activity formats. Non-academic behaviour, that of talking, sitting, walking and waiting occurs about 23 per cent of the time, this estimate being about 10 percentage points higher than the estimate given in Table 5.1.

It is apparent from these data that more detailed information on the context is necessary to understand the importance of particular types of student behaviour in the classroom. The fact that the curricular topic alone determines, to a large extent, the types of activities one typically sees during a lesson, suggests that teacher and student behavioural data should be reported at least within curricular areas. But properties of the activity format also influence behaviour. For example, Stodolsky (1983) reports that the student behaviour pattern of solving problems at the desk accounts for 51 per cent of student occupancy time in mathematics, but only 6 per cent of the time in social studies. This observation is surely a function of the predominance of individual seat-work formats in maths.

Pacing of the Activity

It has been suggested here that properties of the activity format influence the teacher and student role expectations for appropriate behaviour. An important aspect of instructional roles is who or what is responsible for maintaining the pacing of the activity. As used here, pacing does not refer to some kind of rate measure of content coverage, say five workbook pages in an hour. Rather, it refers to whether the teacher, the student, groups of students, or some external inanimate object like a film, is primarily responsible for involvement in the activity and maintenance of the activity flow.

Fisher *et al.* (1978) present some interesting data on the percentage of instructional time that is spent in self-paced activity formats and other-paced activity formats. Self-paced formats are those in which 'the student works independently and determines for himself (within some time limit) the rate at which work gets done' (p. 5-2). Other-paced formats are defined as those in which 'the student must interact with other students or must share the teacher's attention with other students. The pace of instruction is determined by the whole interactive unit and is beyond the control of the individual student' (p. 5-4). These data come from day-long observations of six target students once a week for approximately 15 weeks. Students were observed on a rotating basis about once every 4 minutes and aspects of their behaviour, including whether they were engaged or not, were coded. These codes were then averaged across observations and teachers within grade level and curricular area.

Table 5.8 presents the mean per cent instructional time spent in self-paced and other-paced activity formats, and mean per cent instructional time spent interacting with the teacher within these two formats. Also included in Table 5.7 is a measure of mean student engagement in each of the two formats.

It is apparent that considerably more time is spent in self-paced than in other-paced activity formats in both reading and mathematics. The slight increase in self-paced formats from second to fifth grade is consistent with the Lambert and Hartsough data discussed earlier. It is also apparent the students do not spend a great deal of time interacting with the teacher, the percentages of 'no teacher interaction' being about 67 to 75 for second-grade reading and maths, and about 74 to 79 for fifth-grade reading and maths.

If we look at the engagement data, we find a 13 to 16 percentage point increase as the activity format goes from self-paced to other-paced. It appears that self-paced activity formats are less sustaining attentionally than teacher-paced activity formats. But the issue is probably more complex than it appears at first, and there is some evidence that grouping arrangement influences student involvement. For example, Good and Beckerman (1978) report engagement percentages of 82, 79 and 66 for teacher-directed small groups, teacher-directed large groups, and teacher-directed, whole-class presentations. In fact, their engagement percentage for the self-paced format (what they called 'individual setting') was 71, higher than that reported for the teacher-directed whole-class format. And Stodolsky (1983) reports slightly higher engagement percentages in child-paced activity formats than in teacher-paced formats for maths but not for social studies.

It is likely that student involvement is influenced by a number of the properties of activity formats as well as the type of tasks which are embedded in the activity. How these properties interact to determine student involvement, however, is not clear. Stodolsky (1983) does present an analysis of student involvement that suggests a complex interaction between pacing, type of learning task and curricular topic. More research on the effects of properties of activity formats on student involvement would very likely prove to be fruitful.

Table 5.8: *Mean Per Cent of Instructional Time and Mean Per Cent Engagement Rate in Self-paced and Other-paced Activity Formats*

	2nd Grade				5th Grade			
	Reading		Maths		Reading		Maths	
Activity format	Time	Engagement	Time	Engagement	Time	Engagement	Time	Engagement
Self-paced	64.3	68	73.5	67	68.7	70	76.0	72
Interaction with teacher	6.5		6.6		2.3		3.3	
No teacher interaction	57.8		66.9		66.4		72.7	
Other-paced	35.7	84	26.5	82	31.2	84	24.0	85
Interaction with teacher	26.7		18.6		23.6		18.0	
No teacher interaction	9.0		7.9		7.6		6.0	

Source: Adapted from Fisher *et al.* (1978), Tables 5-2 and 5-6.
Note: Engagement rate is the percentage of observational time students appear to be attending.

Learning Tasks

The learning task embedded within an activity is obviously an important component of the activity. The types of learning tasks that students focus on during activities is not as well documented as one might expect however. The data that exist do suggest that not a great deal of higher-level cognitive behaviour is expected of students in elementary schools. For example, Gansneder, Caldwell, Morris, Napier and Bowen (1977) had 67 elementary school teachers report their instructional objective for three consecutive days. These objectives were then coded according to type and level of expected behaviour. They found that 73 per cent of the objectives were cognitive, 14 per cent were affective, and 8 per cent were psychomotor (5 per cent were not codable). Within the cognitive objectives only 4 per cent were classified above the level of knowledge or comprehension.

It is possible to examine this rather crude analysis in considerably more detail in the study by Calfee and Calfee (1976) discussed earlier. They coded the type of task[4] that students were working on during the lessons they observed, and their data are reported in Table 5.9. Again, their data are reported in percentage of total student minutes averaged across classrooms within grade level and curricular area.

Table 5.9: Per Cent of Total Student Minutes in Reading and Maths Spent in Different Types of Tasks

Task	2nd Grade		5th Grade	
	Reading/language	Maths	Reading/language	Maths
New concept	1.8 (15)	3.2 (12)	4.1 (12)	0.6 (6)
New skill	1.9 (5)	1.3 (5)	1.0 (8)	0.4 (4)
New fact	2.2 (20)	1.6 (5)	3.2 (22)	2.5 (10)
Practise concept	0.3 (7)	2.6 (15)	1.9 (12)	3.9 (14)
Practise skill	54.1 (95)	48.6 (77)	51.1 (88)	55.6 (84)
Practise fact	4.2 (30)	7.6 (20)	4.4 (27)	3.8 (20)
Review concept	0.8 (17)	4.1 (15)	1.6 (18)	1.7 (12)
Review skill	5.1 (30)	15.8 (35)	4.6 (27)	10.4 (37)
Review fact	8.9 (37)	2.6 (15)	4.8 (35)	5.6 (18)
Apply concept	1.6 (17)	0.0 (0)	4.0 (20)	0.6 (4)
Apply skill	4.5 (30)	3.2 (10)	3.7 (29)	3.1 (14)
Apply fact	0.3 (2)	0.0 (0)	4.0 (16)	1.5 (4)
Student time unaccounted for	14.3	9.4	11.6	10.3

Source: Calfee and Calfee (1976), Table 3.
Note: See text for explanation of data. Numbers in parentheses are percentages of classroom in which the tasks were observed.

The amount of student time spent practising skills is striking. This one category accounts for roughly 50 per cent of student time regardless of grade level or curricular topic. Another 11 to 22 per cent of time is spent in reviewing facts, skills, or concepts. Only 3 to 12 per cent of the time are students making applications of the content they are learning. There is a doubling in time spent in application from second-grade to fifth-grade, an increase one might expect, but the absolute levels even after this doubling are low, 12 per cent of student time in fifth-grade reading and 5 per cent of student time in fifth-grade maths. Stodolsky (1983) reports similar data for fifth-grade maths, but considerable more diversity of expected cognitive performance and higher levels of application in fifth-grade social studies.

Data on teacher reports of daily time spent in mathematics tasks somewhat similar to the categories of Calfee and Calfee are given by Graeber, Rim and Unks (1977). They collected questionnaire data from teachers based on a stratified random sample of schools in a three-state area of the Northeast. A 43 per cent return yielded over 1,300 questionnaires from first, third, fifth and seventh-grade teachers. Table 5.10 reports the percentage of teachers at each grade level responding to each duration category for four different types of tasks. These data are somewhat difficult to interpret, given the grouped score intervals of the number of minutes spent, but they do provide some descriptive information on trends across grade level.

The majority of teachers at all grade levels report that they spend between 6 and 15 minutes daily introducing new content to students. In this category there does not appear to be any systematic interaction between number of minutes spent and grade level. This does not appear to be the case for practice tasks, either with new material or review concepts, but the nature of the interaction is far from obvious. Seventh-grade teachers appear to report spending less time practising new material than any of the other grade-level teachers, and there appears to be a systematic decrease from first to seventh grade in reported time spent practising review concepts. The less time spent practising is apparently made up in reviewing homework, as there is clearly a trend in more time spent in this task, and the no-response category can be taken as a rough indicator of whether teachers even assign homework.

Summary of Time-use

There is no easy summary of the data reported in this chapter. Time metrics vary widely across studies, curriculum areas are different, and grade levels change. Perhaps the most difficult aspect of this research

Table 5.10: Reported Number of Daily Minutes Spent in Mathematics in Different Types of Tasks

Number of minutes	Introducing new material Grade				Practising new material Grade				Practising review concepts Grade				Reviewing homework Grade			
	1	3	5	7	1	3	5	7	1	3	5	7	1	3	5	7
0-5	2.1	3.2	0.0	4.8	2.7	1.6	1.6	8.6	16.6	19.2	28.4	48.5	33.9	34.7	18.5	14.8
6-15	73.0	57.0	64.9	64.9	59.7	44.7	47.7	70.5	57.2	58.6	45.8	31.1	14.0	42.7	64.8	75.5
16-25	19.9	28.5	27.6	25.4	30.4	37.7	31.7	14.2	13.7	8.0	7.5	2.5	0.9	3.2	5.3	4.0
Over 25	3.0	5.1	4.6	2.4	4.8	9.3	14.4	3.8	4.8	2.5	4.4	1.7	0.0	0.3	0.6	1.1
No response	2.1	5.8	2.8	2.6	2.7	6.5	4.7	3.4	7.7	11.4	13.8	16.4	51.3	18.8	10.7	4.7

Source: Adapted from Graeber et al. (1977), Tables 3, 4, 5 and 6.
Note: Numbers are percentages of teachers responding to each category.

and data is that definitions of the observational-category codings combine and confound different properties of activities. It is clear that a better conceptualization of the context of teaching and the classroom environment would result in better observational data in general, and better time-use data in particular. *Post hoc* conceptualizations, as attempted in this paper, are fraught with difficulties.

Still, a picture of elementary classrooms does emerge from the data reported in this chapter, although it is a vague picture. Students spend a great deal of their instructional time in whole-group recitation and individual seatwork activity formats where direct teacher interaction occurs less than one might expect, even with 30 to 1 student-teacher ratios. For a sizeable percentage of this time, students have primary responsibility for the pacing of the activities they are engaged in, yet the tasks embedded in these activities are predominantly practice and review tasks, where the expected cognitive behaviour is largely low-level processing of skills they have been taught. This general picture of elementary classrooms is similar to that drawn by Goodlad, Klein and associates (1974):

> The instructional environment of the classes we visited, more in grades one through three than in the kindergarten, were characterized by telling, teachers' questioning individual children in group settings, and an enormous amount of seemingly quite routine seatwork. Rather than probing, seeking, inquiring, children were predominantly responding and covering. Even when using the materials of curriculum projects presumably emphasizing 'discovery' methods, pupils appeared bent on covering the content of textbooks, workbooks, and supplementary reading material. (p. 79)

Somewhere in this mosaic of time-use in the elementary classroom exists what may be termed 'quality of instructional time'. Even though the same activities take place in a multitude of classrooms, some teachers are simply better at providing more productive instructional time and promoting learning than others. I would like to close this chapter by suggesting that it is not the activities that fill the time in elementary schools that are important, but the way in which those activities flow in time. The hypothesis to be offered is that flow of activity influences the quality of instructional time.

Activity Flow and Lesson Flow in Classrooms

The thesis that the flow within and between activities influences the quality of instructional time is not based on any direct evidence. Rather, it is based on the simplistic reasoning that since there is not a great deal of diversity in classrooms in the types of activities which occur (as evidenced by the data presented in this chapter), then the way in which teachers direct and maintain the flow of those activities must be important. Some indirect evidence does exist which supports this thesis.

Activity flow, as defined here, refers to the psychological and procedural continuity of a particular activity. Psychological continuity is the consistency of students' concentration and involvement in the task component of the activity. As such, it is an internal state of the learner. Procedural continuity refers to the absence of external distractions and interruptions during the activity. As such, it is a characteristic of the learning environment. The two types of continuity are interrelated. If few distractions occur, then the procedural continuity of the activity provides support for psychological continuity. If many distractions occur, then the procedural continuity is absent and no support is provided for psychological continuity. This latter condition does not mean psychological continuity will be absent; it simply means that the activity will not provide external support for internal concentration and involvement on the part of the students.

Although activity flow is important, it is only part of a complex picture. Since most lessons consist of a sequence of activities, the continuity between activities within the lesson must also be considered if we are to understand the quality of instructional time. Let me refer to such continuity as lesson flow.

As might be expected, there are psychological and procedural parameters of lesson flow, but they are slightly different from those discussed in the context of activity flow. With respect to lessons, procedural continuity refers to an orderly transition between activities with relatively little loss of instructional time. Psychological continuity is closely related to the accomplishment of the goal of the lesson. To the extent that concentration and involvement in the task components of the sequence of activities lead to the attainment of the goal of the lesson, then psychological continuity exists in the lesson.

Consider the following analysis. When a teacher begins a lesson, the teacher usually has a goal or purpose in mind for that lesson. It might be, for example, mastery of a skill or concept, or coverage of a specific number of pages in a textbook. To attain this goal in the available time, the psychological and procedural parameters of activity flow and lesson flow must exist. Teacher concerns during the lesson are related to these parameters, and a number of cues in the classroom environment can be used by teachers to monitor the activity and lesson flow. These teacher concerns and cues are presented in Figure 5.2 for activities and for lessons, and for psychological and procedural continuity. Each of the four teacher concerns are numbered in the order that they might normally occur during a lesson, and the discussion that follows will treat each in turn.

Figure 5.2: Some Parameters of Activity Flow and Lesson Flow

		Activity	Lesson
Psychological Continuity	Teacher Concern	1. Concentration on task component of activity	4. Completion of lesson goal on time
	Teacher Cues	Involvement	Pace of lesson Steering groups
Procedural Continuity	Teacher Concern	2. Minimize distraction and interruptions	3. Orderly and time-saving transitions between activities
	Teacher Cues	Cooperation	Orderliness Noise level Duration of transition

Once the first activity of a lesson is underway, a major concern of teachers is to maintain student concentration on the task component of the activity. A primary cue which teachers use to gauge the extent of psychological continuity during an activity and to assess how an activity is progressing is student involvement (see Clark and Yinger, 1979; Jackson, 1968; Joyce, 1978-9; Morine-Dershimer, 1978-9; Zahorik, 1982). It is likely that student involvement is an immediate and easily recognizable cue for teachers that learning is going on.

To help maintain this psychological continuity, it seems natural to assume that there should be minimal interruptions and distractions during the activity. A second concern of teachers, therefore, although I have little data to support this contention, is to provide the procedural continuity to support this involvement in learning. The work of Kounin (1970) clearly suggests there are substantial individual differences among teachers in their ability to maintain the procedural continuity of the activity. Furthermore, a recent observational study by

Behnke, Labovitz, Bennett, Chase, Day, Lazar and Mittleholtz (1981) documents dramatically that interruptions are a common occurrence in classrooms, while at the same time providing further support for Kounin's findings. Behnke *et al*. recorded the number of distractions (defined as 'those events which take teachers and/or their students off the intended instructional tasks' (p. 136)), and the coping responses of teachers to those distractions during nine 60-minute observations in each of eight elementary classrooms during reading lessons. The average number of distractions per 60-minute observation was 42, and the range between classrooms was 30 to 61 per hour. That is, twice as many distractions occurred in some classrooms as in others.

Doyle (1979) has argued persuasively that a primary task of teachers is to 'gain and maintain co-operation in classroom activities' (p. 47). It is suggested here that teachers use co-operation as a major cue to gauge the extent to which the procedural continuity of the activity is being maintained. A lack of co-operation in the activity on the part of students would obviously cause more interruptions and distractions during the activity. That students are the primary source of distractions is clear from the Behnke *et al*. (1981) study cited above. Fully 89 per cent of all the distractions which occurred were student generated, and 25 per cent of all distractions were students verbally interrupting the teacher.

Since activities are embedded within lessons, the movement from one activity to another requires some sort of transition. Speculating again, a third concern of teachers during a lesson would seem to be an orderly, short transition between the end of one activity and the beginning of the next. This procedural continuity between activities within a lesson suggests that orderliness, noise level and transition duration may be some of the cues used by teachers to gauge how well transitions are occurring. Arlin (1979) discussed at length some of the techniques that teachers use, or do not use, which influence the quality of transitions. In this vein it is interesting to note that Evertson (1982) found that even though there were more transitions in higher-ability junior high maths and English classes, the duration of transitions and total time spent in transitions were greater in lower-ability classes. She suggests that teachers may not change activities as much in lower-ability classrooms because it takes longer for these students to get involved in the new activity after the transition.

Once the transition is completed and a second activity is underway, teachers return to the first and second concerns and cues shown in Figure 5.2. Sometime during the lesson, however, teachers would likely begin to assess the progress of students toward the goal of the lesson, whether that be mastery of specific objectives, coverage of specific content, or some other purpose. This fourth and final concern in Figure 5.2 suggests that the pacing of the lesson may be a cue by which teachers derive information as to the extent to which students are achieving the goal of the lesson. How salient pacing cues are, however, is unclear. Barr (1975) reports that teachers, although aware of pacing differences between reading groups, were unaware of the cues used to set instructional pace. One hypothesis is the concept of a 'steering group' (see Barr and Dreeban, 1977; Dahloff, 1971; Good, Grouws and Beckerman, 1978), which is defined as some subgroup of the class whose progress is monitored by the teacher and used to modify the rate of instruction and learning.

Regardless of the cues that might be used by teachers for this final concern of lesson-goal attainment, the attainment of the lesson goal itself seems crucial to the psychological continuity of the lesson. Teachers who consistently fall short of achieving their lesson goals and end lessons prematurely, either because too much time is lost in distractions and/or transitions, or because of their inability to maintain student involvement, are not providing the activity flow and lesson flow hypothesized here to characterize good instruction. Students who experience closure to lessons on a consistent basis must surely have an easier time learning than students who do not experience such closure.

The thesis presented here that activity flow and lesson flow are two important indicators of the quality of instructional time is admittedly speculative. It does, however, suggest a common denominator for two of the major interactive teaching tasks that confront teachers in the classroom; namely the management of learners and the management of their learning. To the extent that teachers are able to use the cues available to them and provide procedural continuity to a lesson through effective management skills, they will be better able to support the psychological continuity necessary for effective instruction. And to the extent that psychological continuity can be maintained, student learning will be enhanced.

How the temporal distribution of activities within a lesson influence the ability of teachers to provide such continuity seems a relevant first question. And how procedural and psychological continuity come together and interact to produce quality instructional time in classrooms seems a potent agenda for future research. Such understanding is essential since, as was suggested at the beginning of this chapter, the meaning of time, not the amount *per se*, needs to be the focus of time research in classrooms.

Notes

1. Time is a dimension which humans scale arbitrarily for measurement purposes. In educational research time can be used to quantify a wide variety of classroom activities and events. Researchers have been somewhat remiss in accurately reporting what events they are measuring and what time metric they are using for quantification. Several potentially informative studies could not be used here bcause it was impossible to determine what time the researchers were writing about, or there were major inconsistencies in their reported data (e.g. they did not explain why the percentages of codes from supposedly mutually exclusive and exhaustive coding categories did not sum to 100 per cent).

2. This view of learning task is consistent with Doyle's (1979, 1980) discussion of tasks, but it is less restricted than Doyle's emphasis on the information-processing operations necessary to achieve a goal, and his placement of tasks within a formal performance-grade exchange framework. Doyle (1979, p. 46) is correct when he states that most classroom observational research focuses on time-on-activity rather than time-on-task. Activity is observable; information-processing is not. But time-on-activity still provides a measure for time-on-task to the extent that an activity contains a relevant task. One other analytic note is in order. In discussing tasks, it is important to be clear from whose perspective one is speaking. From a teacher's perspective, an activity need not contain a learning task, as in the case when teachers assign activities for no other reason than to fill time or occupy students' attention. From a student's perspective, this same activity does contain a task component, since the student is expected to attempt or complete whatever the requirements of the activity are. In this sense then, Figure 5.2 presents a view of the task from the student's perspective.

3. The typical practice in instructional research is to treat opposing teaching methods as being qualitatively distinct. But as Cooley and Lohnes (1976, Chapter 5) and Leinhardt (1980) argue, different teaching methods often share attributes in common, and merely differ on certain dimensions. The analysis of activities presented here suggest that different teaching methods often share common activity formats and the properties of those formats.

4. Strictly speaking, the use of term 'task' is inappropriate here. It is not directly apparent what type of cognitive behaviour is occurring from coding categories such as 'practice concepts' or 'review skills'. Still, some inferences can be made, and that is the reason for the use of the term.

References

Arlin, M. (1979) 'Teacher Transitions Can Disrupt Time Flow in Classrooms', *American Educational Research Journal, 16*, 42-56

Barr, R. (1975) 'How Children Are Taught to Read: Grouping and Pacing', *School Review, 83*, 479-98

—— and Dreeben, R. (1977) 'Instruction in Classrooms' in L. Shulman (ed.), *Review of Research in Education, vol. 5*, Itasca, Ill.: F.E. Peacock

Behnke, G., Labovitz, E., Bennett, J., Chase, C., Day, J., Lazar, C. and Mittleholtz, D. (1981) 'Coping With Classroom Distractions', *The Elementary School Journal, 81*, 135-55

Berliner, D. (1979) 'Tempus Educare' in P. Peterson and H. Walberg (eds), *Research on Teaching: Concepts, Findings, and Implications*, Berkeley, California: McCutchan

—— and Gage, N. (1976) 'The Psychology of Teaching Methods' in N. Gage (ed.), *The Psychology of Teaching Methods*, Chicago, Ill.: The University of Chicago Press

Blumenfeld, P. (1980) 'An Initial Model of the Relation Between Work Form, Content and Process'. Paper presented at the Annual Meeting of the American Educational Research Association, Boston

——, Pintrich, P., Meece, J. and Wessels, K. (1982) 'The Formation and Role of Self-perceptions of Ability in Elementary Classrooms', *The Elementary School Journal, 82*, 401-20

Bossert, S. (1979) *Tasks and Social Relationships in Classrooms*, Cambridge: Harvard University Press

Brady, M., Clinton, C., Sweeney, J., Peterson, M. and Poyner, H. (1977) *Final Report of the Instructional Dimensions Study, 1976-77*, Washington, DC: National Institute of Education

Brophy, J. (1980) *Teachers' Cognitive Activities and Overt Behaviors. Occasional Paper No. 39*, Michigan State University: Institute for Research on Teaching

Caldwell, J., Huitt, W. and Graeber, A. (1982) 'Time Spent in Learning: Implications from Research', *The Elementary School Journal, 82*, 471-80

Calfee, R. and Calfee, K. (1976) *Beginning Teacher Evaluation Study: Phase II, 1973-74, Final Report*, Princeton: Educational Testing Service

Clark, C. and Yinger, R. (1979) 'Teachers' Thinking' in P. Peterson and H. Walberg (eds), *Research on Teaching*, Berkeley: McCutchan

Cooley, W., and Lohnes, P. (1976) *Evaluation Research in Education*, New York: Irvington

Dahloff, U. (1971) *Ability Grouping, Content Validity and Curriculum Process Analysis*, New York: Teacher's College Press

Denham, C. and Lieberman, A. (eds), (1980) *Time to Learn*, Washington, DC: National Institute of Education

Doyle, W. (1979) 'Making Managerial Decisions in Classrooms' in D. Duke (ed.), *Classroom Management*, Chicago: University of Chicago Press

—— (1980) *Student Mediating Responses in Teacher Effectiveness, Final Report*. Washington, DC: National Institute of Education

Erickson, F. (1982) 'Classroom Discourse as Improvisation: Relationships Between Academic Task Structure and Social Participation Structure in Lessons' in L. Wilkinson (ed.), *Communicating in the Classroom*, New York: Academic Press

Evertson, C. (1982) 'Differences in Instructional Activities in Higher- and Lower-Achieving Junior High English Classes', *The Elementary School Journal, 82*, 329-50

Fisher, C., Filby, N., Marliave, R., Cahen, L., Dishaw, M., Moore, J. and Berliner, D. (1978) *Teaching Behaviors, Academic Learning Time and Student Achievement: Final Report of Phase III-B, Beginning Teacher Evaluation Study*, San Francisco: Far West Laboratory for Educational Research and Development

Frederick, W. and Walberg, H. (1980) 'Learning as a Function of Time', *Journal of Educational Research, 73*, 183-94

Gansneder, B., Caldwell, M., Morris, J., Napier, J. and Bowen, L. (1977) 'An Analysis of the Association Between Teachers' Classroom Objectives and Activities', *Journal of Educational Research, 70*, 175-9

Good, T. and Beckerman, T. (1978) 'Time on Task: a Naturalistic Study in Sixth-grade Classrooms', *The Elementary School Journal, 78*, 193-201

——, Grouws, D. and Beckerman, T. (1978) 'Curriculum Pacing: Some Empirical Data in Mathematics', *Journal of Curriculum Studies, 10*, 75-81

Goodlad, J., Klein, M. and associates. (1974) *Looking Behind the Classroom Door*, Belmont, California: Wadsworth

Graeber, A., Rim, E. and Unks, N. (1977) *A Survey of Classroom Practices in Mathematics: Reports of First, Third, Fifth, and Seventh-grade Teachers in Delaware, New Jersey, and Pennsylvania*, Philadelphia: Research for Better Schools, Inc.

Green, J. (1983) 'Research on Teaching as a Linguistic Process: a State of the Art', *Review of Research in Education, 10*, 151-252

Gump, P. (1967) *The Classroom Behavior Setting: Its Nature and Relation to Student Behavior, Final Report*, Washington, DC: US Department of Health, Education and Welfare, Office of Education

—— (1969) 'Intra-setting Analysis: the Third-grade Classroom as a Special But Instructive Case' in E. Willems and H. Raush (eds), *Naturalistic Viewpoints in Psychological Research*, New York: Holt, Rinehart & Winston

—— (1971) 'What's Happening in the Elementary Classroom?' in I. Westbury and A. Bellack (eds), *Research into Classroom Processes: Recent Developments and Next Steps'*, New York: Teachers College Press

Herman, W. (1967) 'The Use of Language Arts in Social Studies Lessons', *American Educational Research Journal, 4*, 117-24

Hoetker, J. and Ahlbrand, W. (1969) 'The Persistence of the Recitation', *American Educational Research Journal, 6*, 145-267

Jackson, P. (1968) *Life in Classrooms*. New York: Holt, Rinehart & Winston

—— and Lahaderne, H. (1967) 'Inequalities of Teach-Pupil Contacts', *Psychology in the Schools, 4*, 204-8

Joyce, B. (1978/9) 'Toward a Theory of Information Processing in Teaching', *Educational Research Quarterly, 3*, 66-77

Karweit, N. and Slavin, R. (1981) 'Measurement and Modeling Choices in Studies of Time and Learning', *American Educational Research Journal, 18*, 157-71

Kounin, J. (1970) *Discipline and Group Management in Classrooms*. New York: Holt, Rinehart & Winston

Lambert, N. and Hartsough, C. (1976) *Beginning Teacher Evaluation Study: Phase II, 1973-74, Final Report*, Princeton: Educational Testing Service

Leinhardt, G. (1980) 'Modeling and Measuring Educational Treatment in Evaluation', *Review of Educational Research, 50*, 393-420

Lomax, R. and Cooley, W. (1979) 'The Student Achievement-Instructional Time Relationship'. Paper presented at the annual meeting of the American Educational Research Association, San Francisco, April

MacDonald, J. (1965) 'Myths About Instruction', *Educational Leadership, 22*, 571-6, 609-17

McDonald, F. and Elias, P. (1976) *Beginning Teacher Evaluation Study: Phase II, 1973-74, Final Report*, Princeton: Educational Testing Service

Mehan, H. (1979) *Learning Lessons: Social Organization in the Classroom*, Cambridge: Harvard University Press

Morine-Dershimer, M. (1978/9) 'How Teachers "see" their pupils', *Educational Research Quarterly, 3*, 43-52

Philips, S. (1972) 'Participant Structures and Communicative Competence: Warm Springs Children in Community and Classroom' in C. Cazden, V. John, and D. Hymes (eds), *Functions of Language in the Classroom*, New York: Teachers College Press

Roehler, L., Schmidt, W. and Buchman, M. (1979) *How Do Teachers Spend Their Language Arts Time? Research Series No. 66*, Michigan State University: The Institute for Research on Teaching

Rosenshine, B. (1978) 'Academic Engaged Time, Content Covered, and Direct Instruction', *Journal of Education, 160*, 38-66

—— (1981) 'How Time is Spent in Elementary Classrooms', *The Journal of Classroom Interaction, 17*, 16-25

Shavelson, R. and Stern, P. (1981) 'Research on Teachers' Pedagogical Thoughts, Judgements, Decisions and Behavior', *Review of Educational Research, 51*, 455-98

Smith, L. and Geoffrey, W. (1968) *The Complexities of an Urban Classroom*, New York: Holt, Rinehart & Winston

Stallings, J. (1980) 'Allocated Academic Learning Time Revisited, or Beyond Time on Task', *Educational Research, 9*, 11-16

Stodolsky, S. (1981) 'Subject Matter Constraints on the Ecology of Classroom Instruction'. Paper presented at the Annual Meeting of the American Educational Research Association, Los Angeles, April

——— (1983) 'An Ecological Perspective on Classroom Instruction: Implications for Teacher Education'. Proceedings of the Bat-Sheva Seminar on Pre-service and In-service Education of Science Teachers, Israel, January

Whipple, G. (ed.) (1934) *The Activity Movement*. Bloomington, Ill.: Public School Publishing Company

Yinger, R. (1979) 'Routines in Teacher Planning', *Theory into Practices, 18*, 163-9

Zahorik, J. (1982) 'Learning Activities: Nature, Function and Practice', *The Elementary School Journal*, 309-17

6 TIME, ACHIEVEMENT AND TEACHER DEVELOPMENT

W. John Smyth

Issues raised in previous chapters highlight the fact that time is indeed the 'coin of the realm' in schooling. Far from being a variable that is merely consumed or used up in the process of schooling, instructional time has important quantitative and qualitative dimensions and consequences for teaching as well as learning. Neither is time in school learning a simple variable capable only of calibration, as some commentators suggest. Rather, time in the context of schooling is far more complex. Time has a transactional quality for students and teachers — both are required to 'invest' time if learning is to occur. This common currency between teaching and learning makes possible something which is quite unusual in research and discussion about schooling — a medium through which both can be examined simultaneously.

Discussion in this chapter starts by endorsing the view that time has an important enabling quality that facilitates teaching and learning. Consideration is given to the current state of research knowledge about the relationship between time and school learning as reflected through measures of student achievement. Research is first reviewed that focuses on the nexus between allocated time and school learning. The second section of the chapter presents research evidence about the relationship between the more refined concept of engaged time or time-on-task and achievement. This section also includes a review of what some of the descriptive research suggests about variability across classrooms. The utility of learning time as a variable in the study of teaching becomes especially obvious in this section as the connection is traced among variables under the teacher's control that influence pupil engagement in learning.

The final section of this chapter addresses the often neglected dimension of how to make best use of research knowledge about instructional time. The suggestion is made that teachers should be encouraged and assisted to explore their own teaching through the collection and analysis of, and reflection upon, data on instructional and learning time. Some research on teacher development is canvassed that suggests the implementation of existing knowledge about the effects of instructional and learning time, and the pursuit of new and interesting research questions, might usefully be served by a collaboration between and among teachers in natural classroom settings. The research on teacher development provides a useful and valuable linkage with the substantive findings from research on learning time.

Research on Allocated Time

At the risk of being accused of stating the obvious, I believe there is something comforting and appealing to both teachers and researchers about the commonsense notion that 'students learn when teachers teach'. Behind this obvious revelation is the often overlooked dictum that 'commonsense does not necessarily imply widespread or common practice'. Where there is an expectation that learning shall occur, students must be provided with adequate opportunity to learn. Teachers have not always been sensitive to the importance of monitoring the extent to which students are provided with opportunities to interact with specific learning activities and content.

Quite apart from its relationship to student achievement, allocated time is interesting because of its potential as a 'teacher controllable variable' (Bloom, 1980). In the context of schooling where so many variables are subject to the conflicting and confounding influence of external constraints, it is encouraging to find at least some factors over which teachers and administrators can exercise some control. This is not to suggest that the overall impact of such control is necessarily large. Rather, the fact is that schools and individual teachers can have some *control* over the learning outcomes of students. Allocating more time is not a panacea for all manner of educational ills. While time is certainly an influential mechanism in gaining an understanding of classroom life, Jackson's (1977) caveat is a relevant one:

> There has been a lot of talk about the importance of time in the determination of educational outcomes . . . Certainly, we should take a look at how time is being used or misused in our schools. It may indeed turn out to be the culprit that critics claim it is. As we test this possibility, however, we must keep in mind that time itself is valueless. It acquires value chiefly because it marks the expenditure of a precious commodity — human life . . . Let us not seize too quickly at remedies for our educational ailments that call for little more than adding days or hours to our present efforts (p. 38).

Expressed in these terms, allocated time clearly has important qualitative as well as quantitative dimensions. Depending upon how it is actually used, equal units of allocated time can have very different impact on student-learning outcomes.

Research on allocated time has either been descriptive, in an attempt to sketch the extent of variations in the way teachers apportion time in and across different curriculum content areas, or correlational in seeking to establish a relationship between time and achievement. Indeed, one of the earliest reported pieces of educational research in the USA was undertaken by Rice in 1897 to investigate the differential impact of allocated time on spelling achievement. The fact that Rice failed to find a significant relationship between time allocated to spelling and spelling achievement does not seem to have deterred the large number of studies that have subsequently pursued the connection between allocated time and student achievement.

Evidence from the descriptive research is clear enough; as we might expect, there is an enormous variability between classrooms in the amount of time teachers allocate to curriculum areas, even where mandatory requirements do exist. Berliner (1979) found that some second-grade teachers allocated twice as much time to language arts and mathematics instruction as did other teachers. In practical terms some youngsters received fewer than 130 hours in total of reading and mathematics instruction over the course of a school year. This variability has also been documented by Garner (1978) and Harnischfeger and Wiley (1977) at the fifth-grade level. Much the same evidence also appears to emerge from similar studies in the UK.

Before we become overly concerned about what may appear to be inequalities in the distribution of allocated time, we should think about some of the realities. Schools being the kind of 'loosely linked' institutions they are, it is not surprising that considerable variation exists in the way learning time is allocated. Given the importance of local needs and contexts in learning, this flexibility should not only be preserved, but encouraged. Schools and teachers, however, should be aware of the way they disburse their time across various curriculum aspects, and be sensitive to the likely consequences. It becomes problematic when teachers and school administrators are unaware of the way they allocate learning time, and are therefore ignorant of the likely impact of their decisions on pupils' opportunity to learn.

The research evidence on the relationship between allocated time and achievement is not altogether clear. Existing research has tended to focus mainly on elementary schools, and in the cognitive areas of reading and mathematics. Several studies (Guthrie, Martuza and Seifert, 1976; Welch and Bridgham, 1968; Felsenthal and Kirsch, 1978; Smith, 1976) have been unable to show that students who receive greater allocations of time in these subject areas performed any better than other students. This finding probably reflects more about the way the studies were conducted than anything else. The tendency was to rely on teacher self-reports of time allocations – a practice which is notoriously inaccurate, given the complexity of life in classrooms. Other studies (Fisher, Filby and Marliave, 1977; Wolf, 1979; Vivars, 1976; Kidder, O'Reilly and Kiesling, 1975; Husen, 1972), however, have shown a sufficiently strong relationship between allocated time and achievement for this to be a legitimate domain for concern. To *what* should time in schools be allocated? To *whom* should time in schools be allocated? Such value-laden questions about equity of treatment and the extent to which schools (and classrooms in particular) reflect and respond to the aspirations of their communities are difficult ones indeed. Evidence about the allocated time-achievement nexus seems to be consistent enough for schools to carefully consider the methods and strategies they have to assist teachers in examining their allocations of in-class time to competing curriculum areas, and to students who compete for the precious commodity of teacher attention.

Research on Time-on-task

A point *not* to be overlooked in the discussion about the relationship between allocated time and achievement is that the research is *not* saying that 'time makes no difference'. On the contrary, the research suggests that global measures of learning time are *not* always consistent predictors of achievement, especially when data are collected by means of teacher self-reports. Establishing a relationship between time and achievement, therefore, requires a much more proximal measure of time. Engaged time, or pupil time-on-task (Smyth, 1983), has long been regarded as such a variable. Because it refers to the amount of time during which pupils are actively involved in learning, rather than the time during which they are exposed to learning activities and materials, time-on-task has been regarded as a useful proxy variable for learning. There is a long-standing belief, accurate or not, that time-on-task is a reliable predictor of pupil achievement; recently a great deal of empirical support has been garnered.

Early research on pupil-engaged learning time (French, 1924; Morrison, 1926), conducted under the guise of class-attention studies, really aimed to establish a basis for the assessment of teacher effectiveness. Pupil attention seemed a logical and measurable way for rating teacher performance. Quite apart from their intended purpose, these studies did provide some important methodological pointers for later observational studies of pupil engagement.

A spate of studies commencing in the 1950s and continuing to the mid-1970s (Morch, 1956; Edminston and Rhoades, 1959; Lahaderne, 1968; Ozcelik, 1973; Stallings and Kaskowitz, 1974; Samuels and Turnure, 1974; McKinney, Mason, Perkerson and Clifford, 1975; Cobb, 1972; Anderson, 1976) found, not expectedly, that the time pupils spent actively engaged was predictive of learning. This relationship was consistent across a range of pupils, in various curriculum areas, and in a variety of different educational settings. According to research summarized by Bloom (1974), variations in pupil engagement were highly predictive of student achievement, and accounted for as much as 20 per cent of the variation in achievement.

What these studies have done, apart from the relationship they established, is to lay a groundwork for further intensive research into teacher-behaviour variables and classroom settings that impact upon pupil engagement. While several recent studies have broadened and elaborated upon the engaged time-achievement relationship (Lee, Carriere, MacQueen, Poynor and Rogers, 1981; Stallings, 1980), there are still unanswered questions about the strength and pervasiveness of the connection (Lomax and Cooley, 1979; McNamara, 1981). While supporting the notion that classes with more engagement had higher levels of achievement, Rim and Coller (1978) found that gains in student achievement and engaged time tended to level off, and actually became negative beyond a certain amount of engaged time. This finding concurred with Karweit's (1978) finding that the relationship of time-on-task and achievement is apparently currilinear; furthermore, different students may exhibit markedly different relationships between time and learning.

These findings suggest that there may be substantial variability between classes, pupils and subject areas in terms of student-engaged time (Stodolsky, 1979). Rusnock and Brandler (1979) and Smyth (1979) both found distinctive patterns of off-task behaviour for different types of students. Whereas low-ability students tended to continually interrupt academic activity, high-ability students tended to finish a task before becoming involved in distractive behaviour. Similarly,

Good's and Beckerman's (1978) naturalistic study confirmed that pupil-engaged time varied substantially according to the ability level of the students, the curriculum content, the type of learning activity and the mode of class grouping. Although prefacing their findings with the need for research to look at the involvement of pupils across a variety of school situations, Good and Beckerman found that levels of engagement for elementary students were highest in more-structured-content areas, such as mathematics and spelling, where the learning task demanded a more active pupil response. They also found pupil engagement to be lowest during whole-class activities and individual seatwork, and highest during small-group (less than 8) and large-group (8 to 15) work with a teacher.

Grannis's (1978) findings from an ecological study of differently structured classroom settings questioned the simplicity of findings such as those of Good and Beckerman. Grannis found that learner-controlled settings could also be associated with high levels of engaged time. According to Grannis, high levels of engaged time were more likely to be an artifact of learners' judgements and feelings about the appropriateness of the learning tasks. Task appropriateness, he argued, was likely to be related to the ability of the teacher to acknowledge the learners' concerns, language and learning styles. He regarded engagement as an outcome of the extent to which joint teacher-learner control of the setting existed, and the congruence among the various demands imposed by that setting.

One of the more enterprising recent studies that has sought to escape the simplistic approach to time-on-task has been the Beginning Teacher Evaluation Study (BTES). While that study certainly added to what we know about the relationship of time-on-task and achievement, it also focused on a unique and frequently overlooked dimension of the study of teaching and learning. As Marliave (1980) pointed out, the association of time-on-task with classroom-learning outcomes was not the core of the BTES nor its more important implication. In his words, 'there exists an entirely different (although not separate) set of findings examining the relationship of instructional functions to student behavior and achievement outcomes' (p. 2). What Marliave was clearly emphasizing was that the real significance of the BTES study goes considerably beyond the notion of time-on-task and its relation to achievement.

The overwhelming importance of the BTES research lies in the group of teacher-alterable variables that emerged from the study, and the possibilities they suggested for monitoring and possibly altering classroom practice. The significance of academic learning time (an amalgam of allocated time, engagement rate and success rate) is not, and never was intended to be, for slavish prescription in all classroom situations. Rather, the significance lies in increased awareness of some areas of classroom teaching whose relationship to academic learning time (ALT) has been empirically validated, and that teachers might incorporate into their classroom practice. Bloom (1980) neatly captured the intent:

> Teachers are frequently unconscious of the fact that they provide more favourable conditions of learning for some students in the class than for others. Generally, they are under the impression that all students are given equal opportunity for learning. When teachers are helped to secure a more accurate picture of their own teaching methods and styles of interacting with their students, they are increasingly able to provide learning conditions for most of their students. (p. 385)

The 'more favorable conditions of learning' referred to by Bloom and isolated in the BTES research, include the monitoring of short-term outcomes of pupil classroom learning. In particular, these researchers (Fisher, Berliner, Filby, Marliave, Cahen and Dishaw, 1980) found that high levels of interactive teaching, where teachers provided frequent feedback to pupils about the correctness of responses, produced high levels of ALT. Likewise, clarity of teacher directions to pupils on how to proceed with learning tasks and what to do when finished, were associated with greater levels of pupil involvement in learning. Where teachers were adept at accurately diagnosing student skill levels, and capable of designing learning experiences of appropriate difficulty, pupils were found to spend more time engaged in assigned learning tasks.

Structure, clarity, direction and feedback are, therefore, elements that emphasize an underlying academic focus within teaching. The BTES research found that pupils were able to understand and respond to that implicit message. Where lessons were unstructured, aims and objectives not communicated to students, and where teachers spent considerable time trying to counteract and rectify deficiencies in planning and exhorting students 'to get back to work', levels of ALT were noticeably lower. Structural defects of this kind were clear indicators of a need for teachers to examine the level of their interactive teaching and its precision, the difficulty level of tasks they prescribed for students, or the frequency and adequacy of feedback provided to pupils.

What is interesting about these findings, and similar ones corroborated in other research, is that they are not novel. For many teachers they are a comforting endorsement of what they already do. We should not, therefore, be too hasty in rejecting these findings merely because they appear to be pedestrian or 'common sense' (cf. McNamara, 1981). It is important to provide teachers with evidence that tried and tested practices grounded in their own theories of classroom practice do, in fact, stand up under empirical scrutiny. As I have noted elsewhere:

> Confirmation of common sense notions, however, does not necessarily imply widespread or common acceptance. While research and the visions of some practitioners may both point to pupil work involvement as a logical concomitant to learning, let us not delude ourselves into believing that all classroom practitioners possess the necessary skills required for implementation. Many of the requisites *can* be acquired, but only as a consequence of careful observation and extensive practice. (Smyth, 1981, p. 142)

Research on Instructional Time and Teacher Development

The brief review of research on instructional time included in this section is clearly incomplete, and the interested reader is referred to extensive reviews elsewhere (Smyth, 1980, 1981, 1983). While some suggestions for further research will be offered at the end of this chapter, attention will now turn to what might usefully be done with what is already known about research on instructional time. So far, the research has indicated three closely related aspects.

First, allocated time or opportunity to learn represents the outer boundary within which classroom learning by students might be expected to occur. Schools and teachers are able to exercise at least some discretionary control over this aspect. At a school-wide level both teachers and principals can be mindful of the implications of allocated time through timetabling and scheduling decisions and the possible effects upon students' opportunity to learn. At the level of the classroom, individual teachers can be sensitive to how they allocate time to particular segments of the curriculum and the likely cumulative effect on students' opportunity to learn. Decisions about whether to assign out-of-school learning, in the form of homework, although often ignored (Coulter, 1979) can also be considered in the light of implications about enhanced opportunity to learn.

Secondly, time-on-task provides teachers with an in-class observational index of apparent involvement by students in substantive learning content. Monitoring a variable such as pupil involvement (or engagement), which has been shown to consistently relate to achievement, means that teachers are no longer forced to rely solely upon outcome measures, such as tests, as indicators that learning is occurring. As Marliave (1980) noted, it is a valuable indicator of on-going learning because it allows for the monitoring of learning 'without disrupting or actually displacing those events [as testing does]' (p. 20). Probably its greatest utility lies in its heuristic value to researchers and teachers as a variable that intervenes between teaching and learning. By looking at what pupils do while ostensibly learning, it is possible to isolate those teaching behaviours and aspects of classroom organization that are associated with that learning. Both teachers and researchers can more readily make the quasi-linkages between teaching 'cause' and classroom 'effect', and monitor both. By looking at the variable of pupil pursuits (or what pupils do) as an element that mediates teaching and learning processes, new research possibilities become apparent (Doyle, 1978). Teaching is no longer conceptualized as somehow mysteriously generating learning. Rather, the way teaching impacts on pupils is considered to be an important and integral part of the analysis of teaching.

Thirdly, research into instructional time has begun to underscore the importance not only of temporal aspects of learning, but of the qualitative aspect of the tasks being attended to. By highlighting this often neglected aspect, research has begun to attend to the issue of appropriateness and meaningfulness of learning experiences for children. While the research knowledge to date is slight, we do know that a high level of success is an important variable in learning (Fisher *et al.*, 1980), particularly for low-ability elementary students. Unless teachers are mindful of this, there is a possibility that learning tasks can be excessively 'easy' or excessively 'difficult', and as a consequence qualitatively impair the time spent engaged. What is being required of teachers here is clearly difficult in the classroom situation. Ensuring that individual pupils interact with learning material geared towards ensuring high levels of learning success places obvious strains upon teachers in terms of diagnosis, prescription and monitoring of learning tasks. While the realities of particular classroom contexts dictate what can realistically occur in this regard, it is nevertheless important that teachers keep the appropriateness and meaningfulness of assigned learning tasks firmly in mind.

Fisher (1980) has noted that knowing *what* and knowing *how* are two very different issues. It is one matter to understand what research on instructional time actually says; it is quite another to actually implement those findings. Indeed, there are serious questions as to whether 'implementation' is the next logical or desired step. Fenstermacher (1980), for example, raises the interesting question as to whether findings from research on teaching should be used as prescriptive rules to alter classroom practice, whether they should be regarded as evidence to be treated as problematic by teachers as they try them out experimentally in their classrooms, or whether they are best regarded as schemata for talking about, classifying and analyzing classroom events and phenomena.

Berliner (1980a) clearly had the latter in mind when advocating that findings from research on instructional time be treated as a group of orienteering variables teachers might keep in mind when monitoring the effect of their teaching. Inglis (1980) also proposed that the findings from the BTES provide teachers with a lens through which to view their own teaching and what is occurring in their classrooms. Given the incomplete nature of research in this area, it would be difficult to take seriously Fenstermacher's (1980) suggestion of using this research as rules or conclusive statements to be applied directly and extensively in classroom situations. Quite apart from the problem of actually converting these findings into actual rules, there are the problems this would create in terms of teachers' self-concept as autonomous professionals (Smyth, 1981).

Possibly the most attractive and useful of Fenstermacher's suggestions for many teachers is that of using the findings on instructional time as a source of evidence from which to derive hypotheses to be tested experimentally in their own classrooms. By researching their own practice, teachers would in effect be collecting and weighing evidence from within their own classrooms, and using this evidence as a basis for deciding as to what changes, if any, are to be made. The practicalities of how teachers might effectively and continuously monitor their own teaching, while simultaneously experimenting with the classroom implications of findings on instructional time, are not as difficult as might be thought.

There is a good deal of interest, discussion and activity at the moment in the concept of 'teacher development'. According to Feiman and Floden (1980) the emergence of this new term in the teacher education lexicon represents a shift in thinking which is away from the technical or delivery system approach to in-service education, and towards the provision of strategies that assist teachers to better understand what they do in classrooms by becoming genuinely reflective about their teaching. This process of extracting meaning from ordinary experience, while not new (Dewey, 1933), comes about as a consequence of upsetting or disturbing the equilibrium of habitual action (Feiman, 1981). In other words, as teachers are assisted in becoming inward-looking about their own practice, difficulties and doubts crystallize into problems capable of being considered in terms of alternative forms of action. This process fits well with what research has shown about how adults, and teachers, learn. Such learning occurs best in a job-embedded context where teachers use trusted colleagues to collect, analyze and reflect upon data about their own performance and experiences (Knowles, 1978; Bents and Howey, 1981; Sprinthall and Sprinthall, 1980; Smyth, Henry and Martin, 1982). The emphasis is clearly upon life-related issues, and involves mutual inquiry and structured feedback rather than the formal transmission of abstract, general or theoretical knowledge.

What is being suggested here, the idea of 'teachers-as-researchers' (Wann, 1952), is not especially new. The proposal that teachers become clinical researchers (Smyth, 1982a, 1982b) of their own and each others' teaching fits both with the intent behind the recent research on instructional time (Berliner, 1980b) and the manner in which teachers should undertake professional renewal. The variables isolated in research on instructional time shown to be related to pupil achievement (especially allocated time, time-on-task, attention, and success rate) provide ideal classroom foci for data collection, analysis, reflection and possible areas for change. The conceptual clarity of these variables and the facility with which data relating to them can be collected makes them especially suitable. There is the added advantage that because teachers continually inhabit the setting in which the variables are operative, they are able to contribute directly to the interpretation of these phenomena and assist in the formulation of new and meaningful research agendas, questions and possible solutions. Whether this occurs through collegial arrangements among teachers for in-class observation, or through partnerships with outside researchers and teacher educators is unimportant. What is of paramount importance is that teachers develop a feeling of being conscious agents in the enhancement of their own learning about teaching.

Fisher *et al.* (1980) suggested that one possibility might lie in the production of ethnographic profiles of attending and non-attending students. Case studies of this kind, done with the assistance of co-operative colleagues, may enable teachers to extract patterns of behaviour that explain how particular students use the allocated time, and why they use this time the way they do. Possession of tacit or personal knowledge of this kind enables teachers to gain control over their actions and act in a deliberate manner. Similarly, profiles of how teachers orchestrate their own time (Stallings, 1980) among competing claims within classrooms, and how they distribute time and attention among individual pupils through interactive teaching (monitoring, feedback, questioning, praise, directives, etc.), provides an important baseline from which teachers can reflect about their practice.

Discussion

One of the persistent difficulties with apparently simple constructs in schooling is that they are invariably misconstrued. Such misunderstanding occurs for various reasons, not the least of which is the cursory way in which research on these variables is read and interpreted. This problem is quite evident with respect to instructional time, especially the components of allocated time and time-on-task. Whereas it is easy to see the former as a 'quick fix' method of alleviating educational ills by increasing it quantitatively, the latter has the problem of being portrayed in the popular educational literature as really amounting to little more than a common-sense notion. Overlooked in these superficial interpretations of instructional and learning times are important questions about educational justice, values and opportunities. Likewise, considerations of teacher self-efficacy and self-control borne out of a greater understanding of classroom contexts rarely rate a mention.

This chapter has attempted to show that there is an articulate body of research that reveals an important and consistent relationship between achievement and facets of instructional and learning time, and that there are distinct aspects of teacher behaviour which can be altered to enhance effective time use by the students and, ultimately, a variety of learning outcomes. Furthermore, empirical support does exist for a mode of teacher development by which teachers can selectively monitor their teaching both to increase their understanding and to improve their classroom performance. To quote from Devaney (1977), teachers who use this approach can 'reach a state of development where they see the teaching act itself as a source of knowledge' (p. 21).

References

Anderson, L. (1976) 'An Empirical Investigation of Individual Differences in Time to Learn', *Journal of Educational Psychology, 68*(2), 226-33

Bents, R. and Howey, K. (1981) 'Staff Development: Change in the Individual' in B. Dillon-Peterson (ed.), *Staff Development/Organizational Development*, Alexandria, Va: Association for Supervision and Curriculum Development, 11-36

Berliner, D. (1979) 'Tempus Educare' in P.L. Peterson and H.J. Walberg (eds), *Research on Teaching: Concepts, Findings and Implications*, Berkeley, Ca: McCutchan

—— (1980a) 'The Teacher-as-executive: Administering a Learning Environment'. Paper presented at the South Pacific Association of Teacher Education Conference, Perth, Australia

—— (1980b) 'Using Research on Teaching for the Improvement of Classroom Practice', *Theory into Practice, 19*(4), 302-8

Bloom, B. (1974) 'Time and Learning', *American Psychologist, 29*(19), 682-8

—— (1980) 'The New Direction in Educational Research: Alterable Variables', *Phi Delta Kappan,*, 382-5

Cobb, J. (1972) 'Relationship of Discrete Classroom Behaviors to 4th-grade Academic Achievement', *Journal of Educational Psychology, 63*, 74-80

Coulter, F. (1979) 'Homework: a Neglected Research Area', *British Educational Research Journal, 5*(1), 21-33

Devaney, K. (1977) 'Warmth, Concreteness, Time and Thought in Teachers' Learning' in K. Devaney (ed.), *Essays on Teachers' Centers*, San Francisco, Ca: Teachers' Centers Exchange, Far West Laboratory for Educational Research and Development, 13-27

Dewey, J. (1933) *How We Think: A Restatement of the Relation of Reflective Thinking to the Educative Process*. Chicago: Henry Regnevy

Doyle, W. (1978) 'Paradigms for Research on Teacher Effectiveness' in L. Shulman (ed.), *Review of Research in Education, 5*, Itasca, Ill.: F.E. Peacock

Edminston, R. and Rhoades, B. (1959) 'Predicting Achievement', *Journal of Educational Research, 52*, 177-80

Feiman, S. (1981) 'Exploring Connections Between Different Kinds of Educational Research and Different Conceptions of Inservice Education', *Journal of Research and Development in Education, 14*(2), 11-21

—— and Floden, R. (1980) *What's All This Talk About Teacher Development?* East Lansing, Michigan: Institute for Research on Teaching, Michigan State University

Felsenthal, H. and Kirsch, I. (1978) 'Variations in Teachers' Management of and Time Spent in Reading Instruction: Effects on Student Learning'. Paper presented to annual meeting of American Educational Research Association, Toronto

Fenstermacher, G. (1980) 'On Learning to Teach Effectively From Research on Teacher Effectiveness', in C. Denham and A. Lieberman (eds), *Time to Learn*, Washington, DC: National Institute of Education, 127-37

Fisher, C. (1980) 'Academic Learning Time as Instructional Feedback'. Paper presented to the annual meeting of American Educational Research Association, Boston

——, Berliner, D., Filby, N., Marliave, R., Cahen, L. and Dishaw, M. (1980) 'Teaching Behaviors, Academic Learning time, and Student Achievement: an Overview' in C. Denham and A. Lieberman (eds), *Time to Learn*. Washington, DC: National Institute of Education, 7-32

———, Filby, N. and Marliave, R. (1977) 'Instructional Time and Student Achievement in Second-grade Reading and Mathematics'. Paper presented to annual meeting of American Educational Research Association, New York

French, W. (1924) 'The Correlation Between Teaching Ability and Thirteen Measurable Classroom Activities. Unpublished MEd thesis, University of Chicago

Garner, W. (1978) 'Resource Equalizing Effects of Student Time Allocation'. Paper presented to annual meeting of American Educational Research Association, Toronto

Good, T. and Beckerman, T. (1978) 'Time-on-task: a Naturalistic Study in Sixth-grade Classrooms', *Elementary School Journal, 78*(3), 193-201

Grannis, J. (1978) 'Task Engagement and the Consistency of Pedagogical Controls: an Ecological Study of Differently Structured Classroom Settings, *Curriculum Enquiry, 8*(1), 3-30

Guthrie, J., Martuza, V. and Seifert, M. (1976) *Impacts of Instructional Time in Reading.* Newark, Delaware: International Reading Association

Harnischfeger, A. and Wiley, D. (1977) 'Time Allocations in 5th-grade Reading'. Paper presented to annual meeting of American Educational Research Association, New York

Husen, T. (1972) 'Does More Time in School Make a Difference?', *Saturday Review, 29,* 32-5

Inglis, S. (1980) 'Commentary: Nascency and the BTES', *BTES Newsletter, 7*

Jackson, P. (1977) 'Looking into Education's Crystal Ball', *Instructor, 87,* 38

Karweit, N. (1978) 'The Organization of Time in Schools: Time Scales and Learning'. Paper presented to National Invitational Conference on School Organization and Effects, San Diego, January 27-9

Kidder, S., O'Reilly, R. and Kiesling, H. (1975) 'Quantity and Quality of Instruction: Empirical Investigations'. Paper presented to annual meeting of American Educational Research Association, Washington, DC

Knowles, M. (1978) *The Adult Learner: A Neglected Species,* Houston: Gulf

Lahaderne, H. (1968) 'Attitudinal and Intellectual Correlates of Attention: a Study of Four 6th-grade Classrooms', *Journal of Educational Psychology, 59*(5), 320-4

Lee, D., Carriere, R., MacQueen, A., Poynor, L. and Rogers, M. (1981) 'Successful Practices in High-poverty Schools'. Technical Report no. 16 from The Study of the Sustaining Effects of Compensatory Education on Basic Skills', Santa Monica, Ca.: System Development Corporation

Lomax, R. and Cooley, W. (1979) 'The Student Achievement-instructional Time Relationship Remains Unsubstantiated'. Paper presented to the annual meeting of American Educational Research Association, San Francisco

Marliave, R. (1980) 'Beyond Engaged Time: Approximations of Task Appropriateness in Terms of On-going Student Learning Behavior'. Paper presented to the annual meeting of American Educational Research Association, Boston

McKinney, J., Mason, J., Perkerson, K. and Clifford, M. (1975) 'Relationship Between Behaviors and Academic Achievement', *Journal of Educational Psychology, 67*(2), 198-203

McNamara, D. (1981) 'Attention Time-on-task and Children's Learning: Research or Ideology?', *Journal of Education for Teaching, 7*(3), 284-97

Morsh, J. (1956) 'Systematic Observations of Instruction Behavior', *Developmental Report AF PTRC-7N-56-52,* San Antonio, Texas: Air Force Personnel and Training Research Centre, Lackland AFB

Morrison, H. (1926) *The Practice of Teaching in the Secondary School,* Chicago, University of Chicago Press

Özcelik, D. (1973) 'Student Involvement in the Learning Process'. Unpublished doctoral dissertation, University of Chicago

Rim, E. and Coller, A. (1978) 'In Search of Non-linear Process-product Functions in Existing Schooling Effects Data: A Re-analysis of the First-grade Reading and Mathematics Data Form the Stallings and Kaskowitz Follow-through Study', Philadelphia: Research for Better Schools

Rusnock, M. and Brandler, N. (1979) 'Time-off-task: Implications for Learning'. Paper presented to the annual meeting of American Educational Research Association, San Francisco

Samuels, S. and Turnure, J. (1974) 'Attention and Reading Achievement in First-grade Boys and Girls', *Journal of Educational Psychology*, 66(1), 29-32

Smith, N. (1976) 'The Relationship Between Time Allotted to Social Studies Instruction and Student Achievement in 5th-grade Classes of the In-county Area of Southern Maryland'. Unpublished doctoral dissertation, University of Maryland

Smyth, W. (1979) 'An Ecological Analysis of Pupil Use of Academic Learning Time'. Unpublished doctoral dissertation, University of Alberta

—— (1980) 'Pupil Engaged Learning Time: Concepts, Findings, and Implications', *The Australian Journal of Education*, 24(3), 225-45

—— (1981) 'Research on Classroom Management: Studies of Pupil Engaged Learning Time as a Special but Instructive Case', *Journal of Education for Teaching*, 7(2), 127-48

—— (1982a) 'A Teacher Development Approach to Bridging the Practice-research Gap'. *Journal of Curriculum Studies*, (in press)

—— (1982b) 'Teaching as Learning: Some Lessons from Clinical Supervision'. Paper presented to the annual meeting Australian Association for Research in Education, Brisbane, November

—— (1983) 'Time and School Learning' in T. Husen and N. Postlethwaite (eds), *International Encyclopedia of Education; Research and Studies*, Oxford: Pergamon (in press)

——, Henry, C. and Martin, J. (1982) 'Clinical Supervision: Evidence of a Viable Strategy for Teacher Development', *The Australian Administrator*, 3(5), 1-4

Sprinthall, N. and Sprinthall, L (1980) 'Adult Development and Leadership Training for Mainstream Education' in D. Corrigan and K. Howey (eds), *Special Education in Transition: Concepts to Guide the Education of Experienced Teachers*, Reston, VA: The Council for Exceptional Children

Stallings, J. (1980) 'Allocated Academic Learning Time Revisited, or Beyond Time-on-task', *Educational Researcher*, 9(11), 11-16

—— and Kaskowitz, D. (1974) *Follow-through Classroom Observation Evaluation, 1972-3*, Menlo Park, Ca: Stanford Research Institute

Stodolsky, S. (1979) 'Ecological Features of Fifth-grade Math and Social Studies Classes and Their Relation to Student Involvement. Paper presented to annual meeting of American Educational Research Association, San Francisco

Vivars, T. (1976) 'The Effect of a Fixed Lower Student-staff Ratio Utilizing Para Professionals and Variable Fixed Time Changes on Reading Scores of Grade Six Students With Deficiencies in Basic Reading Skills'. Unpublished doctoral dissertation, Virginia State University

Wann, D. (1952) 'Teachers as Researchers', *Educational Leadership*, 9, 489-95

Welch, W. and Bridgham, R. (1968) 'Physics Achievement Gains as a Function of Teaching Duration', *School Science and Mathematics*, 449-54

Wolf, R. (1979) 'Achievement in the United States' in H. Walberg (ed.), *Educational Environments and Effects: Evaluation, Policy and Productivity*, Berkeley, McCutchan

7 INSTRUCTION AND TIME-ON-TASK: A REVIEW*

Lorin W. Anderson

Introduction

The birth of interest in time as an essential learning variable and a potentially useful instructional variable can be traced directly to the work of John Carroll (1962, 1963). In his now-classic paper 'A Model of School Learning' Carroll makes two major points concerning the role of time in school learning. First, he suggests that learning is dependent on the extent to which students actually spend the time in learning that they need if they are to learn. Secondly, he suggests that aptitude can be defined in terms of the amount of time students need to spend on a task in order to learn it. (Time refers to the amount of time students are *actively engaged* in learning rather than the amount of time students are *exposed* to learning activities and materials.) While the concept of time used by Carroll in his model is quite clear, several labels have been used to refer to the time during which students are actively engaged in learning. *Time-on-task, engaged time,* and *active learning time* are but three of these labels.

One of the more intriguing aspects of his 1963 paper is his concern with the potential impact of quality of instruction on time. His questions concerning the relationship of the quality of instruction with the other components of the model (e.g. aptitude, perseverance) leaves interested researchers with much food for thought. Fortunately, researchers have indeed investigated these relationships over the past decade. Much of this research has focused on a single relationship: the relationship between instructional variables and time-on-task.

Quite clearly, the interest in this relationship stems from more than an interest in testing Carroll's model. Indeed, research examining the

*From *Journal of Curriculum Studies*, vol. 13, no. 4 (1981): 289-303. Reprinted with permission. This is a revision of a paper presented at the annual meeting of the American Educational Research Association, Boston, April, 1980. The author is grateful to Marvin D. Wyne for his comments on an earlier draft of the manuscript and to Ian Westbury for his suggestions for improvement. The author also wishes to thank Charles W. Fisher, Jacob S. Kounin, Richard S. Marliave and Jane A. Stallings for their comments on specific portions of the manuscript.

relationship between instructional variables and time-on-task is appealing for several reasons. First, there is some speculation that keeping students involved in learning, or on-task, is the primary concern of teachers in classrooms. Perhaps Jackson (1968) stated this point of view most succinctly when he wrote that teachers seemed to be

> making some kind of an educated guess about what would be a beneficial activity for a student or group of students and then doing whatever is necessary to see that participants remain involved in that activity. The teacher's goal, in other words, is *student involvement rather than student learning*. It is true, of course, that the teacher hopes the involvement will result in certain beneficial changes in the students, but learning is in this sense a by-product rather than the things about which the teacher is most directly concerned. (p. 24) (my italics).

Secondly, time-on-task has been conceptualized as an alterable (rather than a fixed or stable) variable, and one which has a significant and possibly causal relationship with school learning. While the latter characteristic of time-on-task (that is, the causal relationship with school learning) is part and parcel of Carroll's model, the former (that is, its alterability) has been contributed recently by Bloom (1980), who indicates that

> time-on-task is . . . one of the variables that account for learning differences between students, between classes, and even between nations. *Time-on-task can be altered positively (or negatively) by the instructional process, and this [alteration] has direct consequences for the learning that will take place*. (p. 383) (my italics)

If the time-on-task is causally related to achievement, and if time-on-task is alterable, the promise for improvement in learning is great indeed. Whether time-on task is viewed as an end in itself (e.g. Jackson) or as a means to an end (e.g. Carroll and Bloom), the prospect of altering and, in fact, optimizing such time is of great instructional importance, for our understanding of classroom procedures.

This chapter is written to accomplish two major purposes. The first purpose is to review and summarize current research on the relationship of instruction and time-on-task. The second purpose is to discuss implications for curriculum and instruction that can be derived from the research evidence. The organization of the paper parallels these two aims.

Research on Instruction and Time-on-task: a Framework

The research described in the next several sections tends to centre around five major approaches taken by groups of researchers who have conducted studies of time-on-task within the context of some larger framework. These approaches and their associated research groups are represented by (1) ecological psychology (represented by Gump and Kounin); (2) learning for mastery (LFM) (represented by Anderson, Arlin and Block); (3) survival skills (represented by Cobb, Hops and Walker; (4) Beginning Teacher Evaluation Study (BTES) (represented by Berliner, Fisher, McDonald and others); and (5) Follow Through Evaluation (represented by Stallings and her colleagues at the Stanford Research Institute).

Ecological Psychology

The ecological psychological approach to the study of classroom instruction originated in Kansas in the middle 1960s. The basic tenets of the ecological psychological approach have been stated quite succinctly by Kounin and Sherman (1979):

> A school may be regarded as an environment consisting of various behavior settings: reading circles, arithmetic lessons, gymnasiums . . . The behaviors of both pupils and teachers are influenced by the behavior setting they occupy. We might further propose that how a teacher manages a group of pupils is dependent upon the behavior setting. (p. 145)

These latter two propositions are based on the belief that behaviour settings are associated with patterns of behaviour that are exhibited by participants in the behaviour setting and which are independent of the people who are in the behaviour setting. These 'patterns' are called standing patterns of behaviour. Reading circles, for example, elicit certain behaviours which are independent of the characteristics of the individual students who occupy the reading circle.

One of the earliest studies representative of this group was conducted by Paul Gump (1967), whose results suggested that students spent differing amounts of time-on-task when they were in different behaviour settings and when different pacing conditions were introduced in the classroom. Specifically, the results indicated that time-on-task was lower in whole-class recitations than in small, teacher-led groups. Furthermore, time-on-task was lower for self-paced activities than for externally-paced activities.

While Gump focused on behaviour settings and pacing, Jacob Kounin (1970) began his work on identifying teacher behaviours which were associated with high levels of time-on-task. Several categories of teacher behaviours were identified by Kounin: (1) 'with-it-ness' (that is, behaviours which communicate that the teacher knows what is going on in the classroom at all times; (2) 'smoothness' (that is, behaviours that maintain the flow of classroom activities, particularly, but not exclusively, at points of transition from one activity to another); (3) momentum (that is, behaviours that maintain the flow of the lesson); (4) variety (that is, providing different contexts and formats for classroom activities); and (5) group focus. Group focus is comprised of two subcategories: group alerting (that is, behaviours which alert students to pay attention even when they are not directly involved in the verbal interchange between teacher and students); and accountability (that is, behaviours that increase the number of students who directly participate in the verbal interchange).

Kounin found that, as expected, different categories of teacher behaviours were associated with high levels of time-on-task in different behaviour settings. Variety was associated with high levels of time-on-task in seatwork settings but not in recitation settings. Momentum and group focus, on the other hand, were associated with high levels of time-on-task in recitation settings but not in seatwork settings. Finally, some categories of teacher behaviours (e.g. 'with-it-ness', 'smoothness') tended to be associated with high levels of time-on-task independent of the behaviour setting.

In the mid-1970s Kounin introduced the concept of the 'signal system of a lesson', which helped to explain and extend both his and Gump's findings. He defined signal systems as the information, materials, and/or nature of behaviour settings themselves that guide the sequence of students' behaviours and activities in classrooms. The results of subsequent research suggested that lessons having a continuous signal input, which insulate participants from distracting signals (therefore providing for sustained attention or participation), and which have low intrusiveness from the behaviour of participants, were associated with high levels of time-on-task (Kounin and Gump, 1974; Kounin and Doyle, 1975).

When results of these studies are combined, a single phrase tends to identify the key instructional variable which is related to time-on-task: *continuity of signal systems*. That is, to the extent that signal systems are continuous, students will exhibit high levels of time-on-task.

Continuity can result from any one (or combination) of three sources. First, continuity can result from the behaviour setting itself. Behaviour settings which are high in continuity are said to have 'holding power' (Kounin and Sherman, 1979). Such settings tend to contain a continuous signal system, permit a variety of possible behaviour patterns, and/or contain clear indicators of something being accomplished as a result of the students' behaviours. Thus, behaviour settings in which (1) groups of students are reading in unison or listening to the teacher read, (2) activities and/or events are being demonstrated, and (3) students can work on materials in individual construction activities are high in continuity.

Secondly, continuity can result from the behaviours of the teacher within the behaviour setting. These behaviours (e.g. 'with-it-ness', smoothness) may or may not depend on the particular behaviour setting in which the learning is to occur. Such teaching behaviours would seem to be especially important in behaviour settings with *low* holding power.

Thirdly, continuity can result from the pacing of the lesson. External pacing conditions tend to provide for continuity across lessons. Student self-pacing may or may not provide continuity, depending on the nature of the behaviour setting.

Continuity is a critical instructional variable since it is related to time-on-task. Lessons and activities that have 'holding power' and are 'paced' by the teacher, and teaching behaviours that promote continuity are associated with high levels of time-on-task.

Learning for Mastery (LFM)

Since the development of learning for mastery as an instructional system was derived largely from Carroll's model (Bloom, 1968), it is not surprising that time-on-task research has been conducted within the LFM framework. In contrast with the ecological psychology research, the focus of the LFM research tends to be more global. Rather than examining specific activities and teacher behaviours, fairly general characteristics of instructional programmes are investigated. As a consequence, it often is difficult to identify the particular characteristics of LFM programmes that are related to and/or influence time-on-task. The consistency of the research results, however, tends to limit the characteristics which are, in fact, related to high levels of time-on-task.

As defined by Bloom (1968), the most critical elements of LFM programmes are as follows: (1) clearly defined instructional objectives; (2) small learning units organized around related sets of the objectives;

(3) highly valid, relatively short tests which are used for the purpose of assessing student learning relative to the objectives (so-called formative tests); (4) preset levels of performance standards on the tests which, when attained, indicate that students have acquired (i.e. mastered) the underlying objectives; (5) clear communication with the students concerning what is to be learned and how they are to learn it; (6) the provision of corrective, supplementary learning activities and materials for those students failing to attain the preset performance standards; and (7) the monitoring of the use of these corrective activities and materials and the use of subsequent formative tests until such time as virtually all students in the class have achieved the performance standard.

In most LFM time-based research, students in both experimental and control classes receive the same objectives, the same instructional units presented in basically the same fashion, and the same formative tests. Thus, the clearest differences between LFM and non-LFM classes lie in the communication of expectations to students (that is, what is to be learned, how it is to be learned, and to what level it must be learned), the provision of corrective learning activities/materials, and the monitoring of the use of the correctives by the teacher and/or student tutor. These instructional activities can be subsumed under two general phrases: 'communication of expectations' and 'feedback and correctives'.

The results of the time-based research within the LFM framework have been summarized by Bloom (1976) and are quite consistent. Students enrolled in LFM classes tend to spend an increasing amount of their time-on-task over a series of learning units as compared with their counterparts in non-LFM classes. In addition, LFM students tend to achieve consistently higher levels of achievement over the same learning units as compared with the non-LFM students.

Perhaps the most intriguing, and most controversial, of the LFM-research results is that students tend to require increasingly *less* time to achieve the *same* performance standards over a series of learning units and, as a consequence, tend to become more similar to one another both in terms of the amount learned and the time needed to learn. The range of differences among LFM students in the amount of time needed to attain the performance standards decreased from approximately 7 to 1, to 4 to 1 in one study (Arlin, 1973), and from approximately 4 to 1, to 2 to 1 in two other studies (Block, 1970; Anderson, 1976).

It is of some interest to note that two of the LFM researchers have conducted research on time outside the framework of the LFM model.

Anderson and Scott (1978) investigated the relationship among teaching methods, students' verbal ability, students' academic self-concept, and students' time-on-task. While the study appears similar to Gump's (1967) early work, it adds one important dimension. Rather than examine overall differences in teaching methods with respect to time-on-task, Anderson and Scott investigated the possibility that different teaching methods can be differentially useful (from a time-on-task perspective) for different types of students.

Briefly, the conclusions reached by the authors are as follows. Teaching methods which emphasize 'one-way communication' (that is, communication from the teacher or other instructional source to the students) are associated with higher levels of time-on-task of students with higher verbal abilities and with lower levels of time-on-task of students with lower verbal abilities. Lecturing and the use of films and filmstrips are examples of such methods. Teaching methods which provide for 'two-way communication' (that is, communication which is largely teacher-directed, but which allows students to participate by responding to questions and raising questions) are associated with similar, relatively high levels of time-on-task for all types of students. Classroom discourse, which consists of a series of mini-presentations or mini-explanations followed by a series of questions and answers, is an example of such a method. Finally, teaching methods which place the burden of responsibility for managing the use of time directly on the student (e.g. seatwork) are associated with higher levels of time-on-task of students with more positive academic self-concepts, and with lower levels of time-on-task of students with less positive academic self-concepts.

Arlin (1979) examined the relationship between the teachers' use and monitoring of transitions, and students' time-on-task. Transitions were defined simply as changes from one classroom activity to another. Since transitions are disruptions in the continuity of the lessons, this study clearly fits within the framework of ecological psychology. On the basis of the results, Arlin concluded that considerably more off-task time occurred during transitions, 'even in schools characterized by "tight discipline" ' (p. 55). More importantly from an instructional perspective, however, Arlin found that transitions can be structured so as to minimize off-task behaviour. This structuring can be accomplished by (1) preplanning for transitions rather than allowing them to happen; and (2) making clear the expectations teachers have concerning the way in which the transitions are to occur.

Survival Skills

The 'survival-skills' approach has its roots in Oregon, with research published between 1972 and 1976. The focus of the research is on teaching what are termed 'survival skills' to elementary school students. Four such survival skills were first identified in a correlational study conducted by Cobb (1972). These survival skills were labelled attending (that is, paying attention to the appropriate instructional source); work (that is, being engaged in behaviours that result in products, such as completed worksheets); volunteering (that is, behaviours which inform teachers of a willingness to participate, such as the raising of hands); and compliance (that is, doing what the teacher asks to be done).

Subsequent research (Cobb and Hops, 1973; Hops and Cobb, 1974; Walker and Hops, 1976) was based on the assumption that reinforcing these survival skills would result in (1) an increase in time-on-task, and (2) a subsequent increase in achievement. Teachers in an experimental group were taught to use several types of reinforcement (such as group non-social reinforcement, social reinforcement, vicarious reinforcement, shaping procedures, and close monitoring). Control-group teachers received no such training.

The results of the three experimental studies were quite consistent. Time-on-task (in the guise of survival-skill behaviours) was positively altered through the appropriate use of reinforcement. Furthermore, in two of the studies (Cobb and Hops, 1973; Walker and Hops, 1976) increases in time-on-task were accompanied by similar increases in achievement on standardized, norm-referenced achievements tests. Thus, from the 'survival-skills' perspective, reinforcement is a critical instructional variable.

Beginning Teacher Evaluation Study (BTES)

The Beginning Teacher Evaluation Study is best conceptualized as occurring in three stages. The first stage involved the overall design of the study; the second and third stages consisted of the conduct of the research itself. The research in the second stage was conducted by Frederick McDonald and his colleagues at Educational Testing Service. The research in the third stage was conducted at the Far West Laboratory for Educational Research and Development (FWLERD). Several researchers (among them David Berliner, Charles Fisher, Nikola Filby and Richard Marliave) were instrumental in the conduct of the third stage of the study.

Three types of learning times were identified by the FWLERD

researchers: allocated time (that amount of time set aside for learning a particular subject matter, content area or instructional objective), engaged time (or time-on-task) and academic learning time (time spent on tasks with which the students experienced a high success rate). While results were obtained for each of these types of learning times, only those results pertaining to engaged time or time-on-task will be discussed.

The results suggest the following classroom settings and accompanying teacher behaviours are related to time-on-task: (1) settings in which students were interacting with a teacher or another adult; (2) seatwork formats in which the teacher circulated, checking work periodically; and (3) seatwork which occurred in conjunction with teacher-directed group work (the researchers inferred that the group work was used to prepare for the seatwork through the teacher's structuring and explaining) (Filby and Cahen, 1977; Fisher, 1978; Fisher, Filby, Marliave, Cahen, Dishaw, Moore and Berliner, 1978). Two other instructional variables also were associated with high levels of time-on-task: successful practice (that is, exercises and questions provided to students after initial learning had occurred, which were intended to help students thoroughly master the material) and academic feedback (that is, information concerning whether answers were right or wrong) (Fisher *et al.*, 1978).

Classrooms associated with low degrees of time-on-task were those (1) in which a variety of activities were occurring simultaneously (because, the researchers suspected, the teacher was unable to monitor all of the activities effectively) (McDonald and Elias, 1976); and (2) in which students spent more of their time (greater than two-thirds) working alone (Fisher *et al.*, 1978).

The results also suggested that time-on-task is high in classrooms in which the value of learning is communicated to the students. This communication can occur when the teacher holds students responsible for their work, and/or states clear expectations concerning the completion of work up to recognized standards of quality.

Finally, the concept of academic learning time has implications for engaged time. The results indicated that students spend more of their time engaged in the learning of tasks that were appropriate for the students' current level of knowledge and/or skill. That is, time-on-task is high when the objective or materials to be learned are at an appropriate level of difficulty for the learners.

Two key instructional variables emerge from these findings. The first can be termed 'monitoring'. Instructional settings in which teachers monitor the flow of information and material, monitor the seatwork of students, monitor the practice of students, and monitor the answers produced by students (by means of academic feedback) are associated with high levels of time-on-task. The second key instructional variable can be termed 'task appropriateness'. That is to say, instructional settings in which the task to be learned is at an appropriate level of difficulty for the students tend to be associated with high levels of time-on-task. According to the FWLERD researchers, an appropriate level of difficulty is one in which the students encounter a high rate of success (Fisher *et al.*, 1978).

Follow Through Evaluation

Quite clearly, Jane Stallings is the identifiable leader of this approach. The time variable used by Stallings is more closely related to allocated time than to time-on-task. The periods of allocated time are broken down into categories such as time spent in academic interactions, time spent in various activities, time spent on various materials, time spent in various groupings, and the like. The dependent variable is achievement rather than time-on-task, although Stallings did find that task persistence (as opposed to child movement, and child co-operation with another child) is positively related to reading and mathematics achievement.

Among the many findings resulting from the Follow Through evaluation and other related studies, the following are representative (Stallings and Kaskowitz, 1974; Stallings, 1975). Time spent working with textbooks and academic workbooks (as opposed to time spent on puzzles, games, toys and the like) is related to achievement. Time spent in mathematics, reading, and academic verbal interactions is related to achievement. Classrooms in which groups of eight or more students worked together with a teacher were found to have higher levels of achievement than classrooms in which students worked in smaller groups or alone. Finally, all types of adult feedback that had an academic focus (e.g. acknowledge, praise, positive and negative corrective feedback) were positively related to achievement.

Stallings's findings can be summed up in the key elements of what Rosenshine (1979) terms 'direct instruction'. According to Rosenshine, direct instruction refers to

> teaching activities where goals are clear to students, time allocated for instruction is sufficient and continuous, coverage of content is extensive, the performance of students is monitored, questions are at a low cognitive level so that students can produce many correct

responses, and feedback to students is immediate and academically oriented. In direct instruction the teacher controls instructional goals, chooses materials appropriate for the student's ability, and paces the instructional episode . . . The goal is to move the students through a sequenced set of materials or tasks. Such materials are common across classrooms and have a relatively strong congruence with the tasks on achievement tests. (p. 38)

In contrast with the aforementioned approaches, the Follow Through evaluation approach cannot be described in terms of one or two key variables. Rather the research generated tends to encompass many of the key factors identified by the other approaches: instruction is continuous (from ecological psychology), goals are clear to students, performance of students is monitored, feedback to students is immediate and academically oriented, and materials and tasks are sequenced (from LFM), social reinforcers, such as praise, are used (from survival skills), and time allocated for instruction is sufficient, students can produce many successes, and materials are matched with students' current knowledge and skill level (from BTES). Thus, Stallings' work tends to synthesize research from the other four groups.

Summary of Key Instructional Elements

What can be made of the results from these five approaches? A summary of the key instructional elements is found in Table 7.1, and as can be seen, these are relatively few in number and, surprisingly, compatible with one another. Effective instruction (from the point of view of increasing time-on-task) may proceed something like this: first, tasks should be chosen which are at an appropriate level of difficulty for the students; secondly, the tasks should be communicated directly to the students; that is, students should know (1) what they are to learn, and (2) how they are to demonstrate that learning. Thirdly, behaviour settings and learning activities should be chosen which have high degrees of continuity (e.g. activities involving small groups working on a common goal, activities in which students must make or do something, activities in which the materials are continuously present, and teacher demonstration activities). Fourthly, teachers (or other adults) should monitor the learning. Such 'monitoring' would involve, among other things, pacing the learning of the students and indicating the nature and purpose of transitions between activities. Fifthly, behaviours such as those described in the categories of 'with-it-ness', 'smoothness', momentum, and group alerting should be exhibited by the teacher during activities in which he or she has a direct involvement (such as recitations or classroom discourse), and during the monitoring of activities in which he or she is not directly involved (such as seatwork). Sixthly, appropriate task-oriented behaviours on the part of the students should be reinforced. Seventh, feedback should be given to students concerning their attainment of the specified tasks. Eighth, and finally, errors and misunderstandings of students should be corrected before they are allowed to accumulate and interfere with subsequent learning. In general, instruction of the nature described above will result in high levels of student time-on-task.

Table 7.1: A Summary of Key Instructional Elements which are Associated with, and Possibly Influence, High Levels of Time-on-task (By Research Approach)

Approach	*Key instructional element(s)*
Ecological psychology	Continuity of signal systems (both across activities and within activities)
Learning for mastery (LFM)	Communication of expectations to students; feedback and corrective instruction
Survival skills	Reinforcement of task-oriented behaviour
Beginning Teacher Evaluation Study (BTES)	Teacher monitoring of learning; provision of tasks appropriate to present knowledge and skill level of students.
Follow Through	All of the above

Curricular Implications of the Research

Curricular implications of these results tend to fall into two general areas: curriculum sequencing and curriculum evaluation. These areas will be discussed separately.

Curriculum Sequencing

The results from the LFM and BTES research clearly suggest the need for careful attention to the sequencing of objectives and/or tasks. In combination, these results suggest that the proportion of time students spend on-task is higher when students are attempting to learn something which is at an appropriate level of difficulty.

Within the LFM framework the level of difficulty of objectives and/or tasks is controlled by ensuring that students possess necessary prerequisite knowledge and skills prior to their attempting to learn new knowledge and/or skills. The mechanism for providing virtually all students with these prerequisites is the feedback and corrective component of LFM programmes. The actual possession of the prerequisites is verified through student performance on so-called formative tests.

Within the BTES framework, objectives and/or tasks are selected that are appropriate for students' current level of knowledge and/or skill. Presumably, teachers formally or informally assess the students' current levels of functioning and assign objectives or tasks accordingly. If anything, the objectives or tasks would be slightly easier than might be expected given the students' current level of functioning, so that students can experience a high degree of success when working on the objective or task.

The two approaches (LFM and BTES) differ in at least one major respect. The LFM approach begins with a concern for the *future* needs of students. Primary questions asked by proponents of this approach would include 'What future tasks are the students going to be asked to perform?' and 'What future objectives are the students likely to be expected to attain?' Thus, the overall curricular goals would be identified first. Next, objectives and tasks would be identified that would help to build a 'bridge' between these overall goals and the current level of functioning of *typical* students at various grade levels. Individual students could be placed at appropriate places in the sequence using appropriate assessment devices.

The BTES approach, on the other hand, would begin with a concern for the *present* needs of the students. Primary questions asked by proponents of this approach would include 'What are the current strengths and weaknesses of these students?' and 'What objectives and/or tasks can I select that will play on the strengths and help to overcome the weaknesses?'

The two approaches will quite likely yield different conceptualizations of curriculum. For a given subject matter the BTES approach could conceivably yield several curricula (one for each category of students with particular strengths and weaknesses). For this same subject matter, however, the LFM approach would produce a single curriculum — a curriculum based on long-term goals.

Whichever approach is preferred, the desirability of careful sequencing of objectives and/or tasks is supported by the research. Additional approaches to curriculum sequencing can be found in a paper by Posner and Strike (1976).

Curriculum Evaluation

With respect to the evaluation of curricula, the research suggests that, at the very least, time is a potential confounding variable. When two curricula are compared, the focus typically is on *qualitative* differences between them (e.g. the types of goals and objectives included, the materials and activities recommended for use in helping students to attain the goals and objectives). Large *quantitative* differences (e.g. differences in allocated time or time-on-task) between the two curricula can, however, obscure *qualitative* differences. If, for example, students in one curriculum spend twice as much time studying problem-solving, qualitative differences in materials and activities used in conjunction with problem-solving may be difficult to detect. It seems likely that such large differences in time would make it seem as though the materials and activities of one curriculum were superior to those of the other. Such a conclusion, of course, would be invalid. Time differences between curricula should be estimated and controlled, if possible, if qualitative differences are to be examined meaningfully.

Instructional Implications of the Research

Three categories of instructional implications follow rather directly from the research on instruction and time-on-task. These categories, to be discussed in the following three subsections, are: (1) the need for instructional planning; (2) the need to consider contextual variables in the planning and implementation of instruction; and (3) the need to monitor student attention and learning. Although the importance of monitoring has been discussed several times earlier in this paper, a summary section on the topic seems necessary.

The Need for Instructional Planning

Anderson and Block (1977) suggest that teachers should be *proactive* rather than *reactive*. That is, in their words, 'the teacher is asked to steer the teaching-learning process rather than be steered by it' (p. 169). The need for proactive teachers and, consequently, careful planning on the part of teachers, is clearly supported by the research reviewed in this paper.

Put simply, instructional planning permits teachers to steer the learning process and to anticipate problems before they arise. Teachers, therefore, know what students should be doing in the classroom at various times and are more likely to be 'with-it', in Kounin's words.

Planned lessons have beginnings, middles and ends. Hence, continuity of lesson presentation is more likely. Transitions between the 'beginning, middle and end' of a lesson and between activities within lessons are expected, and such transitions are 'planned for' and not 'allowed to occur'. As a consequence, students can be informed in advance about the way in which transitions are to occur. The flow of the teaching-learning process is maintained and 'down time' (that is, non-instructional time) is decreased.

Planning permits teachers to be more aware of the relationship between activities and goals and, as a consequence, the relationship between activities themselves. They know, for example, that recitation is to be used for the purpose of re-teaching those facts, concepts, or skills frequently missed on the seatwork assignment. They also know that groupwork can be used to provide supervised practice, while seatwork can be used to provide opportunities for independent practice. Thus, the groupwork is used to introduce the seatwork. As a result, as the BTES results indicate, substantive interaction between teachers and students during groupwork is positively associated with time-on-task during seatwork.

In summary, then, the research quite clearly points to the need for instructional planning. Such planning permits teachers to be proactive, rather than reactive. Characteristics of proactive teachers such as 'with-it-ness' and continuity, well-managed transitions between activities, and clearly understood relationships among activities in terms of their purposes, are associated with high levels of time-on-task.

The Need to Consider Context of Planning and Implementing Instruction

The message from the ecological psychologists, simply put, is that what constitutes effective instruction in one setting may not be effective instruction in another. The results from several studies support the validity of this contention. In order to plan effective instruction, then, one must be sensitive to the context within which the instruction is to take place. Furthermore, in order to manage instruction effectively and efficiently, one must be aware of the relationship between the instructional plan and contextual variables such as the physical setting, behaviour setting, and composition of the class in terms of prior achievement, socio-economic status, and the like.

Ecological psychologists have focused primarily on the relationship between teacher behaviours and behaviour settings. Thus, for example, variety is found to be important in seatwork settings, but not in recitation settings. Similarly, momentum and group-focus behaviours of the teacher are important in recitation settings, but not during seatwork.

The research conducted by Anderson and Scott (1978) focused on the relationship between various modes of instruction and the composition of the classroom in terms of verbal ability and academic self-esteem. Their findings suggest that certain modes of instruction are differentially effective for different types of students. Modes of instruction in which the communication flowed from the teacher to the student were associated with high degrees of time-on-task for high-ability students. Modes of instruction which required some responsibility on the part of the students were associated with high degrees of time-on-task for students with positive self-esteem.

In sum, then, the research suggests that effective instructional planning and implementation must be sensitive to contextual variables. More simply stated, an understanding of what is to be taught, to whom it is to be taught, and the setting within which it is to be taught is necessary if instruction is to be associated with high degrees of time-on-task.

The Need for Monitoring the Teaching-Learning Process

Despite the need for 'contextually sensitive' instructional planning and teaching, one instructional variable tends to be associated with high levels of time-on-task across contexts. This variable is the monitoring of the teaching-learning process. Although the importance of this variable transcends contexts, the form that the variable takes is highly dependent on the context. Furthermore, the form that monitoring takes is dependent on the purpose of the monitoring. Two general purposes of monitoring are suggested by the research.

The first purpose of monitoring is to maintain the attention or task-orientation of the students; the second purpose is to check on the effectiveness of the students' learning *vis-à-vis* the instructional objectives. When the research results from all five groups of researchers are combined, the importance of monitoring, in general, is quite clear, although different groups direct their research efforts toward one or the other purposes of monitoring.

Research findings from BTES, ecological psychology and survival skills groups focus mainly on the first purpose of monitoring. As indicated earlier, the form of the monitoring depends on the context within which the instruction is occurring. According to the BTES findings, seatwork is monitored by teachers circulating and checking students' work. The ecological psychologists' research, on the other hand, indicates that time-on-task during seatwork can be monitored by providing a variety of materials and/or activities during seatwork. It seems reasonable that variety is introduced by teachers when they notice that a certain number of students are off-task. In any case, the need for monitoring seatwork if high degrees of time-on-task are to result is important.

Other classroom contexts or settings may require different approaches to monitoring. During classroom discourse or recitation, for example, the asking of questions which require little in the way of thinking on the part of the students is a form of monitoring. This form of monitoring is included at this point in the discussion (rather than later) because it may well be that these questions monitor task-orientation and not actual learning or achievement. Similarly, group alerting techniques such as those described by Kounin (1970) are used during recitation to monitor the attentiveness of students not *directly* involved in the recitation (that is, those students not overtly responding to the questions).

Some forms of monitoring seem to transcend classroom context or setting. 'With-it' teachers quite certainly are involved in some type of sensory monitoring, even if such monitoring may be unconscious. Various kinds of reinforcers, suggested by the survival-skills research, are used to monitor learner activities such as paying attention during lectures, writing on worksheets during seatwork, and volunteering during classroom discourse or recitation.

Finally, some contexts or settings tend to make monitoring more or less difficult. Classroom discourse, for example, provides teachers with many opportunities to monitor attentiveness and task-orientation while the use of audio-visual materials typically does not. Similarly, behaviour settings possessing 'holding power', as defined by the ecological psychologists may, indeed, require little in the way of teacher monitoring.

On the other hand, classrooms in which several groups of students are performing different activities are difficult for a single teacher to monitor effectively. Several specific findings support this contention. Together, these results suggest that lower levels of time-on-task occurred in classrooms in which (1) a variety of activities were taking place at the same time, (2) students were permitted to pace themselves, and (3) students worked either in groups smaller than eight students or alone.

In contrast to the BTES, ecological-psychology and survival-skills groups, the LFM and Follow Through evaluation groups tend to focus mainly on the second purpose of monitoring; namely, the monitoring of actual student learning or achievement. The major component of the LFM approach to instruction, 'feedback and correction' clearly serves this second purpose of monitoring. Similarly, the findings from the Follow Through evaluators that all types of adult feedback having an academic focus are associated with high levels of time-on-task are supportive of this second purpose of monitoring.

Finally, despite their primary focus on the first purpose of monitoring, the BTES and ecological psychology researchers each have identified a variable which is related to the second purpose of monitoring. From the BTES findings the variable is 'holding students responsible for their learning'. The variable identified by the ecological psychology group, 'accountability', appears synonomous with this BTES variable.

Discussion

The importance of time-on-task as a key variable in understanding and improving classroom instruction has been reinforced by the results presented in this chapter. Implications of this research for curriculum and instruction seem simple, yet profound.

The apparent simplicity of the variable 'time-on-task' increases the likelihood that misapplications of the research findings will occur. One misapplication will result from the focus on 'time' at the exclusion of 'on-task'. Such a misapplication occurs when some educators see the critical factor in the success of the LFM programmes as the provision of extra time. Quite clearly, the use of the term 'correctives' by proponents of LFM programmes implies that students initially failing to attain mastery must become engaged in learning activities designed to correct their errors and misunderstandings. Thus, time *and* task are appropriate and important.

Doyle (1979) generalizes the above concern when he differentiates between time-on-activity and time-on-task. If the activities and/or materials used by students in classrooms are not related to the attainment of the learning goals or instructional objectives, the students may be spending time-on-activity but not time-on-task, since this time will be unlikely to result in task accomplishment.

Finally, it is important to point out that many early researchers viewed time-on-task as an indicator of a variable they called 'student involvement in learning'. Student involvement in learning can best be seen as a more global variable of which time-on-task is the *quantitative* component. There is some evidence that students differ in the *quality* of their time-on-task. That is, some students may be more efficient in their use of their on-task time while others may be involved in learning to such a degree at one point in time that the actual amount of time needed to achieve the learning goal is reduced dramatically. Resnick's (1976) discussion of research on mathematics learning suggests that some students are indeed more efficient in their solving of mathematically oriented problems. This efficiency tends to result from a decrease in the number of steps performed by the students in arriving at solutions to problems. Similarly, Bloom's (1981) conceptualization of peak learning experiences suggests that a single, powerful learning experience can have a profound effect on student learning.

Most of the concerns voiced in this final section deal with potential misapplications of the research findings summarized in this paper. Despite these concerns, time-on-task remains a critical variable in classroom instruction and classroom instructional research. An awareness of time-on-task and the planning and managing of instruction focused on producing high levels of time-on-task in a large number of students is likely to yield the most effective classroom instruction currently possible.

References

Anderson, L.W. (1976) 'An Empirical Investigation of Individual Differences in Time to Learn', *Journal of Educational Psychology, 68*, 226-33
—— and Block, J.H. (1977) 'Mastery Learning' in D. Treffinger, J. Davis and R. Ripple (eds), *Handbook on Teaching Educational Psychology*. New York: Academic Press
—— and Scott, C.C. (1978) 'The Relationship Among Teaching Methods, Student Characteristics, and Student Involvement in Learning', *Journal of Teacher Education, 29*(3), 52-7
Arlin, M. (1973) 'Learning Rate and Learning Rate Variance Under Mastery Learning Conditions'. Unpublished doctoral dissertation, University of Chicago
—— (1979) 'Teacher Transitions Can Disrupt Time Flow in Classrooms', *American Educational Research Journal, 16*, 42-56
Block, J.H. (1970) 'The Effects of Various Levels of Performance on Selected Cognitive, Affective and Time Variables'. Unpublished doctoral dissertation, University of Chicago
Bloom, B.S. (1968) 'Learning for Mastery', *Evaluation Comment, 1*(2)
—— (1976) *Human Characteristics and School Learning*. New York: McGraw-Hill
—— (1980) 'The New Direction in Educational Research: Alterable Variables', *Phi Delta Kappan, 61*, 382-5

—— (1981) 'Peak Learning Experiences, in B.S. Bloom, *All Our Children Learning*. New York: McGraw-Hill

Carroll, J.B. (1962) 'The Prediction of Success in Intensive Language Training' in R. Glaser, (ed.), *Training Research and Education*, Pittsburgh: University of Pittsburgh Press

—— (1963) 'A Model of School Learning', *Teacher College Record, 64*, 723-33

Cobb, J.A. (1972) 'A Relationship of Discrete Classroom Behaviors to Fourth-grade Academic Achievement', *Journal of Educational Psychology, 63*, 74-80

—— and Hops, H. (1973) 'Effects of Academic Survival-skill Training on Low-achieving First Graders', *Journal of Educational Research, 67*, 108-13

Doyle, W. (1979) 'Making Managerial Decisions in Classrooms' in D.L. Duke, (ed.), *Classroom Management*. Seventy-eighth Yearbook of the National Society for the Study of Education. Chicago: University of Chicago Press

Filby, N.N. and Cahen, L.S. (1977) *Teaching Behavior and Academic Learning Time in the A-B Period, Technical Note V-1b*, San Francisco: Far West Laboratory for Educational Research and Development

Fisher, C.W. (1978) 'Teaching Behaviours, Academic Learning Time, and Student Achievement: An Overview of Phase III-B of the Beginning Teacher Evaluation Study'. Paper presented at the Annual Meeting of the American Educational Research Association, Toronto

——, Filby, N., Marliave, R., Cahen, L., Dishaw, M., Moore, J. and Berliner, D. *Teaching and Learning in the Elementary School: a Summary of the Beginning Teacher Evaluation Study, Report VII-1*, San Francisco: Far West Laboratory for Educational Research and Development

Gump, P.V. (1976) *The Classroom Behavior Setting: Its Nature and Relation to Student Behavior*, Lawrence, Kansas: Department of Psychology, University of Kansas, (ERIC ED 015 515)

Hops, H. and Cobb, J.A. (1974) 'Initial Investigation Into Academic Survival-skill Training, Direct Instruction, and First-grade Achievement', *Journal of Educational Psychology, 66*, 548-53

Jackson, P.W. (1968) *Life in Classrooms*, New York: Holt, Rinehart & Winston

Kounin, J.S. (1970) *Discipline and Group Management in Classrooms*, New York: Holt, Rinehart & Winston

—— and Gump, P.V. (1974) 'Signal Systems of Lesson Settings and the Task-related Behavior of Preschool Children', *Journal of Educational Psychology, 66*, 554-62

—— and Doyle, P.H. (1975) 'Degree of Continuity of a Lesson's Signal System and Task Involvement of Children', *Journal of Educational Psychology, 67*, 159-64

—— and Sherman, L.W. (1979) 'School Environments as Behavior Settings', *Theory into Practice, 18*, 145-9

McDonald, F.J. and Elias, P.J. (1976) *The Effects of Teaching Performance on Pupil Learning. Beginning Teacher Evaluation Study, Phase II, Vol. I*. Princeton, NJ: Educational Testing Service

Posner, G.J. and Strike, K.A. (1976) 'A Categorization Scheme for the Principles of Sequencing Content', *Review of Educational Research, 46*, 665-90

Resnick, L.B. (1976) 'Task Analysis in Instructional Design: Some Cases from Mathematics' in D. Klahr (ed.), *Cognition and Instruction*. Hillsdale, NJ: Lawrence Erlbaum Associates

Rosenshine, B.V. (1979) 'Content, Time and Direct Instruction' in P.L. Peterson and H.J. Walberg (eds), *Research on Teaching: Concepts, Findings, and Implications*, Berkeley, Ca.: McCutchan Publishing Corp.

Stallings, J.A. (1975) 'Implementation and Child Effects of Teaching Practices in Follow Through Classrooms', *Monographs of the Society for Research in Child Development, 40*(7-8), 1-119

—— and Kaskowitz, D.H. (1974) *Follow Through Classroom Observation Evaluation: 1972-1973*, Menlo Park, Ca.: Stanford Research Institute,
Walker, H.M. and Hops, H. (1976) 'Increasing Academic Achievement by Reinforcing Direct Academic Performance and/or Facilitative Nonacademic Responses', *Journal of Educational Psychology, 68*, 218-25

PART THREE

PRACTICAL APPLICATIONS OF TIME ALLOCATION AND USE

8 TIME-USE AND THE PROVISION OF ADAPTIVE INSTRUCTION*

Margaret C. Wang

The relationship between student achievement and the manner in which school time is spent by students and teachers has become a subject of growing interest on the part of educational researchers and practitioners. Current concern over the implications of time use for teaching and learning stems largely from a variety of widespread problems facing schools in their improvement efforts as well as from recent research findings.

Enhancing the capability of schools to provide high-quality, yet equitable educational experiences for increasingly diverse student populations has become a critical school-improvement task. Public sentiment, economic realities and recent legislation in the United States have created mandates for the provision of such experiences for students of all races, language groups, social classes and unique educational conditions. Schools at every level of schooling are asked to integrate students having a wide range of educational, physical and emotional characteristics into regular classrooms. As a result, teachers are faced with the task of finding ways to meet disparate student needs within the constraints of the present school organizational systems and available resources. Thus, increased allocation and more effective use of school resources, such as time for instruction and learning, have been given high priority by educators and researchers.

Recent research findings also have generated concern over the relationship between time-use and learning. Although investigations of factors related to the time needed to learn have a long history in experimental psychology (e.g. Suppes, 1964; Underwood, 1949; Woodrow, 1940) and educational research (e.g. Thompson, 1915; Washburne, 1925), systematic studies of time and schooling have gained prominence

*The Research reported herein was supported by the Learning Research and Development Center, supported in part as a research and development center by funds from the National Institute of Education, the National Follow Through Program, and the Special Education Program of the United States Department of Education. The opinions expressed do not necessarily reflect the positions or policies of these agencies, and no official endorsement should be inferred.

only in recent years. This latter work has produced some very useful models for studying classroom instruction and school learning within the context of instructional and learning time (e.g. Bloom, 1974; Carroll, 1963; Wiley and Harnischfeger, 1974; Berliner, Fisher, Filby and Marliave, 1978). A common feature of these models is the increased emphasis on instructional improvement – specifically, detailed analyses of factors related to the amount of time students need for learning, and the conditions under which school time can be optimally used by teachers and students.

Empirical evidence of the important role played by the allocation and use of school time in determining learning outcomes has been reported by many researchers (e.g. Anderson, 1976; Bloom, 1968; Carroll, 1963; Frederick and Walberg, 1980; Stallings, 1975; Wang, 1979b; Wang and Yeager, 1971; Wiley and Harnischfeger, 1974). The specific relationship between the manner in which time is spent in school and student achievement has been suggested by the results from a number of major studies (e.g. Bennett, 1976; Denham and Lieberman, 1980; Rutter, Maughan, Mortimore and Ouston, 1979), as well as by recent reviews of the teacher effectiveness research (e.g. Berliner, 1980; Brophy, 1979; Marshall, 1981; Rosenshine, 1979).

Thus, from both theoretical and pedagogical perspectives, these research and development efforts have resulted in important changes in the ways we think about schooling and its effects. Furthermore, the efforts have suggested ways in which we can improve schools' capabilities to maximize student achievement. Time for teaching and learning has come to be viewed as a critical variable in this process. Increasing the amount of time available for learning, decreasing the time students need to learn, and increasing the amount of time students actually spend learning (or trying to learn), lie at the heart of a potentially viable approach to the improvement of student learning and achievement.

Despite general consensus that the allocation and use of school time are related to various learning outcomes, debates concerning the specific classroom practices that are likely to result in increased time-on-task and improved student learning have taken place (e.g. Brophy, 1979; Peterson, 1979). Debates of this sort can be expected to continue unless the current preoccupation with searching for *the* single educational approach that is the most effective is displaced by a focus on identifying and describing the *variety* of operating features that facilitate time-on-task in actual school settings. Research investigating the processes and contexts which lead to different patterns of productive time-use are likely to result in descriptions of demonstrably effective practices that can be used alternately by school personnel.

The overall goal of the work described in this chapter has been the increased understanding of the 'basics' involved in the design of educational programmes that are adaptive to, or accommodate, student differences. A major emphasis of this work has been the development of programming strategies that effectively *decrease* the amount of time needed for learning by individual students, while at the same time *increase* both the amount of time teachers are able to spend on the provision of adaptive instruction and the amount of time students actually spend learning.

Specifically, discussion in this chapter centres on four major topics. They are: (1) the conceptual and practical issues involved in providing instruction that is adaptive to differences among students and that results in the effective allocation and use of school time; (2) the design of and rationale for an educational programme known as the Adaptive Learning Environments Model (ALEM), that includes features thought to be particularly effective in reducing the amount of time needed by each student for learning, increasing the amount of school time available for instruction and learning, and increasing the amount of time teachers and students actually spend on instruction and learning; (3) the results of a study of the programme's impact on classroom processes, student achievement, and the allocation and use of school time; and (4) a brief discussion of the programme in terms of other approaches to effective classroom instruction.

The Concept and Practice of Adaptive Instruction

Adaptive instruction may be defined conceptually as the use of alternative instructional strategies and school resources to provide learning experiences that meet the needs of individual students. An underlying assumption of adaptive instruction is that students learn in different ways and at variable rates. These differences require the provision of a variety of instructional techniques and learning experiences that match the needs of each student, as well as the allocation of adequate amounts of time so that virtually all students learn. In effective adaptive instruction programmes the match between learning experiences and student needs is based on a knowledge of each student's learning characteristics, his or her past performance and present level of competence, and the nature and types of learning tasks to be performed. Essentially, the primary objective of such programmes is to bring students' abilities into a range of competence that enhances their capabilities to profit from available learning alternatives (Glaser, 1977). Thus, the overall goal of adaptive instruction is to ensure schooling success for each student through the provision of educational experiences that effectively accommodate students' diverse learning needs.

Many practical problems have been encountered in efforts to establish adaptive instruction programmes in school settings. Among those cited most frequently are the sometimes intractable demands on teachers' time, and the lack of supports that would enable teachers to spend more time on instruction-related, rather than management-related, tasks (Bennett, 1976; Rosenshine, 1979; Wang, 1979b; McPartland and Epstein, 1975). In conventional whole-class instructional situations students are required to learn particular lessons in a specified interval of time, and all students are expected to proceed with their learning at essentially the same pace. Each student's progress is judged in terms of the amount or degree of learning he or she achieves within a constant amount of time. Typically, this judgement involves a comparison with what other students in the class have learned in a similar time period.

The adaptive instruction approach, on the other hand, permits students to progress through a given set of learning tasks at individual rates. Thus, the level or degree of mastery, rather than the amount of learning time, is held constant. Each student's performance or progress is assessed in terms of the rate at which programme objectives are mastered (Wang, 1979b, 1980a). The design of adaptive instruction programmes, therefore, requires the development of ways to increase the amount of school time teachers and students devote to their teaching and learning tasks, while at the same time reducing the amount of time students need in order to accomplish their tasks.

The Adaptive Learning Environments Model

The Adaptive Learning Environments Model (ALEM) is an instructional programme designed to provide experiences that accommodate the learning needs of diverse students in regular classroom settings. An underlying premise of the programme's design is that the teaching of basic skills need not be sacrificed to an emphasis on fostering students' involvement in making curricular choices or in planning and evaluating their own learning. Rather, both sets of objectives can be achieved through systematic programming and close monitoring of programme implementation.

Among the expected outcomes of the ALEM are the opportunity for each student to successfully acquire skills in academic subject areas through an individually tailored and optimally paced progress plan, the development of students' competence in taking increased responsibility for managing their own learning and behaviour, and a sense of social and cognitive competence and self-esteem. At the same time as teachers become proficient in implementing the programme, they are expected to be able to spend greater amounts of time providing instruction than managing students (Wang, 1980a).

Essentially, the ALEM is a product of the systematic integration of aspects of prescriptive instruction that have been shown to be effective in facilitating basic skills mastery (Bloom, 1976; Glaser, 1977; Rosenshine, 1979) with aspects of informal education that generate attitudes and processes of inquiry, independence and social co-operation (Johnson, Maruyama, Johnson, Nelson and Skon, 1981; Marshall, 1981; Peterson, 1979). The programme has five major design features. Briefly, they are: (1) a basic skills curriculum aimed at accommodating a wide range of learning needs and interests through the inclusion of highly structured and hierarchically organized prescriptive learning activities, while at the same time providing a variety of more open-ended exploratory learning activities; (2) an instructional-learning management system designed to maximize the use of available class-room and school resources (e.g. curricular materials, students' and teachers' time) and develop students' competence in taking responsibility for managing their own learning and behaviour; (3) a family-involvement programme aimed at optimizing student learning through increased communication and integration of school and home-learning experiences; (4) an organizational pattern that includes multi-age grouping and instructional training, and that is designed to increase the flexible use of teacher and student talents, time and educational resources; and (5) a data-based staff development programme that provides written plans and procedures for increasing the capabilities of individual school staff to initiate and monitor the ALEM's implementation. More detailed descriptions of the design and evaluation of these programme features can be found in a number of documents (e.g. Wang, 1982a, 1982b; Wang and Catalano, 1981). The basic programme design, and the implications for the use of school time by teachers and students, are described briefly below.

Figure 8.1 shows a conceptual model of the hypothesized causal relationships among what are perceived to be the critical dimensions of adaptive instruction programmes, the use of time by teachers and students, and expected student behaviour and learning outcomes. Three sets of critical programme dimensions are identified in the far-left column of the figure. These dimensions are designed to provide adaptive instruction, support adaptive instruction in the classroom, and support adaptive instruction in the schools and school districts. The presence of these dimensions is thought to influence both teachers and students (column 2) in ways that increase the amount of productive teaching time (column 3) and learning time (column 4), and ultimately, in improved student attitudes and achievement (column 4).

Figure 8.1: The Provision of Adaptive Instruction: a Causal Model of Adaptive Instruction and Time-Use

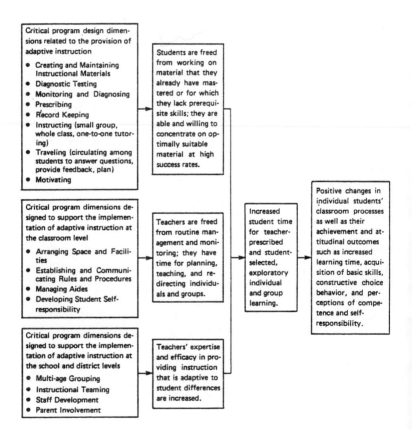

In so far as these critical dimensions represent classroom practices found to be effective by many researchers and practitioners (e.g. Brophy, 1979; National School Public Relations Association, 1981; Walberg, 1983), the *individual* critical dimensions are not unique. The uniqueness lies in the complementary *integration* and *implementation* of the dimensions as part of a comprehensive system that facilitates achievement of desired classroom processes and student outcomes. Obviously there are many ways to group or cluster these dimensions. In Figure 8.1 they are grouped according to what they are designed or intended to do. They also can be grouped in terms of the major components of adaptive instructional programmes. In this regard, four major components have been identified as playing particularly important roles in the effective allocation and use of school time under the ALEM. These components are: (1) an integrated diagnostic-prescriptive process, (2) the systematic provision of a wide range of instructional-learning options, (3) an instructional-learning management system, and (4) a school-wide organizational support system. Table 8.1 shows the alignment of the critical dimensions with the four programme components and the hypothesized relationship of the critical dimensions with three categories of effective allocation and use of school time for instruction and learning: reduction in time needed, increase in available learning time, and increase in actual learning time. Although each of the dimensions potentially contributes to all three of these time categories, an 'X' in the table means that improvement in the specific time category indicated by the column label is most likely attributable to the critical dimension indicated by the corresponding row label. The purpose of the following four subsections is to briefly describe each of the relationships specified in Table 8.1.

Integrated Diagnostic-Prescriptive Process

An integrated diagnostic-prescriptive process has become an essential curricular component of educational programmes aimed at adapting instruction to student differences. Such processes provide for assessment of each student's entering learning behaviours (diagnostic testing), development of individualized learning plans (prescribing), and continuous monitoring and assessment of students' learning progress (monitoring and diagnosing, record-keeping). The critical dimensions included in this component of the ALEM are seen as programme design supports that are particularly effective in reducing the amount of time needed by individual students for learning, and increasing the amount of time students actually spend on learning.

Table 8.1: Hypothesized Relationships Between Programme Design and the Allocation and Use of School Time

Program Components	Critical Program Dimensions Associated with Each Component	Expected Outcomes Related to Effective Allocation and Use of Time		
		Reduction in Time Needed for Learning	Increase in Time Available for Instruction and Learning	Increase in Time Spent on Instruction and Learning
Integrated Diagnostic-Prescriptive Process	Diagnostic Testing	X		X
	Prescribing	X		X
	Monitoring and Diagnosing	X		X
	Record Keeping	X		X
Systematic Provision of a Wide Range of Instructional-Learning Options	Creating and Maintaining Instructional Materials	X		X
	Arranging Space and Facilities			X
	Managing Aides		X	
Instructional-Learning Management System	Establishing and Communicating Rules and Procedures		X	X
	Developing Student Self-responsibility	X	X	X
School-wide Organizational Support System	Multi-age Grouping		X	
	Instructional Teaming		X	
	Staff Development	X	X	X
	Parent Involvement	X	X	X

The diagnostic-prescriptive process essentially is designed as an intervention strategy that ensures predominantly successful experiences in learning, even for those students who are initially the least able. The contentions are that success in school learning is likely to lead to development of students' sense of competence, and that this sense of competence results in self-confidence and a sense of self-efficacy that, in turn, influence the amount of time students actually spend on learning, and their motivation to learn (e.g. Bandura, 1977; Bloom, 1976, 1980; Covington and Beery, 1976; Wang, 1982a).

A major design task for programmes that incorporate a diagnostic-prescriptive process is the development and sequencing of psychologically and pedagogically meaningful learning hierarchies (Resnick, 1973; Wang and Resnick, 1978; Wang, Resnick and Boozer, 1971). Such learning hierarchies form the basis for a criterion-referenced diagnostic system that provides teachers with information on the presence or absence of specific competencies, thereby ensuring each student's placement at an appropriate point in the learning sequence. In addition, learning hierarchies enable teachers to structure learning experiences so that mastery of initial curricular objectives provides the prerequisite learning skills for mastery of later objectives. It is anticipated that in this way students neither repeat tasks they already have mastered, nor work on objectives for which they lack critical prerequisite skills. The fine-grained steps in the learning hierarchies form the natural checkpoints in the curricular continuum, permitting those students who acquire certain skills before entering the programme, or who acquire them quickly, to move ahead to more complex tasks. Thus, inclusion of learning hierarchies can be expected to result in reductions in the amount of time needed by each student for learning.

Systematic Provision of a Wide Range of Instructional-Learning Options

It has been hypothesized that inclusion of a wide range of learning options in the ALEM's design minimizes the amount of time needed by students for learning, and increases the amount of time spent on instruction and learning. In ALEM classrooms instructional and learning choices can be made from a variety of paper-and-pencil and manipulative materials for use by students in independent work, and by teachers in individual or group instruction situations (creating and maintaining instructional materials). Such a wide range of options, combined with adequate and appropriate space and facilities (arranging space and facilities) and effective management and use of the expertise of other paraprofessional and professional adults in the classroom (managing aides) are important conditions for increased instructional and learning opportunities that accommodate both the learning needs of the students and the nature and types of skills to be mastered. It is expected that utilization of a variety of individually adaptive learning options is likely to result in a reduction of time needed and an increase in time spent. The proper arrangement of space and facilities is expected to yield an increase in time spent. Finally, the placement of aides and other paraprofessionals in classrooms is likely to increase the time available for instruction of individual students. That is, more students will have greater access to instruction from adults.

Instructional-Learning Management System

The selection of learning activities, the scheduling of instructional time, and the accessibility of resources and facilities have been major implementation problems for instructional programmes aimed at accommodating student diversity. Typically, scheduling choices have been limited to group instruction versus individual instruction, free-choice versus teacher-prescribed activities, and teacher instruction versus independent student work. Effective implementation of adaptive instruction, however, requires all of these options (Wang, 1974a). To this end, an instructional-learning management system that focuses on the development of student responsibility has been a major component of the ALEM. Known as the self-schedule system, the programme's management system provides teachers and students with the support required to make efficient use of available time, space, and material resources.

Specifically, the self-schedule system is designed to promote flexibility through the establishment and explicit communication of rules and procedures (establishing and communicating rules and procedures), thereby maximizing the distribution of teacher time and instructional resources. By delegating to students increased responsibility for planning and completing their own learning tasks (developing student self-responsibility), and providing teachers with a system for organizing and processing relevant information in the formulation of individualized learning plans, the self-schedule system helps to free teachers from routine classroom and instructional management tasks and allows them to concentrate on teaching (Wang, 1979a, 1980a).

In his review of recent developments in the cognitive sciences, Simon (1981) pointed out that aside from motivation and external opportunities and incentives, the major constraints against performance of demanding cognitive activities are the few items of information that can be held in immediate conscious memory, and the time required to store an item in long-term memory. Thus, attention and memory are limiting factors that must be considered in the provision of adaptive instruction. In order to facilitate learning, then, teachers are required to gather and process information about each student's learning progress on an ongoing basis. They need to evaluate and design alternative plans to foster mastery of learning objectives. Instructional decisions are based not only on student cues, but also on information about the availability of alternative strategies and materials.

The ways in which such information is used is complicated further by each teacher's own beliefs about education, the particular instructional practices in the teacher's repertoire, and the teacher's perceptions of the needs and characteristics of individual students. A major focus in providing support for the ALEM has been the identification of ways to help teachers develop the kind of efficiency in information-gathering and processing that is critical for the successful provision of adaptive instruction. The self-schedule system ensures such support by relieving teachers of some of the burden of routine class-room management by placing more responsibility in the hands of students. Effective implementation of the self-schedule system is expected to decrease the information overload that is bound to occur in the implementation of adaptive instruction programmes in general, and the ALEM in particular.

Research evidence (e.g. Brown, 1978; Phares, 1968) suggests the close relationship between self-management and efficient learning. Pines and Julian (1972), for example, found that students who were competent self-managers showed more initiative and made more use of previously learned principles in problem-solving than did other students. Moreover, teaching students to become effective managers of their classroom learning and behaviour has been found to enable teachers to allocate more time to teaching and related instructional matters (Smith, 1976; Stone and Vaughn, 1976) and less time to managing students (Borg and Ascione, 1982; Kounin, 1970; Evertson and Anderson, 1978).

Effective implementation of the self-schedule system is expected to increase students' motivation and reduce the amount of system-imposed distraction in the learning environment. The development of students' basic academic and self-management skills is viewed as a way of increasing their sense of self-efficacy or personal control over their learning, and thereby increasing willingness to spend the amount of time needed for learning. Furthermore, students' acquisition of self-management skills is seen as a way of maximizing the amounts of time they actually spend on learning. In turn, it is anticipated that increased teacher-instructional time is likely to improve the quality of instruction and, as a result, reduce the amount of time needed for learning.

School-wide Organizational Support System

One of the most frequently cited causes of the unsuccessful implementation of innovative practices in schools is the lack of well-defined organizational supports (Anderson, 1973; Conner, 1976; Decker and Decker, 1977). Adaptive instruction, in particular, requires effective utilization and management of all available resources (e.g. school time, teachers' and students' talents, parents' interest in their children's education) in such a way as to lead to increases in the number and variety of approaches to instruction and learning. Instructional teaming, multi-age grouping, staff development and parent involvement are critical dimensions included in the ALEM's classroom organizational support system. All of these dimensions are intended to increase the amount of time available for instruction and learning. In addition, staff development and parent involvement efforts should increase the time spent in instruction and learning while at the same time reducing the time needed for learning.

Multi-age grouping is a classroom organizational pattern that facilitates effective allocation and use of school time. Essentially, multi-age grouping provides the necessary flexibility to accommodate the differences of individual students, particularly those who tend to make unusually slow or fast progress. For example, through the integration of students who are at different developmental and academic achievement levels, multi-age grouping results in frequent opportunities for both planned and spontaneous peer modelling and peer tutoring (Allen 1976; Wang and Weisstein, 1980).

Aside from the socialization functions that have been attributed to peer groups in the literature (e.g. Allen 1976; Demos and Demos, 1969; Erikson, 1963; Lippit, 1976), cross-age peer tutoring situations have been found to contribute to the school achievement and motivation of tutors and tutees alike (Fogarty and Wang, 1982; Lohman, 1970; Peifer, 1972). Although some spontaneous peer tutoring and modelling might occur in graded classrooms, the greater age span in multi-age grouped classrooms generally tends to result in a wider range of student talents, skills and interests within a single classroom. When viewed as instructional resources, these student characteristics are a source of additional time for instruction and learning. The common occurrence of peer tutoring in multi-age grouped classrooms also enables teachers to spend greater amounts of instructional time with those students who require the most teacher assistance.

Instructional teaming plays an important role in increasing teachers' flexibility to allocate and use school time. Students in classrooms where instructional teaming is implemented have been found to spend more of their school time receiving instruction, compared to students in self-contained classrooms (e.g. Schmuck, Paddock and Packard, 1977; Cohen, 1976). Furthermore, by working together in a team for instructional purposes and sharing their talents and school resources (e.g. instructional materials and time), teachers can provide a wider variety of instructional alternatives (Adams, 1962; Arikado, 1975; Wang, 1976) including different teaching styles (Dawson and Linstrom, 1974). Many studies have found significant differences in students' achievement, as well as in their self-concepts and attitudes toward school (e.g. Klausmeier and Quilling, 1967; Pribble and Stephens, 1976), in classrooms where some forms of instructional teaming were implemented.

The parent-involvement dimension of the ALEM is aimed at providing students with additional instructional resources through increased communication between school and home, and the active participation of parents and other family members in their children's learning. The underlying assumption is that, given the limited amount of time in the school day, students in even the most systematically designed and effectively implemented educational programmes can benefit from additional instructional reinforcement at home. This assumption is corroborated by research evidence which shows that intervention programmes designed to involve parents in significant ways are more effective than programmes aimed exclusively at students (e.g. Bronfenbrenner, 1974; Karnes and Zehrbach, 1977; Lally and Honig, 1977; Levenstein, 1977; Powell, 1979; Schaefer, 1972; Weikart, Epstein, Schweinhart and Bond, 1978). In addition to the increased learning time that is facilitated by parent-involvement activities which are integrally related to students' classroom learning, students' motivation to spend time on their learning should be increased as a result of great parental interest in what they (the students) do in school and in their schooling success.

The inclusion of staff-development efforts as a critical programme dimension in the ALEM's design is based on the premise that the establishment and maintenance of innovative educational programmes require the ongoing support of systematic staff-development activities which promote understanding of the programmes and are directly related to day-to-day implementation efforts. Findings from a number of research and development efforts have pointed to the important supportive role played by ongoing staff development that adapts to the needs and talents of individual staff members (e.g. Cruickshank, Lorish and Thompson, 1979; Griffin, 1979; McLaughlin and Marsh, 1979; McNergney, 1980; Miller and Wolf, 1979; Perry, 1980; Zigarmi, Amory and Zigarmi, 1979). In so far as such programmes contribute to teachers' increased proficiency in the implementation of the other critical dimensions, they will result, at least indirectly, in reductions in the amount of time needed for learning, as well as subsequent increases in time available for, and spent on, instruction and learning. Because of the ALEM's unique programme design and the accompanying fundamental changes in student and teacher roles required to effectively implement the programme, the development of a comprehensive system of staff development that provides school personnel with appropriate technical assistance has been a major focus of programme-implementation efforts. A detailed discussion of the rationale for and design of the Data-based Staff Development Program can be found in Wang (1981b). However, because of the importance of staff development in the proper implementation of the ALEM, the particular approach to staff development used in conjunction with the ALEM will be described briefly at this point in the discussion.

The Data-based Staff Development Programme

The Data-based Staff Development Programme incorporates three levels of training, ranging from initial awareness training to ongoing in-service training, and Figure 8.2 shows the levels and sequential steps of the programme. As outlined in Figure 8.2, Level I is designed to provide basic working knowledge of the curricular content and procedures incorporated in the ALEM. In Level II, more intensive training is provided in specific staff functions. Level III is a clinical-training component tailored to the needs of individual staff members. Training at Level III consists of ongoing in-service training designed to help school staff continually improve and upgrade their classroom implementation. It is primarily at the third level of the Data-based Staff Development Programme that the iterative process of assessment, feedback, planning and training occurs (Wang, 1981b).

As has been mentioned, training at Level I is aimed at providing an overview of the ALEM and a working knowledge of the implementation requirements of the various programme components. The basic training

Figure 8.2: The Data-based Staff Development Programme

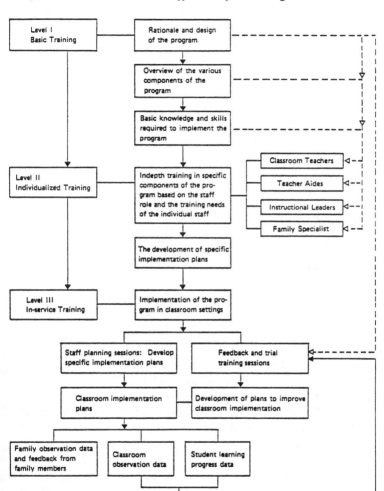

Note: ——→ Training
——▷ Re-training

level focuses on three major topic areas. They are (1) the design and
rationale for the ALEM and relevant programme evaluation results; (2)
an overview of the various programme components; and (3) the knowledge and skills required for programme implementation (e.g. information on the content covered in each of the basic skills and exploratory
learning areas; the procedures for diagnostic testing, prescription
writing and record keeping; the design of the classroom environment;

the management and display of learning materials; and the procedures for self-scheduling). Level I staff-development activities generally are scheduled as pre-implementation sessions. They are designed for all relevant administrative personnel (from central administrative staff to those at the building level), as well as for instructional and other support personnel whose duties affect the implementation of the ALEM and the provision of educational services to students in ALEM classrooms. Staff-development work at the basic training level generally requires two or three days.

Staff-development activities at the individualized training level (Level II) are designed to provide in-depth training that is specific to each staff member's functions, based on analyses of school-specific programme implementation needs. Essentially, training at this level is designed to provide differentiated staff-development activities prior to programme implementation. Specific training activities are designed according to an analysis of the functions to be carried out in the implementation of the ALEM, and the assignment of those functions to the various personnel whose present responsibilities might not include them.

As indicated in Figure 8.2, individualized training is designed to be provided to four basic types of personnel: classroom teachers, classroom aides, instructional leaders and family specialists. The amount of time required for Level II training varies from school to school (depending on an individual school's unique constraints and the staff's understanding of their roles and functions), and a detailed plan for each school's programme implementation is developed. Individualized training sessions, which last two or three days, generally are scheduled immediately after Level I basic training sessions. Experience has shown that the total staff-development work at Levels I and II can be completed in a week-long workshop prior to the opening of school.

Level III, the in-service training component of the Data-based Staff Development Programme, is the culmination of an interactive process of programme assessment, feedback, planning and ongoing staff-development work. Essentially, it provides the technical support required to establish and maintain a high degree of programme implementation at school sites. The in-service-training component is designed to be adaptive to the training needs and expertise of individual staff. As a result, the type and frequency of in-service-training sessions vary for different schools and staff. They range from short meetings (during teacher preparation time) to half-day workshops.

There are two types of Level III training sessions: staff planning sessions, and sessions for feedback and training. Staff planning sessions are designed to develop plans for accomplishing selected instructional-learning objectives, and to determine topics for staff feedback and training sessions. Staff planning is based on information from classroom observations, data on students' learning progress and feedback from family members. Sessions for staff feedback and training are scheduled on a regular basis throughout the school year, according to staff members' needs and interests. They provide opportunities to discuss critical issues related to programme implementation, particularly in terms of programme refinement and improvement in the degree of programme implementation. Feedback and training sessions usually take place during regular staff planning times and/or during schools' scheduled team meetings and in-service training times.

A Description of Adaptive Instruction at Work

Although the effectiveness of the programme components discussed above has been demonstrated in many studies by groups of investigators representing a number of different perspectives, the systematic combination and implementation of these components in a programme such as the ALEM has not been investigated. As an initial step toward filling this gap, and in order to illustrate the type of descriptive database that is critical to furthering understanding of the relationship between programme design, implementation and associated outcomes, major findings from a descriptive study are summarized here. The study focused on investigating (1) the extent to which critical dimensions of the ALEM's design can be implemented in a variety of school sites, and (2) the relationships between the degree of programme implementation, time allocation and use, classroom processes and student achievement and attitudes.

The study was conducted in 138 kindergarten to third-grade classrooms where the ALEM was implemented as the major educational programme. The classrooms were located in 10 school districts in communities with varying ethno-cultural, socio-economic, and geographic characteristics (e.g. inner-city, suburban, rural and Appalachian communities). Six of the school-district sites in the study implemented the ALEM in conjunction with their participation in the National Follow Through Programme, a compensatory education programme sponsored by the United States Department of Education, and four of the sites implemented the ALEM as a programme for mainstreaming mildly handicapped and gifted students in regular classrooms.

Classrooms were selected by district or school administrators for participation in these programmes based on fiscal and administrative considerations (e.g. selection based on the number of students meeting the poverty eligibility requirements for Follow Through funding), and not for any other special reasons. Neither subjective nor objective observations suggest that the teachers or the classrooms were unique in any systematic way other than the preponderance of students from economically disadvantaged backgrounds, students with 'special' learning needs, or both.

Four types of measures were used in the study: degree of implementation, classroom processes, time-use by teachers, and student achievement and attitudes. These measures are described in the following sections.

Degree of Implementation

A key prerequisite for the development of a system for establishing and maintaining a high degree of implementation of an innovative educational programme is the gathering of data on the extent to which the programme is being implemented as designed. The degree of implementation measures for the ALEM consisted of 96 performance indicators for assessing 12 of the critical dimensions of the ALEM programme (see the top two boxes in the first column of Figure 8.1). The Implementation Assessment Battery for Adaptive Instruction (Wang, 1980b), designed to document the presence and absence of these 12 critical dimensions, was used in the collection of degree of implementation data. The battery takes about two hours to administer. The inter-observer generalizability coefficients for the 12 dimensions varied from 0.48 to 0.91, with a median of 0.74 (Strom and Wang, 1982).

Classroom Processes

The Student Behavior Observation Schedule (SBOS) (Wang, 1974b) was used to obtain information on the nature and patterns of inter-actions between teachers and students, the settings in which learning activities occurred, the types of tasks on which students worked, and the manner in which classroom time was spent by students. The SBOS has been used in a number of investigations of classroom processes with inter-observer agreement consistently found to be above 85 per cent (Wang, 1976).

Time-Use by Teachers

The Teacher Behavior Record (TBR) (Wang, Strom and Hechtman, 1981) was used to investigate the nature and patterns of the distribution of time spent on various teacher functions. Information included the purpose (e.g. instruction, behaviour management, checking students' work), subject matter (e.g. reading, maths, exploratory learning, social studies), setting (e.g. individual, small-group, whole-class situations) and target (e.g. whole-class, small-group, individual student, persons other than students) of teacher interactions. Using the TBR teachers were observed for an entire school day whenever they were scheduled to be involved in regular classroom instruction. When teachers left the classrooms for any reasons the amount of time they were out of the classroom was recorded as non-instructional time. Teacher behaviour was not recorded during planning times and at times designated for activities such as recess, between-class breaks and lunch. The mean inter-observer agreement for the TBR was found to be approximately 83 per cent.

Student Achievement and Attitude

Two types of academic-achievement data were used in the analyses: students' progress in the mathematics and reading curricula, and standardized achievement-test results. Data on progress in the mathematics and reading curricula were collected from teachers' records of the skills mastered by each student throughout the year. Scores on standardized achievement tests were provided by participating districts in which the tests are administered routinely at the end of each school year. The decision to use the districts' data, rather than administer additional standardized achievement tests, was made after weighing the time and expense involved. It should be noted, however, that the districts administered different tests, and only the National Follow Through Programme sites administer achievement tests annually.

The Perceived Competence Scale for Children (PSC) (Harter, 1982) was used to collect information on attitudes. Designed to measure students' self-evaluations of their cognitive, social and physical competencies as well as their feelings of general self-esteem, the PSC uses a structured rating-scale format. Because of resource constraints, PSC data were collected only for the first to third-grade students in the mainstreaming schools.

The results of the study pertaining to each type of measure are described below. Following the measure-by-measure presentation an overall summary of the results is given.

Degree of Implementation and Classroom Processes

The primary purpose for examining the overall degree of implementation was to determine the extent to which critical dimensions of the ALEM could be implemented with a high degree of fidelity in a wide range of classroom settings and school sites. Each site's mean degree of implementation scores on the 12 critical dimensions, along with the average scores across sites and dimensions, were calculated and are summarized in Table 8.2.

As shown in Table 8.2, the average degree of implementation across all sites was quite high (92 per cent), with the mean overall degree of implementation for all ten sites at or above 85 per cent (see bottom row of Table 8.2). Similarly, the cross-site averages for individual critical dimensions also were at or above 80 per cent. All but two of the dimensions had a cross-site average degree of implementation of greater than 85 per cent, which was the preset criterion level of a 'high' degree of implementation. The two dimensions were 'Creating and Maintaining Instructional Materials' and 'Developing Student Self-responsibility'. In general, these results suggest that the critical dimensions of the ALEM were able to be implemented with a high degree of treatment fidelity in a large number of classes that included poor and handicapped students, and were located in schools with varying characteristics and constraints.

From both programme design and teacher-training perspectives, it was of interest to investigate whether those classrooms having difficulty implementing the ALEM overall had difficulty with particular dimensions. The 138 classrooms were categorized into three levels of implementation. The *high* implementation classrooms had scores at or above the 85 per cent criterion level on 11 or 12 of the critical dimensions. The *average* implementation classroom had scores at or above the 85 per cent criterion level on 6, 7, 8, 9 or 10 of the critical dimensions. Finally, the *low* implementation classrooms had scores at or above the 85 per cent criterion level on 5 or fewer critical dimensions. A series of analyses of variance were performed to examine differences in degree of implementation of particular dimensions among these three categories of classrooms. The results are reported in Table 8.3.

Some interesting patterns of differences in the implementation of particular dimensions are reflected in the data. The mean scores for all three groups were above the 85 per cent criterion level in four of the critical dimensions: record-keeping, prescribing, testing, and managing aides. This finding suggests that teachers in the ALEM classrooms achieved high performance in the basic mechanics of individualizing

Table 8.2: Mean Degree of Implementation Scores for Each of the ALEM's Critical Dimensions, Spring 1981 (N = 138 Classrooms)

| Critical dimension | Follow Through classrooms | | | | | | Mainstreaming classrooms | | | | Average scores across all sites |
	Site A (N = 22)	Site B (N = 22)	Site C (N = 17)	Site D (N = 19)	(Site E (N = 11)	Site F (N = 26)	Site G (N = 4)	Site H (N = 3)	Site I (N = 5)	Site J (N = 9)	
Arranging space and facilities (0.84)*	97	92	95	94	98	92	100	97	91	96	95
Creating and maintaining ins. mat. (0.83)	85	89	74	80	97	87	71	88	64	76	81
Estab./comm. rules/procedures (0.69)	86	92	90	93	94	89	97	89	91	84	91
Managing aides (0.83)	98	98	100	100	100	99	100	100	93	100	99
Testing (0.48)	100	99	87	100	100	100	100	100	100	100	99
Record-keeping (0.50)	100	100	100	95	100	96	100	89	100	100	98
Monitoring and diagnosing (0.71)	93	98	95	93	93	91	94	100	88	93	94
Prescribing (0.67)	99	97	99	92	100	96	100	100	100	100	98
Travelling (0.91)	75	93	94	95	100	88	75	100	80	94	89
Instructing (0.74)	92	91	93	97	92	87	86	86	76	76	88
Motivating (0.74)	90	92	93	99	98	88	100	87	80	96	92
Developing student self-responsibility (0.66)	88	82	88	84	85	90	58	100	60	96	83
Overall scores per site	92	94	92	94	96	92	90	94	85	93	92

Note. *Inter-observer generalizability coefficients are given in parentheses.

instruction (e.g. making use of paraprofessionals, prescribing work for students).

Table 8.3: Differences in Patterns of Mean Degree of Implementation Scores Among Classrooms at the High, Average and Low Degree of Implementation Levels, Spring 1981 (N = 138 Classrooms)

Critical Dimensions	Mean Percentage Scores			F-Test
	High	Average	Low	
Record Keeping	99	98	87	2.13
Prescribing	100	96	96	3.78
Testing	100	98	95	5.89*
Managing Aides	100	98	100	1.83
Arranging Space and Facilities	98	93	77	6.84*
Establishing and Communicating Rules and Procedures	93	87	79	7.48*
Monitoring and Diagnosing	95	93	83	6.43*
Instructing	96	87	77	8.34*
Motivating	99	89	80	10.11*
Creating and Maintaining Instructional Materials	92	78	62	9.39*
Traveling	100	84	70	7.13*
Developing Student Self-Responsibility	93	81	74	9.17*
Mean Across All Dimensions	97	90	81	7.35*

Note.   *$p < .01$

Dimensions for which mean scores above the 85% criterion level were achieved by all three levels of degree of implementation classrooms.

Dimensions for which mean scores above the 85% criterion level were achieved by the high and average degree of implementation classrooms, but not by the low degree of implementation classrooms.

Dimensions for which mean scores above the 85% criterion level were achieved by the high degree of implementation classrooms, but not by the average and low degree of implementation classrooms.

Teachers in the high and average degree of implementation groups differed from teachers in the low degree of implementation group in the areas of classroom instruction and management. Specifically, low-implementation teachers experienced greater difficulty arranging space and facilities, establishing and communicating rules and procedures, monitoring and diagnosing, instructing and motivating.

Finally, teachers in the high degree of implementation group differed from those in the other two groups on three critical dimensions: creating and maintaining instructional materials; travelling (that is, circulating among students to instruct, assist, evaluate, and answer questions); and developing student self-responsibility. These dimensions include skills in simultaneous analyses of individual students' needs, and accurate assessment of the availability of alternative learning resources and experiences so that efficient instructional matching decisions can be made.

Thus, teachers in classrooms with overall high degrees of implementation can be differentiated from teachers in classrooms with overall average or low degrees of implementation in terms of their competencies in processing and using information about students' ongoing learning behaviour and learning needs, the nature of the tasks to be learned, and the instructional and learning resources that can be used to make instruction more adaptive to each student's needs. These competencies include the ability to identify and create supplementary or new materials and activities that adapt to individual students' learning needs (creating and maintaining instructional materials); the ability to make on-the-spot decisions to alter instruction, provide feedback, and motivate students (travelling); and the ability to help students acquire self-management skills for planning and carrying out their learning plans (developing student self-responsibility). It should be pointed out here that these differences in the patterns of degree of implementation are replications of the findings from a previous study in which the same hierarchy of teacher competencies differentiated high, average and low degrees of implementation of adaptive instruction (Strom and Wang, 1982).

The overall degree of implementation was also examined in relation to a variety of classroom-process variables: teacher-student interactions, peer interaction, the nature of instructional settings, the type of activities, and the manner of time-use by the students. The mean percentages of observed frequencies of these classroom-process variables for classrooms in the three degrees of implementation categories are displayed in Table 8.4.

A statistically significant canonical correlation (0.36 p <0.01) was found between degree of implementation and the various classroom processes. In addition, some distinct patterns in classroom processes were noted among classrooms at the high, average and low degree of implementation levels. As noted earlier, the classroom process data (from the SBOS) were collected only for the first-grade and second-grade classrooms in the study. Therefore, the number of classrooms for this analysis is 72, rather than 138.

Table 8.4: Mean Percentages of Observed Frequencies of Classroom-process Variables for Classrooms at the High, Average and Low Degree of Implementation Levels, Spring 1981 (N = 72 Classrooms)

| | Degree of implementation levels | | | | | | |
| | High (N = 29) | | Average (N = 39) | | Low (N = 4) | | |
Variables	Mean	S.D.	Mean	S.D.	Mean	S.D.	F-test
Interactions between teachers and students							
Instruction	93.3	(2.3)	91.7	(2.0)	90.0	(1.7)	4.83*
Management	6.7	(0.6)	8.3	(0.4)	10.0	(0.4)	1.24
Interactions with peers							
Sharing ideas	99.8	(2.3)	94.4	(2.8)	90.0	(1.8)	1.02
Disruptive	0.2	(0.2)	5.6	(0.3)	10.0	(0.3)	5.01*
Settings							
Group interactive	5.1	(2.1)	3.0	(1.6)	3.0	(1.8)	2.73
Group parallel	5.1	(2.0)	2.0	(1.5)	0.0	(0)	6.13**
Individual	89.8	(2.9)	95.0	(2.4)	97.0	(1.8)	4.98*
Activity types							
Prescriptive	84.7	(3.5)	96.0	(2.1)	98.0	(1.6)	8.94**
Exploratory	15.3	(3.4)	4.0	(1.9)	2.0	(1.3)	6.37**
Manner							
On-task	86.0	(2.5)	81.0	(3.7)	76.0	(3.2)	4.92*
Waiting	8.0	(1.9)	8.0	(2.7)	10.0	(2.3)	3.11*
Distracted	6.0	(1.6)	11.0	(2.2)	14.0	(2.5)	7.49**

Note: *$p < 0.05$
   **$p < 0.01$

As shown in Table 8.4, the differences among the three categories of classrooms in the frequency of instruction-related interactions between teachers and students were found to be statistically significant. Teachers in higher degree of implementation classrooms tend to be involved in a greater number of instructional interactions than teachers in lower degree of implementation classrooms. This finding lends support to the hypothesis that the higher the degree of implementation, the greater the frequency of observed instructional interactions between teachers and students. Also, the peer interactions in classrooms with lower degrees of implementation were significantly more disruptive. Furthermore, students in high implementation classrooms spent significantly less time in individual settings than students in average and low-implementation classrooms. This finding suggests that higher degrees of implementation permit the integration of individual and group settings.

Significant differences were noted in the types of learning activities and the manner in which learning tasks were carried out by students. Students in classrooms at the highest level of implementation were observed to spend less time on teacher-assigned, prescriptive tasks than students in classrooms at the average and low levels of implementation. Conversely, these students were observed to spend significantly more time on self-selected, exploratory learning tasks as compared with students in classrooms at the average and low levels of implementation. Furthermore, students in high-implementation classrooms exhibited more on-task behaviour and were less distracted than their counterparts in the average and low-implementation classrooms. It should be noted that the differences in classroom processes that were not found to be statistically significant also reflected trends in the hypothesized directions.

Overall results from the analyses of the differences in classroom processes among classrooms at three degrees of implementation levels, then, support the general contention that there is a relationship between the extent to which critical dimensions of the ALEM are in place and the nature and patterns of the resulting classroom processes. Specifically, students and teachers in classrooms at the high level of implementation seem to exhibit more of the classroom processes the programme is designed to achieve (e.g. instructional interactions between teachers and students, constructive interactions with peers, and on-task behaviour) as compared with students and teachers in classrooms at the lower levels of implementation.

Time-Use by Teachers

Data from the Teacher Behavior Record were collected in the 28 mainstreaming classrooms. As noted earlier, these data characterize the patterns of the distribution of time among the various teacher functions included in the ALEM's design. In addition to an interest in the overall patterns of teachers' time-use under the ALEM, the data permit three basic questions to be addressed. First, does the actual amount of instructional/non-instructional time vary among three types of instructional settings (individual, small-group, large-group or whole class)?

Secondly, to what extent does the distribution of instructional/non-instructional time vary among classrooms at three different levels of implementation? Finally, do teachers spend varying amounts of instructional/non-instructional time with students classified as handicapped, gifted or regular?

The percentages of time teachers spent on various instructional and non-instructional functions were initially examined. The results are summarized in Tables 8.5 and 8.6.

As shown in Table 8.5, the teachers were observed to spend approximately three-fourths of their time on instruction-related activities. Of this time, approximately 90 per cent was spent providing either instruction to individual students, small groups or the entire class, or giving instruction-related management directions (e.g. going over workbook directions, explaining how to get reference materials for specific learning tasks). Approximately 10 per cent of the instruction-related time was spent on evaluation and planning activities (e.g. prescribing learning tasks, checking student work, recording student progress). About 70 per cent of the time spent providing instruction was spent working with individual students; about 10 per cent was spent providing small-group instruction; and about 20 per cent was spent in large-group instruction. Similar proportions of teacher time for giving instruction-related management directions were observed among the three different types of instructional settings.

Overall results from the analysis of the data on teachers' use of time point to several major patterns. These patterns can be summarized briefly as follows:

On the average, teachers in the ALEM classrooms spent comparatively large percentages of their time on instruction-related activities. Only very small proportions of teachers' non-instructional time were spent on behaviour management.

Some differences were observed in teacher time-use among classrooms at the high, average, and low degree of implementation levels. Teachers in low degree of implementation classrooms, for example, spent comparatively large proportions of their evaluation and planning time on record-keeping, and smaller percentages of this time prescribing and checking student work. These teachers also were observed to spend a comparatively large percentage of time on behaviour management in large-group instructional situations.

Although teachers seemed to spend comparable amounts of total time on interactions with the three different groups of students

Table 8.5: *Summary of Mean Percentages of Time Spent by Teachers on Various Instructional Functions under the ALEM [N = 28 Teachers from the Mainstreaming Classrooms]*

Type of analysis	Instructional functions [77.08]**						Evaluation and planning [10.96]		
	Instruction [89.04]								
	Instructing [70.21]			Giving instruction-related management directions [29.79]					
	Individual	Small group	Large group	Individual	Small group	Whole class	Prescribing work	Checking work	Record keeping
Time spent across all classrooms	72.86* (14.66)	8.56 (9.61)	18.59 (10.27)	77.08 (21.13)	5.03 (8.25)	14.68 (11.26)	14.11 (16.12)	31.69 (25.75)	50.65 (35.52)
Time spent in classrooms at different degree of implementation levels									
High (N = 11)	76.21 (12.10)	7.65 (8.95)	16.15 (10.15)	86.82 (6.95)	2.00 (2.19)	11.18 (6.59)	14.66 (17.70)	29.34 (26.17)	56.07 (35.47)
Average (N = 13)	69.69 (17.96)	8.85 (11.31)	21.46 (11.52)	68.00 (26.61)	8.11 (11.16)	16.97 (13.60)	15.48 (15.84)	37.50 (24.81)	39.32 (31.22)
Low (N = 4)	73.94 (8.31)	10.13 (6.83)	15.94 (2.72)	79.77 (17.61)	3.33 (4.45)	16.90 (13.49)	8.16 (16.12)	19.24 (29.12)	72.60 (44.22)
Time spent with individual students									
Regular	89.96 3.64/Student (11.73)			85.46 3.57/Student (11.94)			52.31 2.19/Student (44.40)	63.38 2.65/Student (42.46)	
Handicapped	8.79 3.20/Student (8.93)			8.99 3.27/Student (8.60)			13.25 4.82/Student (26.48)	6.61 2.40/Student (11.64)	
Gifted	4.25 3.40/Student (5.43)			5.52 4.42/Student (5.66)			2.23 1.78/Student (5.21)	1.79 1.43/Student (4.47)	

Note: * Numbers in parentheses throughout indicate standard deviations.
**Numbers in square brackets indicate mean percentages.
***Mean Number of Observation Minutes Per Teacher = 199.29.

Table 8.6: *Summary of Mean Percentages of Time Spent by Teachers on Various Non-instructional Functions under the ALEM (N = 28 Teachers from the Mainstreaming Classrooms)*

| Total of Analysis | Non-instructional functions [22.92]** | | | | | |
| | Behaviour management [24.86] | | | | Conversations with students (personal or other non-instructional purposes) | Other non-instructional functions |
	Individual	Small group	Whole class	Total percentage		
Time spent across all classrooms	44.66 (34.63)	3.11 (7.12)	44.39 (35.60)	27.01 (25.04)	9.90 (9.33)	63.09 (25.07)
Time spent in classrooms at different degree of implementation levels						
High (N = 11)	47.53 (33.18)	2.41 (5.23)	50.03 (33.92)	22.78 (19.50)	13.86 (12.67)	63.36 (19.99)
Average (N = 13)	51.04 (37.02)	4.66 (9.23)	27.45 (30.74)	25.59 (25.50)	7.29 (5.12)	67.12 (27.43)
Low (N = 4)	16.03 (18.51)	0.00 (0.00)	83.97 (18.51)	43.25 (36.74)	7.49 (6.92)	49.26 (31.44)
Time spent with individual students						
Regular	60.94 2.55/Student (40.27)				85.15 3.56/Student (26.78)	
Handicapped	8.54 3.11/Student (16.32)				2.22 0.81/Student (5.42)	
Gifted	2.97 2.38/Student (6.27)				5.48 4.38/Student (10.01)	

Note: *Numbers in parentheses indicate standard deviations.
**Numbers in square brackets indicate mean percentages.
***Mean Number of Observation Minutes Per Teacher = 199.29.

(regular, handicapped, gifted), some differences in the patterns of time-use were noted. For example, there were some noticeable differences in the distribution of teacher time spent among regular, handicapped, and gifted students for instructional planning and non-instructional functions. Teachers spent more time prescribing work for handicapped students and less time on personal conversations with them. Moreover, teachers spent more time giving instruction-related management directions to gifted students, less time prescribing and checking work for them, and more time on personal conversations with them. It is also interesting to note, however, that teachers spent comparable amounts of time instructing students in the three groups.

Achievement and Attitudes

Findings on student achievement in the basic skills and students' social behaviour and attitudes offer important evidence of the ALEM's effectiveness in accommodating the learning needs and characteristics of diverse student populations. As stated previously and shown in Figure 8.1, positive outcomes in these areas are viewed as being directly related to implementation of critical programme dimensions and the resulting effects on the allocation and use of school time and classroom processes.

Data on the Follow Through student's achievement in the basic skills were analyzed in terms of national and estimated population norms, as well as cross-cohort and grade-level comparisons over the 1979-80 and 1980-1 school years (Wang, 1981a). Results of the analyses show that, on the average, reading and maths achievement scores for the ALEM students were consistently above both the population norms for students from low-income families (see Branden and Weis, 1977) and the national norms established by the publishers of the standardized tests.

The relationship between programme implementation and student achievement is suggested by data that show improvements in achievement scores from one year to the next. This improved achievement is manifested in *increased* percentages of students scoring with the upper quartile of the distribution of scores, and *decreased* percentages of students scoring in the lower quartile.

In addition to the achievement results from the Follow Through sites, the ALEM's positive effects on the basic-skills achievement of regular, handicapped, and gifted students in the mainstreaming classrooms are also suggested (Wang, Thompson and Meece, 1982). Results from analyses of the data from these sites show that regular students in the ALEM mainstreaming classrooms achieved as well in reading and mathematics as similar students in comparison classrooms. Furthermore, achievement gains in reading and mathematics of handicapped and gifted students favoured those in the ALEM over their comparison classroom counterparts. It is important to point out here that the achievement findings for the ALEM and non-ALEM mainstreaming classrooms should be interpreted in light of the differences in the amounts of instructional time and the student-adult ratios (in so far as they dictated the amount of time teachers spent with individual students) in the two types of classrooms. Handicapped students in the non-ALEM comparison classrooms received reading and maths instruction in a pull-out, resource-room programme throughout the entire morning of each day. The resource room had a student-teaching staff ratio of 5 to 1, compared to a ratio of 15 to 1 in the ALEM classrooms. In addition, the non-ALEM handicapped students spent the entire morning of each school day receiving instruction in reading and maths, while the activities of the ALEM handicapped students during the same period consisted of a variety of student-selected exploratory learning tasks, as well as teacher-prescribed tasks in spelling, perceptual skills, and other academic subject areas (in addition to reading and maths work).

Attitudinal data consisted of students' self-ratings in three domains: cognitive competence, social competence and general self-esteem (Harter, 1982). As noted earlier, these data were collected only in the mainstreaming classrooms. Attitudinal outcomes are particularly important in the ALEM classrooms in light of the inclusion of systematic diagnostic-prescriptive procedures in the programme's design to ensure that instruction is adapted to the student's individual needs, and that regular progress is made by each student. Although a wide range of ability levels is found, and even expected, in the ALEM classrooms (particularly in the mainstreaming classrooms), all students are expected to be able to make regular progress. When individual learning needs are diagnosed on an ongoing basis, appropriate learning activities are provided, and sufficient amounts of time to complete the activities allocated, students will likely experience learning success and, as a consequence, develop perceptions of competence and a general sense of self-esteem. In this way, they are expected to be less likely to view themselves as 'exceptional'.

The overall results indicate some quite positive attitudinal outcomes.

When the students' self-ratings on the four-point scale were compared, the ALEM handicapped students showed higher self-ratings of cognitive and social competence than the handicapped students in the non-ALEM classrooms. It is also noteworthy that greater percentages of the self-ratings of the handicapped students in the ALEM classrooms fell into the highest interval (the 3-4 interval) of the four-point scale in all three domains. In the non-ALEM classrooms, on the other hand, handicapped students had consistently lower percentages of self-ratings in the highest interval (Meece and Wang, 1982).

Discussion

There are some interesting areas of agreement and contrast between the findings reported in this chapter and those from the extant research literature on effective teaching. Perhaps the most controversial is the challenge posed by the evidence presented here to the predominant data-base on the efficacy of educational practices that attempt to accommodate the learning needs of individual students, and the educational benefits of students' active role in the planning and management of their learning and behaviours. On the whole, there is little evidence in the literature to support either the efficacy or the practicability of implementing adaptive instruction programmes in school settings. In contrast, the results presented in this chapter suggest a composite scenario of learning environments that differs significantly from traditional classrooms.

Of particular interest are the findings related to time-on-task and student achievement. Among the most frequent criticisms of adaptive instruction programmes is that they tend to lead to ineffective use of teacher and student time and, consequently, lower student achievement. Many argue that a major design flaw of such programmes is the expectation that students work alone most of the time, resulting in fewer instruction-related interactions with teachers, lower rates of time-on-task, and lower rates of achievement than in more conventional programmes. However, the data presented in this chapter suggest that, along with quite positive student achievement outcomes, desirable classroom processes (e.g. time-on-task, instructional interactions with teachers) that have been identified in the research literature on effective teaching, can indeed be attained under adaptive instruction programmes such as the ALEM.

Findings from the study also challenge current opinion on the 'implementability' of adaptive instruction programmes (i.e. the potential for widespread implementation of programmes such as the ALEM in school settings). The general consensus is that effective implementation of adaptive instruction requires considerable teacher expertise and resources. Many have come to the conclusion that even if adequate school organizational and resource supports could be provided, the knowledge-base on how to develop the teacher expertise required to effectively implement an adaptive instruction approach is sorely lacking. Based on the assumption that it is extremely difficult to 'clone' the special sort of teacher required by such programmes, findings of successful demonstration of adaptive instruction have been attributed to unusual teachers, students, or both. In the ALEM classrooms in which the present study was conducted, however, most of the teachers (more than 95 per cent) were able to develop the expertise, or use the expertise they already possessed, to effectively provide adaptive instruction. In fact, it is noteworthy that results from a study conducted concurrently show significant improvements in programme implementation from autumn to spring as the result of the utilization of a data-based, individualized staff-development programme (Gennari, Tomich and Zajac, 1982). Results such as these clearly point to the feasibility of a large proportion of school teachers providing the kind of adaptive instruction that generally is believed to be a rare occurrence in many schools today.

The overall results presented in this chapter suggest four major conclusions:

1. As critical features of the ALEM are established, so are classroom processes hypothesized to facilitate effective allocation and use of instructional and learning time. Classrooms at various levels of implementation can be characterized by differences in classroom processes, particularly in the nature and patterns of the use of school time by students and teachers, the interactions between teachers and students, and the interactions between students and their peers.

2. In classrooms in which the ALEM is implemented, teachers spend a significant part of their day (approximately 90 per cent) on instructional activities. Furthermore, when non-instructional time was analyzed, teachers were found to spend less than 6 per cent of their time on behaviour management.

3. In classrooms where the ALEM is implemented as a mainstreaming programme for exceptional students, teachers do not seem to

consistently distribute more or less of their time to any specific group of students (handicapped, regular, or gifted).

4. The implementation of the ALEM on a large-scale basis can be established and maintained by a variety of teachers in a variety of school settings.

Despite the limitations of generalizing implications of a single study, the available evidence supports the contention that it is not necessary to trade off high achievement in basic skills for student growth in dimensions such as independence, self-responsibility and social co-operation. Furthermore, attainment of both sets of educational skills is shown to be possible through the integration of programme design features that are known to facilitate the effective allocation and use of instruction and learning time. Finally, if such a programme is to be implemented appropriately and successfully an ongoing staff-development programme must be in place, and one that adapts to the implementation needs of individual school personnel.

References

Adams, A.S. (1962) 'Operation Co-teaching. Date line: Oceano, California', *The Elementary School Journal, 62*, 203-12

Allen, V.L. (1976) (ed.), *Children as Teachers: Theory and Research on Tutoring*, New York: Academic Press

Anderson, R. (1973) 'Mainstreaming is the Name for a New Idea', *School Management, 17*(7), 28-30

Anderson, L.W. (1976) 'An Empirical Investivation of Individual Differences in Time to Learn', *Journal of Educational Psychology, 68*, 226-33

Arikado, M. (1975) 'Team-teaching: What Makes it Work', *Education Canada, 15*(2), 26-9

Bandura, A. (1977) *Social Learning Theory*, Englewood Cliffs, NJ: Prentice-Hall

Bennett, N. (1976) *Teaching Styles and Pupil Progress*, Cambridge, Mass.: Harvard University Press

Berliner, D.C. (1980) 'Using Research on Teaching for the Improvement of Classroom Practice', *Theory into Practice, 19*, 302-8

——, Fisher, C.W., Filby, N.N. and Marliave, R. (1978) *Executive Summary of Beginning Teacher Evaluation Study*. San Francisco: Far West Laboratory for Educational Research and Development

Bloom, B.S. (1968) 'Learning for Mastery', *Evaluation Comment*, May, *1*

—— (1976) *Human Characteristics and School Learning*, New York: McGraw Hill

—— (1980) *All Our Children Learning*, New York: McGraw Hill

Borg, W.R. and Ascione, F.R. (1982) 'Classroom Management in Elementary Mainstreaming Classrooms', *Journal of Educational Psychology, 74*, 85-95

Branden, A. and Weis, L. (1977) 'Alternative Presentation of the MAT Data: Follow Through National Evaluation'. Paper presented to US Office of Education, Office of Planning and Evaluation, Elementary and Secondary Programs, Washington, DC

Bronfenbrenner, U. (1974) 'Is Early Intervention Effective?' in H.J. Leichter
(ed.), *The Family as Educator*, New York: Teachers College Press
Brophy, J. (1979) 'Teacher Behavior and its Effects', *Journal of Educational
Psychology, 71*, 733-50
Brown, A. (1978) 'Knowing When, Where and How to Remember' in R. Glaser
(ed.), *Advances in Instructional Psychology* (vol. 1), Hillsdale, NJ: Erlbaum
Carroll, J.B. (1963) 'A Model for School Learning', *Teachers College Record, 63*,
723-32
Cohen, E.G. (1976) *Problems and Prospects of Teaming* (Memorandum No. 143),
Stanford, Ca: Stanford University, Center for Research and Development in
Teaching
Conner, L.E. (1976) 'Mainstreaming a Special School', *Teaching Exceptional
Children, 8*, 76-80
Covington, M.L. and Beery, R. (1976) *Self-worth and School Learning*. New
York: Holt,Rinehart & Winston
Cruickshank, D.R., Lorish, C. and Thompson, L. (1979) 'What We Think We
Know About In-service Education', *Journal of Teacher Education, 30*(1),
27-31
Dawson, D.T. and Linstrom, R. (1974) 'The Expanded Self-contained Classroom',
The Elementary School Journal, 74, 203-9
Decker, R.J. and Decker, L.A. (1977) 'Mainstreaming the LD Child: A Cautionary
Note', *Academic Therapy, 12*(3), 353-6
Demos, J. and Demos, V. (1969) 'Adolescence in Historical Perspective', *Journal
of Marriage and the Family, 31*, 635-42
Denham, C. and Lieberman, A. (1980) (eds), *Time to Learn*, Washington, DC:
National Institute of Education
Erikson, E.H. (1963) *Childhood and Society*, New York: W.W. Norton
Evertson, C. and Anderson, L. (1978) *Interim Progress Report: the Classroom
Organization Study* (Report No. 6002), Austin, Tex.: University of Texas,
Research and Development Center for Teacher Education
Fogarty, J. and Wang, M.C.(1982) 'An Investigation of the Class-age Peer Tutoring
Process: Some Implications for Instructional Design and Motivation', *The
Elementary School Journal, 82*, 451-69
Frederick, W.C. and Walberg, H.J. (1980) 'Learning as a Function of Time',
Journal of Educational Research, 73, 183-94
Gennari, P.A., Tomich, N. and Zajac, M. (1982) *The Data-based Staff Develop-
ment Program to Improve Program Implementation*, University of Pittsburgh,
Learning Research and Development Center
Glaser, R. (1977) *Adaptive Education: Individual Diversity and Learning*, New
York: Holt, Rinehart & Winston
Griffin, G.A. (1979) 'Guidelines for the Evaluation of Staff Development Pro-
grams' in A. Lieberman and L. Miller (eds), *Staff Development: New Realities,
New Perspectives*, New York: Teachers College Press
Harter, S. (1982) 'The Perceived Competence Scale for Children', *Child Develop-
ment, 53*, 87-97
Johnson, D.W., Maruyama, G., Johnson, R., Nelson, D. and Skon, L. (1981)
'Effects of Cooperative, Competitive, and Individualistic Goal Structures on
Achievement: A Meta-analysis', *Psychological Bulletin, 89*, 47-62
Karnes, M.B. and Zehrbach, R.R. (1977) 'Educational Intervention at Home' in
M.C. Day and R.K. Parker (eds), *The Preschool in Action* (2nd edn), Boston:
Allyn & Bacon
Klausmeier, H.J. and Quilling, M.R. (1967) *An Alternative to Self-contained, Age-
graded Classes*, Madison, Wis.: Wisconsin University, Research and Develop-
ment Center for Cognitive Learning

Kounin, J.S. (1970) *Discipline and Group Management in Classrooms*, New York: Holt, Rinehart & Winston

Lally, J.R. and Honig, A.S. (1977) 'The Family Development Research Program' in M.C. Day and R.K. Parker (eds), *The Preschool in Action* (2nd edn), Boston: Allyn & Bacon

Levenstein, P. (1977) 'The Mother-child Home Program' in M.C. Day and R.K. Parker (eds), *The Preschool in Action* (2nd edn), Boston: Allyn & Bacon

Lippit, P. (1976) 'Learning Through Close-age Peer Tutoring: Why and How' in V.L. Allen (ed.), *Children as Teachers: Theory and Research on Tutoring*. New York: Academic Press

Lohman, J.E. (1970) 'Age, Sex, Socioeconomic Status and Youth's Relationships With Older and Younger Peers', *Dissertation Abstracts International, 31*, (5-A), 2497

Marshall, H.H. (1981) 'Open Classrooms: Has the Term Outlived its Usefulness?', *Review of Educational Research, 51*, 181-92

McLaughlin, M.W. and Marsh, D.D. (1979) 'Staff Development and School Change' in A. Lieberman and L. Miller (eds), *Staff Development: New Demands, New Realities, New Perspectives*, New York: Teachers College Press

McNergney, R.F. (1980) 'Responding to Teachers as Individuals', *Theory into Practice, 19*, 234-9

McPartland, J. and Epstein, J. (1975) *The Effects of Open School Organization on Student Outcomes*, (Report No. 195), Baltimore, Md: The Johns Hopkins University, The Center for Social Organization of Schools

Meece, J.L. and Wang, M.C. (1982) 'A Comparative Study of Social Attitudes and Behaviors of Mildly Handicapped Children in Two Mainstreaming Programs'. Paper presented at the annual meeting of the American Educational Research Association, New York, March

Miller, L. and Wolf, T.E. (1979) 'Staff Development for School Change: Theory and Practice' in A. Lieberman and L. Miller (eds), *Staff Development: New Demands, New Realities, New Perspectives*, New York: Teachers College Press

National School Public Relations Association. (1981) *Good Teachers: What to Look For*, Arlington, Va.: National School Public Relations Association

Peifer, M.R. (1972) 'The Effects of Varying Age-grade Status of Models on the Imitative Behavior of Six-year-old Boys', *Dissertation Abstracts International, 32*, (11-A), 6216

Perry, R.H. (1980) 'The Organizational/Environmental Variables in Staff Development', *Theory into Practice, 19*(4), 256-61

Peterson, P. (1979) 'Direct Instruction Reconsidered' in P. Peterson and H.J. Walberg (eds), *Research on Teaching: Concepts, Findings, and Implications*, Berkeley, Ca.: McCutchan

Phares, E.J. (1968) 'Differential Utilization of Information as a Function of Internal-external Control', *Journal of Personality, 36*, 649-62

Pines, H.A. and Julian, J.W. (1972) 'Locus of Control Differences in Motivational Arousal and Predecisional Cognitive Processing', *Journal of Personality, 40*, 407-16

Powell, D.R. (1979) *A Social Interaction Approach to Parent Education: An Overview of the Child and Family Neighborhood Program*, Detroit, Mich.: The Merrill-Palmer Institute

Pribble, D. and Stephens, E. (1976) 'IGE and the Multi-unit School: an Examination of its Influence on an Upper Elementary Reading Program'. Paper presented at the annual meeting of the International Reading Association, Anaheim, California

Resnick, L.B. (1973) (ed.), 'Hierarchies in Children's Learning: a Symposium', *Instructional Science, 2*, 311-62

Rosenshine, B.V. (1979) 'Content, Time and Direct Instruction' in P. Peterson and H.J. Walberg (eds), *Research on Teaching: Concepts, Findings, and Implications*, Berkeley, Ca.: McCutchan

Rutter, M., Maughan, B., Mortimore, P. and Ouston, J. (1979) *Fifteen Thousand Hours: Secondary Schools and Their Effects on Children*, Cambridge, Mass.: Harvard University Press

Schaefer, E.S. (1972) 'Parents as Educators: Evidence from Cross-sectional, Longitudinal and Intervention Research', *Young Children*, April, 227-39

Schmidhammer, J. (1980) *A Computer Program for the Analysis and Reporting of Degree of Implementation Data*. University of Pittsburgh, Learning Research and Development Center

Schmuck, P., Paddock, S. and Packard, J. (1977) *Management Implications of Team-teaching*, Eugene, Or.: University of Oregon, Center for Educational Policy and Management

Simon, H.A. (1981) *The Sciences of the Artificial*, Cambridge, Mass.: MIT Press

Smith, E. (1976) 'Implementation of the Self-schedule System: The teacher's Perspective' in M.C. Wang (ed.), *The Self-Schedule System for Instructional-learning Management in Adaptive School Learning Environment (LRDC) Publications Series 1976/9)*, Pittsburgh, Pa.: University of Pittsburgh, Learning Research and Development Center

Stallings, J. (1975) 'Implementation and Child Effects of Teaching Practices in Follow Through Classrooms', *Monographs of the Society for Research in Child Development, 40*(7-8, Serial No. 163)

Stone, R. and Vaughn, L. (1976) 'Implementation Evaluation of the Self-schedule System in an Adaptive School-learning Environment' in M.C. Wang (ed.), *The Self-schedule System for Instructional-learning Management in Adaptive School Learning Environments (LRDC Publications Series 1976/9)*, Pittsburgh, Pa.: University of Pittsburgh, Learning Research and Development Center

Strom, C.D. and Wang, M.C. (1982) 'A Validation Study of a Degree of Program Implementation Assessment Instrument'. Paper presented at the annual meeting of the National Council on Measurement in Education, New York, March

Suppes, P. (1964) 'Modern Learning Theory and the Elementary School Curriculum', *American Educational Research Journal, 1*, 79-94

Thompson, F.E. (1915) 'Typical Experiments for Economizing Time in Elementary Schools', *The Fourteenth Yearbook of the National Society for the Study of Education*, Chicago, Ill.: University of Chicago Press

Underwood, B.J. (1949) *Experimental Psychology: An Introduction*, New York: Appleton-Century-Crofts

Walberg, H.J. (1983) 'Teaching Strategies', *International Encyclopedia of Education*, Oxford, England: Pergamon Press

Wang, M.C. (1974a) *The Rationale and Design of the Self-schedule System (LRDC Publications Series 1974/5)*, Pittsburgh, Pa.: University of Pittsburgh, Learning Research and Development Center

—— (1974b) *The Use of Direct Observation to Study Instructional-learning Behaviors in School Settings (LRDC Publications Series 1974/9)*, Pittsburgh, Pa.: University of Pittsburgh, Learning Research and Development Center

—— (1976) 'The Use of Observational Data for Formative Evaluation of an Instructional Model', *Instructional Science, 5*, 365-9

—— (1979a) 'Implications for Effective Use of Instruction and Learning Time', *Educational Horizons, 57*, 169-74

—— (1979b) 'Maximizing the Effective Use of School Time by Teachers and Students', *Contemporary Educational Psychology, 4*, 187-201

—— (1980a) 'Adaptive Instruction: Building on Diversity', *Theory into Practice, 19*, 122-7

—— (1980b) *The Degree of Implementation Measures for the Adaptive Learning Environments Model*, University of Pittsburgh, Learning Research and Development Center

—— (1981a) *The Individualized Early Learning Program: 1980-81 Sponsor's End-of-year Report*. Technical report submitted to the National Follow Through Program of the US Department of Education, University of Pittsburgh, Learning Research and Development Center

—— (1981b) *The Use of the Data-based Staff Development Program to Improve Program Implementation*, University of Pittsburgh, Learning Research and Development Center

—— (1982a) 'Development and Consequences of Students' Sense of Personal Control' in J. Levine and M.C. Wang (eds), *Teacher and Student Perceptions: Implications for Learning*, Hillsdale, NJ: Erlbaum, (in press)

—— (1982b) 'Provision of Adaptive Instruction: Implementation and Effects'. Symposium paper presented at the annual meeting of the American Educational Research Association, New York, March

—— and Catalano, R. (1981) *The Adaptive Learning Environments Model: An Overview*, University of Pittsburgh, Learning Research and Development Center

—— and Resnick, L.B. (1978) *Primary Education Program (PEP): Introductory Handbook*, Johnstown, Pa.: Mafex Associates, Inc.

——, Resnick, L.B. and Boozer, R. (1971) 'The Sequence of Development of Some Early Mathematics Behaviors', *Child Development, 42*, 1768-78

——, Strom, C.D. and Hechtman, J. (1981) *The Teacher Behavior Record*, University of Pittsburgh, Learning Research and Development Center

——, Thompson, M.D. and Meece, J.L. (1982 'Provision of Effective Learning Experiences for Mainstreamed Mildly Handicapped and Gifted Students'. Paper presented at the annual meeting of the American Educational Research Association, New York, March

—— and Weisstein, W.J. (1980) 'Teacher Expectations and Student Learning' in L.J. Fyans, Jr (ed.), *Achievement Motivation: Recent Trends in Theory and Research,* New York: Plenum

—— and Yeager, J.L. (1971) 'Evaluation Under Individualized Instruction', *The Elementary School Journal, 71*, 448-52

Washburne, C.N. (1925) 'Adapting the School to Individual Differences', *The Twenty-fourth Yearbook of the National Society for the Study of Education*, Chicago, Ill.: University of Chicago Press

Weikart, D., Epstein, A.S., Schweinhart, L. and Bond, J.T. (1978) *The Ypsilanti Preschool Curriculum Demonstration Project: Preschool Years and Longitudinal Results*, Ypsilanti, Mich.: Monographs of the High/Scope Educational Research Foundation

Wiley, D.E. and Harnischfeger, A. (1974) 'Explosion of a Myth: Quantity of Schooling and Exposure to Instruction, Major Educational Vehicles', *Educational Researcher, 3*, 7-12

Woodrow, H. (1940) 'Interrelations of Measures of Learning', *Journal of Psychology, 10*, 49-72

Zigarmi, P., Amory, J. and Zigarmi, D.A. (1979) 'A Model for an Individualized Staff Development Program' in A. Lieberman and L. Miller (eds), *Staff Development: New Demands, New Realities, New Perspectives*, New York: Teachers College Press

9 TIME AND INSTRUCTIONAL IMPROVEMENT: AN R AND D-BASED APPROACH*

William G. Huitt and Janet H. Caldwell

Several previous chapters have indicated that student engaged time, or time-on-task, is an important factor influencing student achievement. Thus, it seems reasonable for teachers and administrators to try to optimize students' use of time in school. How can this best be done? The answer to this question forms the basis of this chapter.

Time is one of several factors addressed by the Achievement Directed Leadership (ADL) programme, a research-based programme developed by Research for Better Schools, Inc. (RBS), a Philadelphia-based regional educational laboratory. The programme was developed in cooperation with over fifty teachers and administrators in schools in Delaware, New Jersey and Pennsylvania. The programme provides a means of helping educators translate into practice the important implications of recent classroom research on effective schools and school districts, as well as on educational change (RBS, 1976, 1978, 1979; Graeber, 1980; Helms, 1980; Huitt and Rim, 1980). In essence, the ADL programme provides an overall, district-wide approach to instructional leadership focusing upon the following four primary classroom teaching and learning variables:

(1) prior learning – knowledge students possess or acquire which helps their learning of a new subject matter;

(2) student engaged time – amount of time students actually spend working on and trying to accomplish assigned academic tasks;

*Preparation of this paper was supported in part by funds from the National Institute of Education (NIE). The opinions expressed do not necessarily reflect the position or policy of NIE, and no official endorsement should be inferred. This chapter discusses a strategy for managing instructional time in the classroom that is one element of a comprehensive training programme for administrators, supervisors, and teachers called Achievement Directed Leadership (ADL). David Helms and Anna Graeber conceptualized the programme and its major elements at Research for Better Schools, Inc. (RBS) and led development efforts. Development of the programme also benefited from the co-operative assistance of educators in Delaware, New Jersey and Pennsylvania. This work is recorded in RBS documents which have been submitted to the National Institute of Education and are listed at the end of this chapter.

(3)   coverage of criterion content — students' opportunities to learn the content on which they are to be tested;

(4)   academic performance — students' success with daily learning tasks, mastery of content units, and review of recently learned subject matter.

This chapter illustrates ways in which the ADL programme uses research findings on students' use of time to improve basic skills instruction. The programme draws upon two types of research: (1) correlational studies relating time and student achievement (see Chapter 6), and (2) correlational and experimental studies relating teaching behaviours to improved student engaged time (see Chapter 7). The first section of this chapter describes the process of managing students' use of time, and this is followed by one which explains the materials and procedures used in this process. In the third and final section of the chapter data relating to participants' experiences with the programme are presented, and the potential significance of the time component of the ADL programme is discussed.

Management Process

Recent research indicates that teachers need skills in decision-making as well as certain effective teaching techniques (McDonald, 1977). In the ADL programme instructional improvement is achieved through a knowledge-based decision-making process for managing critical schooling factors or influences. This process, a four-phase instructional improvement cycle, is used by classroom teachers to manage several critical classroom variables, one of which is students' use of time. The process (see Figure 9.1) relies on the collection of classroom data, the comparison of classroom data with relevant research findings, the making of decisions about appropriate instructional modifications, and the implementation of these modifications. Since the cycle is iterative, subsequent collections of classroom data permit the evaluation of the effectiveness of these instructional changes.

Information Collection

In order to make knowledge-based improvements in classrooms, educators must first be able to measure present levels of student engaged time. As a consequence, the first phase of the instructional improvement cycle calls for the collection of descriptive data on students' use of time.

Two types of data are collected. First, the teacher completes a log indicating the amount of time allocated for instruction in a subject area. Secondly, an observer systematically collects data on the extent to which students are actively involved in academic work during that allocated time. The data collection procedures were established by RBS in such a way as to assure the equivalency of the data collected in the selected classrooms with the data collected in a variety of relevant research studies (Huitt, Caldwell, Traver and Graeber, 1981).

Figure 9.1: Four-phase Instructional Improvement Cycle (RBS, 1979)

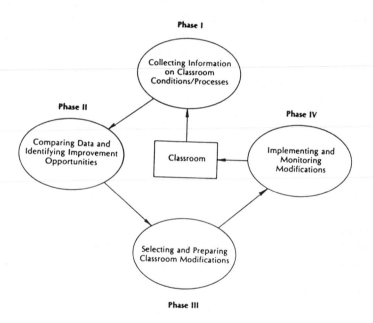

Comparison and Identification

If teachers are to treat instructional improvement as a decision-making process, they must be able to compare their own classroom instruction with available evidence obtained from other classrooms. Summaries of research that are readily available to teachers provide general information about the research, but seldom include sufficient detail to permit valid comparisons with existing classrooms. The complete reports of these studies, on the other hand, are usually voluminous and difficult to obtain. Furthermore, most of these studies report relationships between classroom variables such as student engaged time and student achievement as correlation coefficients. These coefficients do indicate that there is a positive relationship between classroom variables such as student engaged time and achievement, but do not indicate the *levels* of the variable that are associated with the highest achievement gains.

While some researchers suggest that more student engaged time is appropriate for all classrooms, others (e.g. Rim and Coller, 1978) indicate that in some cases, moderate amounts of student engaged time are associated with the highest achievement gains. Thus, correlation coefficients alone are insufficient for determining whether or not the level of student engaged time in a specific classroom is appropriate or should be increased. In the comparison phase of the process teachers use graphs which have been generated from the original research studies of the relationship between engaged time and achievement to help them decide whether there is an opportunity or need to increase student engaged time in their classrooms. If a teacher decides to change student engaged time, the research findings are used to assist the teacher in setting appropriate goals.

Selection and Preparation

If a change in student engaged time is desired, then a teacher moves on to the third phase of the instructional improvement cycle. In this phase the teacher further analyzes the data collected in the classroom, and reviews research findings on teaching behaviours found to be related to improvement in student engaged time. The teacher then selects a modification that is appropriate to his or her classroom situation, and that reasonably can be expected to produce the desired change. A plan is then developed for implementing and monitoring the selected improvement strategy.

Implementation and Recycling

The planned modification is implemented by the teacher in his or her classroom and when monitoring indicates that the modification is properly in place data collection begins anew. On the basis of this monitoring teachers may decide to continue, modify or discontinue use of the selected modification.

Educators using the time component of the ADL programme make repeated observations of students' use of time over the course of an entire year. This information continually aids the teacher in making instructionally-relevant decisions. Such periodical recycling assists teachers in attaining and maintaining optimal levels of student engaged time which, in turn, will hopefully have significant and positive effects on students' achievements.

Materials and Procedures

In order to use the improvement cycle to manage students' use of time, teachers and administrators need to acquire several skills. First, they need to learn specific procedures for collecting classroom data. Then, they must be able to compare those data with data obtained from other research studies. Finally, they must be able to select, prepare and implement appropriate improvement strategies. The materials and procedures used to accomplish these tasks are described in this section.

Procedures for Collecting Data

From the beginning of the project, the developers thought that the data collection instruments and procedures used in available research studies would probably need to be simplified if they were to be used by teachers and administrators. For example, the observers, using an instrument in the Stallings and Kaskowitz (1974) study, collected information on over one hundred variables by scanning the classroom every 15 minutes on three school days. A more practical, feasible observation system seemed needed. The first modification of the instrument involved simplifying the form so as to focus only on students' use of time; however, the complexity of the resulting calculations and the time requirements for observations necessitated further adaptation.

Re-examination of the procedures used in the original study revealed that student engaged time could be defined as a function of two separate variables: allocated time (that is, amount of time provided to students for instruction) and engagement rate (that is, the proportion of allocated time that students were observed to be actively involved in an assigned academic task). More specifically, student engaged time can be estimated by multiplying allocated time by engagement rate. Simplified instruments and procedures were then designed for collecting data separately on allocated time and engagement rate.

First, teachers collected data on allocated time for their own classrooms by completing a log (see Figure 9.2). Such data are essentially equivalent to those obtained by a trained observer (Marliave, Fisher and Filby, 1976) and, in addition, the log is fairly simple to complete.

A systematic observation process for collecting data on the percentage of students in the class actually working on assigned academic tasks was then developed, using categories similar to those found in existing research studies. Observers were trained to use this system before they collected data in classrooms. The nature of the data, the collection process, and the local circumstances determined who collected the classroom process data. Peer teachers, principals, district personnel, substitute teachers, aides and student teachers were used as data collectors.

Figure 9.2: Complete Allocated Time Log

ALLOCATED TIME LOG				
STATE _Atlantic_ DISTRICT _Eastern_ SCHOOL _New Delpen_ TEACHER _Demetrios_	STATE # _03_ DISTRICT # _47_	SCHOOL # _08_ TEACHER # _X105_	DATE _10-5_ GRADE _3_	SUBJECT _Reading/Lang._ NO. OF STUDENTS PRESENT _30_

	ACTIVITY	BEGINNING TIME	ENDING TIME	TIME IN MINUTES
1	Reading groups	8:51	10:13	82
2	Reading groups & seatwork	10:30	10:57	27
3	Spelling	12:59	1:16	17
4	Sustained silent reading	2:30	2:50	20
5				
6			TOTAL	146

Observation training included both written and videotaped exercises, and required between three and five hours. Much of this time was spent coding videotapes of actual classrooms. Of more than 300 teachers and administrators trained in 18 different sessions, approximately 90 per cent were able to code selected videotapes at an acceptable criterion level by the end of training.

The observer used an Engagement Rate Form (see Figure 9.3) to code engagement rate, typically making about fifteen scans during each classroom observation at intervals of from 1 to 3 minutes. Students were coded as being engaged or not engaged. *Engaged* students were those involved in or attending to instruction. For example, an engaged

Figure 9.3: Completed Engagement Rate Form

			ENGAGEMENT RATE FORM				SUBJECT Rdg/Lang	

STATE Atlantic
DISTRICT Eastern
SCHOOL New Delpen
TEACHER Demetrios
CODER Allen

STATE # __03__   SCHOOL # __08__   DATE __10-5__
DISTRICT # __47__   TEACHER # __X105__   CODER # __K14__

GRADE __3__
STUDENTS PRESENT __30__

PART OF CLASS OBSERVED
Beg. ✓
Mid. ___
End ___

TIME	1	2	3	4	5	6	7	8	9
	9:01	9:02	9:03	9:04	9:05	9:06	9:07	9:08	9:09
ASSIGNED	30	30	30	30	30	30	30	30	30
MANAGEMENT/ TRANSITION	IIII	HHt	II	II					I
SOCIALIZING	II						II		
DISCIPLINE	I								
UNOCCUPIED/ OBSERVING	I		I	I					I
OUT OF ROOM	I							I	I
TOTAL UNENGAGED	9	5	3	3	0	0	2	1	3
ENGAGED	21	25	27	27	30	30	28	29	27

TIME	10	11	12	13	14	15	TOTAL	ENGAGEMENT RATE
	9:10	9:11	9:12	9:13	9:14	9:15		
ASSIGNED	30	30	30	30	30	30	450	ENGAGED ASSIGNED
MANAGEMENT/ TRANSITION	I	I		III	IIII		23	
SOCIALIZING				II	II		8	
DISCIPLINE	II	III	III			HHt HHt HHt HHt HHt HHt	39	$\frac{360}{450}$ =
UNOCCUPIED/ OBSERVING			III	IIII	III		14	
OUT OF ROOM	I	I	I				6	80%
TOTAL UNENGAGED	4	5	7	9	9	30	90	
ENGAGED	26	25	23	21	21	0	360	

student may have been reading, writing, answering a teacher's question, watching a student answer a problem on the board, listening to a teacher's academic presentation, or doing anything else that would indicate that he or she was involved in academic tasks. *Unengaged* students, on the other hand, are *not involved in the assigned academic tasks*. The following five categories were used to code different types of unengaged behaviours so that teachers could make more precise analyses of their classrooms:

(1) management/transition – getting ready for instruction, waiting, listening to non-academic directions, or changing activities;

(2) socializing — interacting with other students or watching others do so;
(3) discipline — being reprimanded or punished by an adult or watching another student being disciplined or punished;
(4) unoccupied/observing — wandering about with no apparent purpose or goal, watching other people, or playing with materials; and
(5) out of room — being temporarily out of the classroom.

At the beginning of each scan the observer recorded the time and number of students assigned to the subject or topic of interest. A tally mark was made in one of the five unengaged categories each time an unengaged student was observed. At the end of each scan the number of engaged students was computed by subtracting the number of tallies from the number of assigned students (that is, 'Assigned' minus 'Unengaged' equal 'Engaged'). After all 15 scans had been completed, the observer added each row and found the engagement rate by dividing the total number of engaged students by the total number of assigned students. If, for example, there were 30 students in a class during 15 scans of the classroom, the total number of assigned students would be 450 (i.e. 30 x 15). If the total number of engaged students over all these observations was 360 students, the engagement rate would be computed by dividing 360 by 450, a rate of 80 per cent.

Since student engaged time is a better predictor of achievement than either allocated time or engagement rate alone, teachers need to use their collected classroom data to calculate student engaged time before comparing classroom data to the research evidence. In order to make valid comparisons, such data on student engaged time should be equivalent to those obtained from research studies. RBS conducted a small study to determine if practitioners could collect data that are essentially equivalent to those collected by a trained observer using the Stallings and Kaskowitz instrument in the same classroom.

Eleven teachers from three different schools were observed for two days in both reading/language arts and mathematics. Each day's estimate of student engaged time, as calculated by an observer using the Stallings and Kaskowitz instrument, was compared with the estimate of student engaged time obtained by teachers using the instruments and procedures developed by RBS. The Pearson Product-moment Correlation between these two estimates of student engaged time was 0.92. Thus, the data collected from the simplified observation system developed by RBS were comparable to those collected using the research-based instrument and procedures.

Teachers used a single form to record student engaged time data throughout the year. The amount of student engaged time was calculated for each day an observation took place. This amount was obtained by multiplying the total allocated time (see Figure 9.2) by the engagement rate computed on the observation form (see Figure 9.3). If data from several days were available, then an average student engaged time was also calculated. Data for three observations are shown in Figure 9.4. Student engaged times were calculated for each day (e.g. 70% x 100 minutes = 70 minutes), and an average student engaged time for the three days was computed.

Figure 9.4: Completed Summary Sheet

State Atlantic ____   COMPLETED SUMMARY SHEET FOR TIME
District Eastern ____
School New Delpen ___   State # 03   School # 08   Grade 3
Teacher Demetrios ___   District 47   Teacher X105   Year 1981-82

Date	Coder #	Part of Period	Engagement Rate	Allocated Time	Student Engaged Time	Average Student Engaged Time
10-2	M010	End	70%	100 min.	70 min.	✕
10-4	A294	Middle	80%	90 min.	72 min.	71 min.
10-5	K14	Beg.	80%	146 min.	117 min.	86 min.

Comparing Data to Research

In the comparison phase of the instructional improvement cycle, teachers compare their own classroom time data with the results of previous research in order to identify opportunities for improvement. The classroom observational data do not by themselves give teachers an adequate basis for making decisions about what changes might be made to increase student achievement. For example, these observations may reveal to the teacher that in his or her third-grade class the students spend 100 minutes of time engaged in reading. Such information does not tell the teacher whether increasing, decreasing or sustaining this level of student engaged time would be most beneficial to student achievement. Only when the classroom information is compared to research data relating student engaged time to student achievement can the teacher begin to make a data-based decision about the probable effect of a change in student engaged time upon student achievement.

To assist teachers in making knowledge-based decisions regarding student engaged time, RBS prepared reference graphs from existing research data. Figure 9.5 presents an example of a reference graph. The information in this figure is based on a reanalysis of data from Stallings and Kaskowitz (1974) by Rim and Coller (1978) and shows the relationship between student engaged time in reading/language arts classes and student achievement gains in reading/language arts. The horizontal axis represents student engaged time in reading/language arts as the number of minutes per day; the vertical axis represents the difference between the actual end-of-year achievement-test scores, and the achievement-test scores predicted from the beginning-of-year achievement-test score.

On each graph, student engaged time (horizontal axis) is marked with three kinds of zones (bars) which correspond to the positive, zero and negative zones on the student achievement scale. These zones are determined by first examining the point(s) on the horizontal axis that correspond with no difference between actual and predicted (expected) achievement scores. A minimum-change unit based on the standard error of prediction is specified for each graph. This minimum-change unit is the smallest amount of change in student engaged time that is likely to produce a change in student achievement. In Figure 9.5, for example, the minimum-change unit is 13 minutes. Generally, if the student engaged time of a classroom in the research study fell within the range marked by a zone on the horizontal axis, then it is likely (at least two out of three times) that student achievement would fall in the corresponding range on the vertical axis. Next, zones around each of the two zero points in Figure 9.5 are determined by adding and subtracting the minimum-change unit at the appropriate points on the horizontal axis. These are termed zero zones. Finally, positive and negative zones are created by examining the nature of the curved line on either side of each zero zone.

The data from two research studies (Stallings and Kaskowitz, 1974; Fisher, Filby, Marliave, Cahen, Dishaw, Moore and Berliner, 1978) were reanalyzed to generate all these reference graphs. The graphs were then summarized (see Figure 9.6) by reporting information relating to the horizontal axes only.

Figure 9.5: Examples of Graph Relating Student Engaged Time to Student Achievement (Rim, Caldwell, Helms and Huitt, 1981)

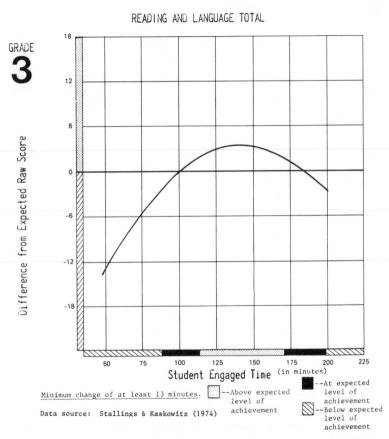

Teachers who have collected data on student engaged times in their classrooms first select a graph appropriate for their subject and grade-level. They then recall the amount of student engaged time for their classroom, locate that amount on the appropriate graphs, and determine the corresponding predicted-achievement zone. The teachers then decide (1) whether to attempt to make changes in student engaged time; (2) in what direction any such change ought to be made; and (3) the extent of the change. For example, the average student engaged

Figure 9.6: Summary of Graphs for Student Engaged Time (Rim, et al., 1981)

STUDENT ENGAGED TIME AS RELATED TO STUDENT ACHIEVEMENT

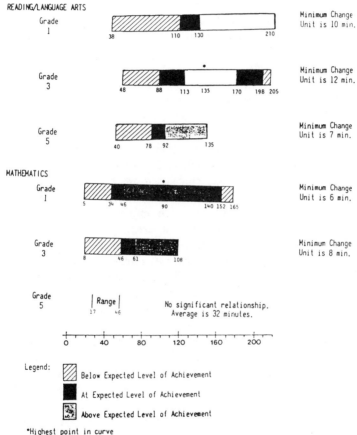

Legend:
- Below Expected Level of Achievement
- At Expected Level of Achievement
- Above Expected Level of Achievement

*Highest point in curve

time calculated on the illustrative summary sheet presented in Figure 9.4 is 86 minutes. Let us assume this is a reading class. According to the third-grade reading/language arts graph (Figure 9.6), this level of student engaged time would probably be associated with less-than-optimal student achievement. Based on this information the teacher might decide to try to increase student engaged time. The minimum-change unit for this graph indicates that a change of at least 12 minutes should be made. Depending upon the particular circumstances, then, a reasonable goal for this teacher might be 100 minutes of student engaged time; this level of student engaged time falls near the middle of the zero zone. Quite obviously, a larger increase would be needed if the goal was to attain student-achievement scores which would fall in the positive zone.

After setting a goal for student engaged time for their classrooms, teachers need to decide whether to change allocated time or engagement rate. Research relating to each of these variables can help teachers in making their decisions.

Most teachers will probably want to increase allocated time to correspond with the average amount of time allocated for the subject at the particular grade-level. Average amounts of time allocated to elementary reading/language arts has been found to be from 120 to 130 minutes; for secondary, the average is 40 minutes. Average allocated time for elementary mathematics is from 40 to 45 minutes; for secondary the average ranges from 40 to 60 minutes. In general, if the engagement-rate for a class of students is average (60 per cent), then allocating an average amount of time for a subject is not sufficient to enable a class to reach a level of student engaged time associated with achievement at or above the expected level. For example, an average amount of allocated time for elementary reading/language arts coupled with an engagement rate of 60 per cent, yields student engaged time which is in the negative zone for all grades (120 minutes x 60% = 72 minutes). Some educators are recommending increases in allocated time beyond the current averages. The National Council of Teachers of Mathematics, for example, now recommends daily time allocations for mathematics of 60 minutes in the primary grades and 85 minutes in the intermediate grades.

In setting engagement-rate goals most teachers will probably want to set a tentative goal of at least the average engagement-rate for their situation; that is, 60 per cent for elementary classrooms and 65 to 70 per cent for secondary classrooms, when calculated using methods comparable to those developed by RBS. Most teachers probably will not want to set goals above the highest average engagement-rates found (90 per cent). In the 60 to 85 per cent range, teachers will usually want to try to increase the engagement-rate by at least 5 per cent (again based on the standard error of prediction), if possible.

In setting all time goals, teachers should use their own judgement as well as research evidence in considering the feasibility of tentative goals for their own particular situations. It is this combination of research evidence and professional judgement which forms the foundation of the problem-solving, decision-making process.

Identifying and Selecting Appropriate Improvement Strategies

Teachers who have decided that a change in student engaged time is desirable and have set specific goals to make such a change, next review existing research-based strategies. The focus of this review is on ways in which either allocated time or engagement-rate can be changed.

There are few research-based suggestions as to how allocated time might be increased since such suggestions are often school specific. Thus, most of the principles presented here are suggestions from teachers and administrators involved in developing the ADL programme. The strategies can be grouped into three general themes: (1) use all of the scheduled allocated time, (2) reduce the amount of non-academic time, and (3) reorganize the time scheduled for academic work. A sampling of these principles follows:

USE ALL OF SCHEDULED TIME
   Adhere to the schedule more closely.
REDUCE AMOUNT OF NON-ACADEMIC TIME
   Shorten opening exercises.
   Reduce the time spent moving between classrooms by scheduling 'special' subjects for longer time periods on fewer days.
   Instead of having a single ten or fifteen-minute break let students go to the bathroom or get a drink of water individually during instructional periods.
REORGANIZE ACADEMIC TIME
   Add sustained silent reading, mathematics drill, or mathematics problem-solving activities during class periods other than those devoted to the teaching of reading/language arts and mathematics. Integrate reading/language arts or mathematics activities with activities in other subject areas, such as science or social studies. Assign homework as additional independent practice.

Quite often the application of these principles for improving allocated time results in increases of only 5 or 10 minutes. Over the course of the year, however, these small amounts of time add up to many additional hours of instruction. For example, a 5-minute increase when considered over 180 days results in a total increase of 15 hours of allocated time.

The number of specific teacher behaviours that research has shown to be significantly related to high engagement-rates is quite large. In order to facilitate teachers' use of this research, the findings have been divided into two areas: *management behaviours*, which deal mainly with skills and techniques designed to control students' behaviour; and *instructional behaviours*, which deal with improving the quality of students' learning.

Three themes emerge from an examination of *management behaviours*: selecting and arranging activities, monitoring student behaviour, and dealing with misbehaviour. A review of those management strategies associated with high engagement-rates yields the following generalizations (see Caldwell, Huitt and French, 1981).

SELECTING AND ARRANGING ACTIVITIES
    Use *routines* to reduce confusion.
    Establish clear and consistent *rules*.
    Plan for *transitions* between activities; have materials ready.
    Foster good *student work habits*.
    Structure the physical environment to facilitate learning.
MONITORING
    Move around the room to *monitor* behaviour.
    Pace activities appropriately.
STOPPING MISBEHAVIOUR
    Anticipate consequences; head off misbehaviour before it occurs.
    State *expectations* for behaviour clearly.
    Hold students *accountable* for behaviour.
    Give *feedback* on behaviour, perhaps privately.

To facilitate teachers' use of these generalizations, they are specified in terms of ways in which teachers can employ them in their classrooms. For example, the following suggestions can be given to teachers wishing to use the generalizations concerning selecting and arranging activities.

Have materials and supplies *ready in advance* of activities.
Use more *routines and procedures* to handle daily business such as turning in completed work, noting student progress and checking attendance.
Shorten *transition* times whenever possible. Specifically,
    plan specifically how to change activities;
    establish clear and consistent rules for transitions;
    provide clear starts and stops for activities;
    alert students to upcoming transitions;

economize movement. For example, have all of the students in a small group move at the same time rather than calling them individually.

Teach students classroom rules and procedures as they are needed, with special emphasis on this area in the first weeks of school. You may wish to rehearse procedures, use incentive systems to shape behaviour, or teach students to respond to specific signals such as the bell or the teacher's call for attention.

Teach students the skills needed to perform school work, skills such as following directions, copying assignments from the chalkboard, finding pages in the book, using programmed materials.

Even though research evidence on specific instructional behaviours reveals numerous and complex relationships with student engaged time (as well as with student achievement) a number of teacher behaviours seem to be consistently mentioned as facilitating student engagement (Anderson, 1981; Medley, 1977; Rosenshine and Furst, 1973). A synthesis of relevant research and theory (e.g. Bloom, 1976; Good and Grouws, 1979; Hunter and Russell, 1977; Medley, 1977; Rosenshine, 1976) has led to the development of a sequence of important instructional events. These events can be grouped into four major categories: presentation, practice, feedback and monitoring (see Figure 9.7).

Figure 9.7: Overview of Critical Instructional Events (from Helms, Graeber, Caldwell, and Huitt, 1982)

INSTRUCTIONAL EVENTS

PRESENTATION — Introduce, develop, or review concepts and skills.

- Review
- Overview — what, why
- Explanation
- Student demonstration of understanding

PRACTICE — Strengthen, apply, or give additional experience with concepts and skills.

- Guided or controlled practice
- Independent practice

FEEDBACK — Let students know whether their answers were right or wrong and why.

MONITORING — Assess and maintain student's knowledge and application of concepts and skills.

- Daily work (including new and review content)
- Unit or topic tests

As in the case of management generalizations, these instructional generalizations can be made more meaningful to teachers by associating specific teaching practices with each generalization.

Teachers must identify the specific behaviours they believe to be the most useful to them, and organize them into a cohesive approach or strategy. This strategy will be employed to achieve the specified goal of optimizing the amount of allocated time, engagement rate or both. After designing such a strategy for reading these goals, teachers must *plan* to implement the strategy. It also is important to *plan* how to monitor the use of the strategy so teachers and administrators are certain the planned change has taken place.

Implementation and Recycling

In the final phase of the improvement cycle, teachers implement their selected strategy and monitor that implementation to ensure that the strategy is in place before a second round of data collection begins. In the recycling phase teachers also generate data for formative evaluation of their use of the approach. This evaluation has two aspects which occur simultaneously: (1) a subjective judgement as to the degree of success, based on discussions with other teachers, supervisors or both; and (2) a data-based judgement as to the status and change of student engaged time.

Implementation procedures allow teachers to subjectively share their experiences with their colleagues and supervisors in a set of regularly scheduled meetings. During these meetings teachers provide their answers to questions such as:

(1) What was the strategy and to what extent was it implemented as planned?
(2) Was the strategy modified during its implementation, and, if so, how was it modified?
(3) What happened that was either expected or unexpected?
(4) What can you tell others who might wish to implement the strategy?

Implementation procedures also permitted teachers to examine observation data collected in their classroom. One such data-based procedure calls for teachers to plot collected data on specially prepared graphs (see Figure 9.8). The vertical axes for these graphs were produced from the graphs used for comparing collected data to research evidence as shown in Figure 9.6. Thus, there are separate graphs for maths and reading/language arts and for grades 1, 3 and 5. The horizontal axis on

Figure 9.8: Example of Completed Observation Record

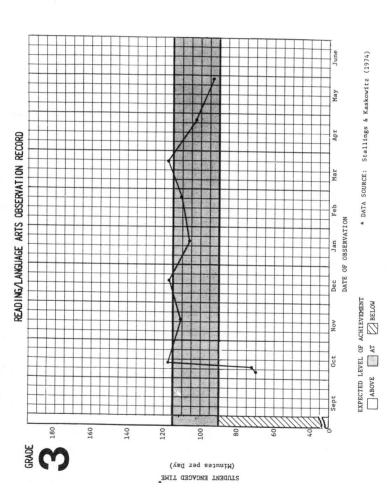

READING/LANGUAGE ARTS OBSERVATION RECORD

GRADE **3**

STUDENT ENGAGED TIME* (Minutes per Day)

DATE OF OBSERVATION

EXPECTED LEVEL OF ACHIEVEMENT
☐ ABOVE   ▨ AT   ▨ BELOW

* DATA SOURCE: Stallings & Kaskowitz (1974)

each graph is simply a time-line for the school year. Use of these graphs focuses attention on both the status of the class in terms of expected student achievement as well as changes in student engaged time over the entire school year (see Huitt, Segars and Caldwell, 1982).

For example, Figure 9.8 shows that the first two observations were in the 'below expected' level of achievement zone. The remainder were in either the 'at expected' or 'above expected' level of achievement zone. These data would indicate that the teacher had been relatively successful in increasing and maintaining an appropriate level of student engaged time.

Experiences and Implications

As of May 1982 more than 1,000 teachers and 500 administrators in sixty districts in ten states had been trained in the time component of the ADL programme. While the evaluation data presented here cannot appropriately be used as summative data for the ADL programme since they relate only to the time component, the data nevertheless provide encouragement as to the success of this portion of the programme. Some of RBS's experiences in developing and implementing the time component of the ADL programme as well as the programme's implications for teachers and administrators are reported in this section.

A basic skills instructional improvement programme may be considered successful for many reasons. Perhaps teachers and administrators like the programme and perceive it as helpful. Similarly, a programme may be considered successful if it actually changes teachers' behaviours or students' behaviours as intended. Or, a programme may be considered successful if student achievement improves. Experiences with the time component of the ADL programme indicate that success defined in each of these ways was attained. A brief description of each of these 'successes' is discussed below. More complete descriptions of the outcomes of the programme are available elsewhere (Graeber, Huitt, Helms and Segar, 1981).

Attitudes and Perceptions

Although systematically collected data on perceptions of programme benefits are not available in large quantity, the following generalizations are consistent with the anecdotal evidence.

Participation gives teachers a chance to use research findings in the classroom.

The programme brings consultants, administrators, specialists and teachers together with a common purpose and goals — to improve instruction.

The programme has provided individualized in-service training. It has let teachers look at the use of time in their classrooms and personalize the training they receive in order to meet classroom needs. But more than that, it has helped to identify school-wide and, in some cases, district-wide, opportunities for improvement.

One of the advantages of this programme is getting to work closely with other teachers in each other's classrooms.

Using the observation instrument has helped shift the focus during observations from looking at what the teacher is doing to concentrating on what the students are doing.

In addition to the above generalizations, a more structured questionnaire was administered to fifteen teachers in a single school. These teachers responded to the questionnaire which grew out of the school's special interest in using its work on student engaged time to improve staff relations. These teachers reported changes in their own behaviour and that of the principal. The principal was reported as becoming more willing to help teachers, more open to teachers' suggestions and ideas, more interested in working together with teachers in school improvement, and more interested in teachers' professional improvement. Eleven of the fifteen teachers also reported that they received adequate support to make the needed changes in their classrooms. Teachers developed an awareness of the activities of other teachers; a willingness to discuss educational problems with other teachers and the principal; a willingness to help, share, and work with other teachers, and increased feelings of importance as a professional.

Teacher Behaviour

Some data have been collected on changes teachers have reported making in their own teaching behaviours. Most teachers implementing the programme reported making changes in their own behaviours to improve students' use of time. Some of the implemented strategies were:

More whole-class instruction.
Increased feedback to students on written work.
Less time spent giving directions.

Keeping books in desks instead of distributing them and picking them up each class period.

Less independent seatwork.

Many teachers seemed to begin the improvement process by implementing management strategies and then considering instructional strategies. Furthermore, teachers have reported improvements in their knowledge of effective instructional practices, increased awareness of students' use of time, and increased sensitivity to classroom management and quality of instruction.

Some strategies have also been implemented at the school and district levels. Schedules have been changed, for example, so as to increase allocated time, and times for pullouts, and special subjects have been co-ordinated to minimize disruptions to classrooms.

Student Behaviours

Preliminary data from a complete implementation of the ADL programme inn three districts provides an indication that the programme is effective in helping educators attain and maintain appropriate levels of student engaged time. Of 343 classrooms involved in the study, 59 per cent had engaged times corresponding with achievement above the expected level, 26 per cent had engaged times corresponding with achievement at the expected level, and only 15 per cent had engaged times corresponding with achievement below the expected level.

In one school 7 teachers used a team-teaching approach with groups of third and fourth-grade students and worked on increasing student engaged time. Three measures of student engaged time were obtained at the beginning of the programme, and one measure was obtained two months later. When individual teacher data were plotted on the third-grade reference graphs, student engaged time in reading/language arts was initially in the 'below expected' (2 teachers) or 'at expected' (5 teachers) zones. Two months later student engaged time was in the 'above expected' zones in three classrooms and in the 'at expected' zones in four classrooms. For mathematics, the initial measures were in the 'below expected' (4 teachers) or 'at expected' (3 teachers) zones, and two months later all 7 teachers were in the 'at expected' zone.

The changes between the average of the three initial measures and the ending measure were calculated for all seven classes. On the average, student engaged time increased by 15 minutes per day in reading/language arts (from 98 to 113 minutes) and by 7 minutes per day in mathematics (from 45 to 52 minutes). This increase may seem small, but if the increased number of minutes had been maintained over one-half off the school year, students would be engaged in learning an additional 22 hours in reading/language arts and an additional 10 hours in mathematics.

Student Achievement

Although RBS personnel believe that achievement gains are more likely to result from proper implementation of all components of the ADL programme rather than emphasizing the time component alone, some data are available which suggest that significant achievement gains may occur when implementation of only the time component is emphasized.

Third and fourth-grade students at one school were tested using the Stanford Achievement Tests (Primary II, Primary III and Intermediate I) in March 1979 and May 1980. A norm-referenced model (similar to Model A for Title I evaluation) was used to analyze reading and mathemtics test scores (Graeber *et al.*, 1981). The results show that these students made an average gain of 4 percentiles in reading (55th to 59th percentile) and 12 percentiles in mathematics (from 47th to 59th percentiles). The gain in mathematics is statistically significant ($t = 3.58$ with 136 degrees of freedom, $p < 0.01$) and approaches the level of educational significance (one-third of the standard deviation of the national norm group) as defined by the Rand Corporation for Title I evaluation.

Significant gains in achievement were also made by students in seven classes in grades 1-5 at another school where administrators and teachers were involved in the development of the entire ADL programme. Previously unreported test results from the California Achievement Tests indicate average gains of 10 percentiles in reading (from 55th to 65th percentile) and 12 pecentiles in mathematics (from 51st to 63rd percentile) from the spring of 1979 to the spring of 1980. These gains were statistically significant ($t = 2.61$ for reading, $t = 3.43$ for maths with 133 degrees of freedom, $p < 0.01$). Students in nine classes in the same school continued to gain the next year, although these gains were less substantial; average gains were 3 percentiles in reading (from the 59th to the 62nd percentile), 8 percentiles in language (from the 68th to the 76th percentile), and 6 percentiles in mathematics (from the 59th to the 65th percentile). Thus, achievement gains slowed, but continued as the programme was expanded and institutionalized.

Discussion

The ADL programme, developed by Research for Better Schools, provides teachers and supervisors with a feasible approach to the use of existing research on student engaged time in order to improve instruction. While conclusions about the effectiveness of the approach are forthcoming, early experiences are promising. Research evidence on student engaged time can be used by teachers and administrators as the basis for an instructional improvement programme. Both teachers and administrators tend to find the programme beneficial. Furthermore, teachers report changes in their own behaviours and teaching practices. Changes in student engaged time also seem to occur in classes taught by teachers who participate in the programme.

The use of a four-stage instructional improvement cycle offers an opportunity for schools to build in-service experiences around needs identified by the teachers themselves. Principals and central office staff, working with teachers, can design in-service sessions for small groups of teachers who have identical or similar needs. The basis for designing effective in-service programmes for these teachers rests in the proper understanding and use of a research-based, decision-making process to effect changes in the classroom, school and district that improve students' use of a valuable resource, time.

References

Anderson, L.W. (1981) 'Instruction and Time-on-task: a Review', *Journal of Curriculum Studies, 13*(4), 289-303

Bloom, B.S. (1976) *Human Characteristics and Student Learning*, New York: McGraw-Hill

Caldwell, J., Huitt, W. and French, V. (1981) 'Research-based Classroom Modifications for Improving Student Engaged Time' in D. Helms, A. Graeber, J. Caldwell and W. Huitt (eds), *Leader's Guide for Student Engaged Time*, Philadelphia, Pa.: Research for Better Schools

Fisher, C.W., Filby, N.N., Marliave, R.S., Cahen, L.S., Dishaw, N.M., Moore, J.E. and Berliner, D.C. (1978) *Teaching Behaviors, Academic Learning Time and Student Achievement: Final Report of Phase III-B, Beginning Teacher Evaluation Study*, San Francisco, Ca.: Far West Laboratory for Educational Research and Development

Good, T.L. and Grouws, D.A. (1979) 'The Missouri Mathematics Effectiveness Project: an Experimental Study in Fourth-grade Classrooms', *Journal of Educational Psychology, 71*(3), 355-62

Graeber, A.O. (1980) 'A Basic Skills Instructional Improvement Program: Utilizing Research to Facilitate Implementation and Dissemination. Paper presented at the annual meeting of the American Educational Research Association, Boston, April

——, Huitt, W., Helms, D. and Segars, J. (1981) *1979-80 Interim Evaluation Report*, Philadelphia, Pa.: Research for Better Schools, Inc.

Helms, D.C. (1980) 'A Basic Skills Instructional Improvement Program: an Overview'. Paper presented at the annual meeting of the American Educational Research Association, Boston, April

——, Graeber, A., Caldwell, J. and Huitt, W. (1982) *Leader's Guide for Student Engaged Time* (revised edition), Philadelphia, Pa.: Research for Better Schools, Inc.

Huitt, W., Caldwell, J. Traver, P. and Graeber, A. (1981) 'Classroom Observation System for Student Engaged Time' in D. Helms, A. Graeber, J. Caldwell and W. Huitt (eds), *Leader's Guide for Student Engaged Time*, Philadelphia, Pa.: Research for Better Schools, Inc.

—— and Rim, E.D. (1980) 'A Basic Skills Instructional Improvement Program: Utilizing Research to Improve Classroom Practice'. Paper presented at the annual meeting of the American Educational Research Association, Boston, April

——, Segars, J. and Caldwell, J. (1982) 'Monitoring and Evaluating the Critical Dimensions of Effective Classrooms'. Paper presented at the annual meeting of the American Educational Research Association, New York, April

Hunter, M. and Russell, D. (1977) 'How Can I Plan More Effective Lessons?', *Instructor, 87*(2), 75-6, 88

Marliave, R., Fisher, C. and Filby, N. (1976) 'Alternative Procedures for Collecting Instructional Time Data: When Can You Ask the Teacher and When Must You Observe for Yourself? Paper presented at the annual meeting of the American Educational Research Association, New York, April

McDonald, F.J. (1977) 'Research and Development Strategies for Improving Teacher Education', *Journal of Teacher Education, 28*(6), 29-33

Medley, D.M. (1977) *Teacher Competence and Teacher Effectiveness*, Washington, DC: American Association of Colleges for Teacher Education

(RBS) Research for Better Schools, Inc. (1976) *A Cooperative Research and Development System for Improvement of Instruction and Achievement in Basic Skills*, Philadelphia, Pa.: Research for Better Schools, Inc.

—— (1978) *A Collaborative Research and Development Effort to Improve Basic Skills Instruction in Delaware, New Jersey and Pennsylvania*, Philadelphia, Pa.: Research for Better Schools, Inc.

—— (1979) *Continuation of a Program of Regional School Improvement Activities: Basic Skills* (Technical Proposal), Philadelphia, Pa.: Research for Better Schools, Inc.

—— (1982) *Program of Regional School Improvement Activities: Basic skills* (Technical proposal), Philadelphia, Pa.: Research for Better Schools, Inc.

Rim, E.D., Caldwell, J., Helms, D. and Huitt, W. (1981) 'Comparing Student Engaged Time to Research Data' in D. Helms, A. Graeber, J. Caldwell and W. Huitt (eds), *Leader's Guide for Student Engaged Time*, Philadelphia, Pa.: Research for Better Schools, Inc.

Rim, E.D. and Coller, A. (1978) *In Search of Nonlinear Process-product Function in Existing Schooling Effects Data: I. A Reanalysis of the First-grade Reading and Mathematics Data from the Stallings and Kaskowitz Follow Through Study*, Philadelphia, Pa.: Research for Better Schools, Inc.

Rosenshine, B. (1976) 'Recent Research on Teaching Behaviors and Student Achievement', *Journal of Teacher Education, 23*(1), 61-4

—— and Furst, N. (1973) 'The Use of Direct Observation to Study Teaching' in R. Travers (ed.), *Second Handbook of Research on Teaching*, Chicago: Rand McNally

Stallings, J.A. and Kaskowitz, D. (1974) *Follow Through Classroom Observation Evaluation, 1972-1973*, Menlo Park, Ca.: Stanford Research Institute

10 BREAKTHROUGHS AND BREAKDOWNS: A CASE STUDY OF THE IMPLEMENTATION OF THE STALLINGS EFFECTIVE TEACHING PRACTICES TRAINING PROGRAMME

Ward J. Ghory

During the 1979-80 school year the Cincinnati (Ohio) public schools pilot-tested the in-service training programme developed by Jane Stallings and her associates at Stanford Research International (SRI). This training programme addresses three general aspects of classroom instruction in the basic skills: classroom organization, behaviour management, and 'direct instruction' techniques. The programme begins by having teachers review specific recommendations for instructional improvement based on research on the effective use of time in urban school classrooms. They then set personal targets for improvement. By means of classroom observations teachers were helped to identify the current level of their use of various instructional practices discussed in a series of workshops. Post-observation data, compared with pre-observation data, permitted assessment of teacher change. Thus, one could determine whether teachers had acted on the research-based recommendations and improved their performance.

The Stallings Effective Teaching Practices (ETP) training programme was chosen for pilot-testing in Cincinnati, based on its record of significant teacher improvement and accelerated student achievement in a variety of urban schools. Thirty-one teachers in three schools participated in the first year of the project. At the end of the first year a formal evaluation of project effectiveness was conducted. The results were as positive as those obtained in previous projects and schools using the ETP programme.

During the second year of the project, however, problems arose. Only one-half as many teachers participated in the project. During the winter an administrative decision was made to discontinue the programme at the end of the second year. Furthermore, key personnel were transferred from the project to other positions within the Cincinnati public schools. As a consequence, the training component of the programme was not continued during the spring. In addition, a formal evaluation of the second year of the project was not completed

228

since appropriate personnel were not available. At the end of the second year the programme was in fact terminated with some parts of the programme being incorporated into a new funded project on a somewhat larger scale.

This chapter begins with a paradox: programme-development efforts have become increasingly sophisticated and effective, but the longevity of successful innovation based on such development is short, and the art of implementing *and sustaining* successful programmes remains stubbornly problematic. The chapter is organized into four major sections. First, an overview of the ETP programme is provided; secondly, a summary of the context within which the programme was implemented is presented; and thirdly, the implementation process is analyzed in terms of nine practical objectives that need to be achieved if an innovative programme is to be sustained. In this section alternative approaches to achieving each objective will be suggested. Fourthly, results from the evaluation of the first year of the project are summarized, and reflections on the implementation process based on the results described.

An Overview of the ETP Programme

Phases of Development

The continually evolving nature of the ETP programme is partially explained by its origins in a series of correlation and quasi-experimental research studies whose momentum still continues to cause frequent refinements in the programme (see, for example, Stallings, 1977, 1980). Stallings and Needels have identified four phases of their research and dissemination efforts. In Phase I, 'Correlational Research', they observed 46 secondary reading classrooms in urban districts to examine the relationship between teacher behaviour and student reading gains. The results of this study provided specific guidelines for efficient instruction that were incorporated in Phase II, 'Experimental In-service Training'. One-half of the Phase II teachers were trained, and the other half were in a control group that did not receive training until the end of the study. The treatment teachers did change their behaviours in recommended ways, and their students did gain substantially more in reading achievement than did students in the control group.

In Phase III, 'Extended Teacher Training', Stallings monitored previously trained teachers as these teachers conducted similar in-service workshops in their own districts. In Phase IV, 'Dissemination

Training', she prepared apprentices to return to their districts and function as trainers of classroom observers and as workshop leaders. Each apprentice's work was monitored by Stallings through tape-recorded sessions, written reports and telephone consultations. After this system had been in place for one year and judged satisfactory, the apprentice was approved and eligible to train other, new apprentices. In this fashion the Stallings system continues to expand with carefully selected and approved teacher trainers. Since I was one of the first apprentices trained, the current study offers an opportunity for me to critically analyze the effectiveness of this dissemination approach (see also Meehan and Sullivan, 1982).

The purpose of the training programme was to increase the basic skills achievement of low and medium-skilled urban youth by improving teachers' skills in the three aspects of classroom instruction mentioned earlier: classroom organization, behaviour management, and 'direct instruction' techniques. The two key elements were an interactive data collection and teacher training processes. The two processes were co-ordinated in an observe-train-implement-observe sequence as pictured in Table 10.1.

Table 10.1: Key Elements and Sequence of Activities in the Implementation of the Stallings Effective Teaching Practices (ETP) Programme

Data-collection process	Teacher training process
1a. recruiting observers	1b. recruiting teachers
2. training observers	
3. conducting classroom observations	
4. processing data	
5. analyzing and interpreting data	
	6. planning sessions based on data
	7. conducting teacher workshops
	8. implementing recommended practices
9. conducting classroom observation	
10. processing data	
11. analyzing and interpreting data	
	12. conducting summary workshops
13a. conducting periodic follow-up	13b. maintaining skills developed

Data-collection Process

One of the reasons the ETP training programme has made sense to teachers is that it begins in their own classrooms with three days of systematic observation of classroom activities and materials, teacher-student interactions, and student grouping patterns. The observation system used in this study was initially developed at SRI in response to a 1969 request by the US Office of Education to evaluate the implementation of educational models in the Follow Through programme. This system has been modified over time and adapted to the secondary school level. The observation system contains two sections: the 'Snapshot' and the 'Five Minute Interaction' (see Stallings, 1977 for details). An observer training programme also has been developed.

In Cincinnati, observers were trained with the ETP programme for seven days. At the completion of training observers watched and listened to a videotape of a teacher in a classroom. They coded what they heard and saw on a standard observation checklist, and the way in which each observer coded the videotaped classroom activities was compared with predetermined codes. If at least 85 per cent of an observer's codings matched the predetermined codes the observer was certified as a qualified observer. Cross-validity checks between the two sections of the observation system helped establish the validity of the instruments. In general, observation results have been widely accepted by teachers as accurate throughout the entire history of the use of this instrument.

After being selected for the programme, teachers were observed during the same class period on three consecutive days. Every 10 minutes the groupings, activities and materials in use in the classroom were recorded on the 'Snapshot' section of the instrument. A total of fifteen such observations were recorded for each teacher, five per day. Following each 'Snapshot', the verbal interactions of teachers and students were coded continuously for 5 minutes (hence, the name for the 'Five Minute Interaction' section). Verbal interactions were recorded for 5 minutes in each of the three observation periods. All observer records were made on sheets contained in a data collection booklet. The results were then summarized in computer-generated profiles of teacher behaviours.

The information contained in these profiles was the heart of the training process. In an objective, straightforward manner, the profiles were interpreted to the teachers. Such an interpretation allowed project teachers to compare themselves with teachers who had been found to be highly effective with students similar to those in their own classrooms. When interpreted and presented properly the profile data left little room for evasion or excessive rationalization on the teachers' parts; they were given a summary of three periods in their own classrooms as compared to three periods in 'effective' teachers' rooms. Early in the workshops, these profiles provided a firm basis for goal setting; after the workshops, a second profile based on additional observations provided an opportunity to examine the extent to which those goals had actually been accomplished. In short, in this training programme data collection was transformed from an auxiliary evaluation tool into a motivational and accountability process promoting serious commitment to improved teaching practices.

Teacher Training Workshops

As has been mentioned earlier, the purpose of the training workshops was to familiarize teachers with research recommendations related to teaching basic skills to students of varying skill levels. The workshops were also designed to include supportive, problem-solving sessions where teachers could identify their individual needs and could attempt to improve their own teaching performance relative to specific, observable variables. If successful, the workshops provided teachers with an opportunity to define a more precise and demanding set of personal standards for their own teaching.

Five 2-hour workshops were held on a weekly basis after school for small groups of five to seven teachers. In Workshop I teachers read and analyzed a report of Stallings' study, 'Teaching Basic Reading Skills in Secondary Schools'. In this report the practices of teachers effective with low, medium and high-skilled students were summarized. In Workshop II the teachers received a profile of their own teaching practices, based on the three days of observation. The variables reported on the individual profile were the same as those studied in Stallings' research. As a consequence, teachers could compare their own level of performance with that of teachers who were effective in teaching students having skill levels about the same as their own students. Based on the information provided, teachers selected a limited number of teaching behaviours they intended to alter.

The remainder of the training focused on identifying, practising and revising strategies for making these changes in teacher practice. In Workshop III teachers discussed and learned to implement methods of classroom organization designed to increase student time-on-task. In Workshop IV teachers analyzed preventive and motivational techniques for managing student behaviour. In Workshop V teachers reviewed techniques of direct instruction found to be effective with poor readers.

One or two months after the workshops, teachers were observed for three days in the same class. Afterwards they convened for a follow-up workshop in which they received and discussed their new profiles. In short, the workshop series was a self-improvement process for teachers based on research-derived recommendations and an objective summary of an individual's teaching techniques.

The Context for Implementation

This brief description of the context for implementation of ETP in Cincinnati presents background data on the funding agency and the participating schools. This context is then contrasted with the conditions under which Stallings' original research was conducted.

Funding Agency – the Urban Education Pilot Project

In 1977 the Cincinnati public schools were awarded $2 million by the State of Ohio for the biennium 1977-9 to develop a model educational programme in one inner-city school district consisting of one high school, two junior high schools and fourteen elementary schools. The district was chosen because it had the lowest achievement, lowest attendance and highest suspension and expulsion rates in Cincinnati. For example, only 20 per cent of elementary students scored at or above the national average in reading; only 25 per cent in mathematics. Similarly, at the junior high level, approximately 4 per cent of the students scored at or above the national average in either subject. The overall student population was predominantly from poor and working-class backgrounds, with 81 per cent of the students black, and eight schools containing more than 90 per cent of a single race.

The Urban Education Pilot Project (UEPP) was organized as a broad-based school-improvement project, with the principals of the schools acting as the key decision-makers. In addition there was a small central-office management staff. Eighty-eight per cent of project funds were spent on personnel costs. The project's goals were: (1) to increase the percentage of students scoring at or above the national average on achievement tests by 3 per cent each year; (2) to increase student motivation (as measured on student surveys) through curriculum enrichment programmes; (3) to improve student conduct (as measured by an increased district attendance of 1 per cent each year and a reduction in suspensions and expulsions of 5 per cent each year); (4) to increase parent and community involvement; (5) to sponsor staff-development programmes. Administratively, UEPP was assigned to the Department of Curriculum and Instruction, in the Planning and Development branch (see Ghory, 1980).

The Stallings Effective Teaching Practices training programme was one of *twenty-five* in-service programmes offered that year, most of which were locally developed and based on expressed needs of the teachers. Its teacher stipend budget of $3,000 represented 15 per cent of the staff-development budget for the year, although its 31 partici-pants represented only 8 per cent of those attending in-service training. The training programme was directed by the author, a former teacher in the district, and then Assistant Director of UEPP responsible for evalua-tion and programme development.

Participating Schools

When participation in the training programme was proposed, there was considerable scepticism among the principals, primarily related to three issues. Firstly, principals perceived that classroom observation would be resisted by teachers. Secondly, the programme was not viewed as cost-efficient, since the time and cost of extended observation and the small size of training groups limited the number of participants. Thirdly, the programme was viewed as a secondary school programme, at a time when there was tension in the project over the distribution of resources among elementary and secondary schools. Still, with the support of the Council of Principals, a pilot-test year involving the senior high school, one of the junior high schools and one of the elementary schools was approved. The choice of the specific junior high and elementary schools was based on the interest shown by their princi-pals.

A profile of the three schools is provided in Table 10.2. The high school and junior high school populations were relatively large for their buildings, resulting in serious attendance, discipline and achievement problems. Although the elementary school was also large, it had a recent history of steady improvement in achievement and attendance.

Table 10.2: Selected Characteristics of Participating Schools

School	Grades	Size	Per cent black	Average daily attendance %	Number of suspensions	Per cent in lowest three Stanines in reading
Senior high	9-12	2,078	85	64	1,383	no testing
Junior high	7-8	636	84	69	203	65.5
Elementary	K-6	571	99	91	26	34.0

A Comparison of Implementation Contexts

Cincinnati's training conditions diverged from Stallings's in at least four aspects. While it should be expected that any model will be implemented in many different ways, divergences should be noted since they necessarily influence the comparability of results.

First, the Cincinnati public school district is larger than any district in Stallings's Phase II studies, and has a higher percentage of low-income and black students. Secondly, while Stallings's training focused on secondary reading teachers, 40 per cent of the teachers trained in Cincinnati taught at the elementary level. Thirdly, the focus of this project was on changing teacher behaviour. No relevant student-achievement data were available or collected; no control group of teachers was observed. Instead, the relation of the selected teaching variables to student achievement was predicated on previous research. Fourthly, whereas Stallings's teachers were all volunteers in the early stages of the research, Cincinnati teachers were recruited from two groups: (1) those who volunteered after a brief presentation to a school staff meeting; and (2) those who were nominated by assistant principals, discipline personnel and department heads as needing assistance with classroom organization and behaviour management.

Implementation Criteria

To properly implement the Stallings programme, nine criteria were considered. These criteria, presented in two columns in Table 10.3, were used as the framework for description and analysis of the implementation year. The first column lists criteria that must be in place at the system level. The second column lists criteria that must be in place at the individual school level. The criteria at both levels are quite parallel; hence the numbering of activities as 1a, 1b, etc. As a consequence, the criteria are discussed in the subsequent sections in the order in which they would likely appear in developing and sustaining a successful training programme.

Criterion 1a: A Commitment Among District Leaders to the Training Programme as a Priority School-improvement Strategy Must be Built

Awareness and commitment from top decision-makers are necessary to permit any extra-cost innovation to gain entry and persist. In Cincinnati the key person was the Director of Planning and Development, who organized a two-day workshop for Cincinnati administrators led by

Stallings. It was during a hectic time of year and the weather was bad, and as a consequence attendance was spotty: no board members, assistant superintendents, or area directors attended. Furthermore, but a single principal, two instructional supervisors, two directors (of Evaluation and of Staff Development), and an assortment of project directors and teachers attended.

Table 10.3: A List of Implementation Criteria at the System and School Level

System level	School level
1a. A commitment among system leaders to the training programme as a priority school-improvement strategy must be built	1b. A commitment to the training programme by the principal and recruited teachers must be built
2a. The capability for observing teachers must be developed	2b. Teachers must be observed both before and after exposure to training
3. The capability for summarizing data and creating teacher profiles must be developed	
4a. The capability for leading teacher training workshops must be developed	4b. Teacher training workshops must be conducted
5a. The capability for implementing the training programme must be extended	5b. A maintenance strategy must be implemented

The workshop introduced participants to the research base on the effective use of time in the classroom, and reviewed the data-collection and teacher training aspects of the model. Its purpose was to establish that researchers had organized promising, empirically supported approaches to the improvement of basic-skills instruction and achievement. My own reaction was enthusiastic, both to the content and to the presenter, but the experience was viewed as a one-time educational treat with no serious implications for the future. In short, despite admirable intentions and an appropriate plan, the initial orientation workshop seemed like another bust: compelling ideas cast uselessly into an already over-committed and resistant educational system.

When the Director of Planning and Development a month later suggested that I travel to California to be trained as an apprentice in the Stallings system, I did not take him seriously. Our schools were going to shut down for six weeks the following November because of a lack of money. None the less, negotiations with SRI concerning a training contract went forward, and a contract for two (rather than three) weeks of training was signed.

With the initial commitment level of the district relatively shallow, it was essential upon return from California to map out a strategy to guarantee ongoing support. The strategy had three parts. First, a steering committee was formed; consisting of the Director of Evaluation, the Director of Staff Development, the Director of Planning and Development, the most respected technical evaluator, the district's Reading Coordinator and the UEPP Director. This group met three times for the purpose of reviewing evaluation results and approving future plans. More importantly, however, a vehicle was established for providing information, seeking assistance, and attaining visibility for the training programme. Secondly, discussions with UEPP principals and support personnel were held in order to build internal support from the most likely funding source. Thirdly, a series of speeches was made to groups such as the instructional supervisors and the union's steering committee, and research summary articles appeared in in-house journals. A monthly series of video presentations was made to all teachers.

In summary, innovative programmes in schools must struggle for recognition and acceptance. At least a temporary shelter needs to be provided by key decision-makers.

Criterion 1b: a Commitment to the Training Programme by the Principal and Recruited Teachers Must be Built

In many ways the principal acts as the primary gatekeeper to the changes in his or her school. Thus, the principal must be committed to the programme if it is to succeed. In this regard, the programme was introduced to interested principals and a request made to discuss the programme at a staff meeting. The principal also was asked for the names of teachers whom he or she would recommend for training. Unfortunately, immediate principal support was not forthcoming: no principals visited our workshops, although invited; none requested information for teacher appraisal; none tried to influence workshop content, even though, as an outcome of the workshops, teachers at the junior high school suggested changes in administrative procedures. If the principals were available, they were visited briefly on each visit, and given complimentary copies of the workshop handouts.

A second gatekeeper whose toll is paid in our programme is the Teacher Building Committee (TBC), a school-based union organization. Their primary concern was with the confidentiality of observation results; and when informed that observation results would not be used as part of the formal appraisal process, they provided their support.

Next began one-on-one recruitment of the teachers who expressed tentative interest, and of the teachers whose names were recommended by the principal, assistant principal or discipline dean. One assistant principal told all teachers to take part. One teacher was approached by three different administrators about joining the programme. In discussions with these 'coerced volunteers', they were asked to describe a classroom-management problem of general interest to them. They then discussed the approach, if any, that might be recommended by researchers. Roughly 70 per cent of those approached in this way agreed to join the workshops.

At a second meeting, interested teachers were given a clear-cut list of expectations and the criteria for final selection of teachers. The five expectations were: (1) to be observed before and after the in-service training; (2) to attend six, 2-hour, after-school meetings; (3) to voluntarily attempt to alter or improve aspects of your teaching; (4) to prepare for each meeting by completing the required reading and/or homework; (5) to assist other teachers in resolving their concerns about their own classrooms. From all who were interested, information about preferred times for observation and workshop training was obtained.

In summary, building commitment was viewed primarily as a question of gaining entry and credibility. Essentially, the programme was run as a technical assistance programme originating outside the school.

Criterion 2a: the Capability for Observing Teachers Must Be Developed

Teacher observation is probably the most difficult element for school systems to assimilate. Teacher autonomy, time constraints preventing principals and supervisors from getting into classrooms, lack of familiarity with formal data-collection procedures, contractual limitations on observation for teacher appraisal, time necessary to observe and record classroom data in an objective manner — these and other reasons tend to make from five to seven full days of observer training, the observation of 6 hours of classroom instruction per teacher, 2 hours of data editing, travel time, and $45 per teacher in data-analysis costs appear prohibitive initially. Still, it is unlikely that classroom practice will improve substantially until those responsible for the supervision of instruction develop expertise at analyzing and solving problems through work in specific classrooms.

In a sense, this process could be compared to language training. At the same time as an observer's facility at using the language accurately was increasing, the observer's ability to 'think in the language' — to perceive and respond to the cues of effective teaching — was also developing. Finally, the opportunity to observe closely both effective and ineffective teachers during a concentrated two week period provided sufficient time for personal judgements to develop concerning the value of the research recommendations. In short, the apprentice had to develop a technical expertise related to the structure and use of the observation instrument, and at the same time begin to gain experience related to the identification of effective teaching and profile interpretation. After two full weeks in close consultation and training with national experts in the field, however, it was determined that further assistance would be necessary before I could lead observer training workshops on my own. As a consequence, Cincinnati contracted with one of Stallings's associates to spend a week in Cincinnati to begin the training of local observers.

The goal for the first year in Cincinnati was to train a cadre of ten reliable observers, five in September, five more in January. In order to select observers, four general criteria were set: (1) sufficient classroom teaching experience; (2) availability to conduct observations; (3) a personal orientation to details; and (4) an overall racial/sexual balance within the group. Stallings has used substitute teachers, graduate students and secretaries on a paid basis with great success. Since no money had been appropriated for observers, they were recruited primarily from the ranks of project teachers who had been assigned to instructional support roles outside the classroom. Despite repeated efforts to invite instructional supervisors and assistant principals to be trained, none agreed to participate until the second project year. With the support of their director, two evaluators also participated in the training, and developed into superior observers and future workshop leaders.

In summary, the capability to observe teachers includes: (1) a local trainer, use of an outside trainer, or both; (2) observers with aptitude, experience and availability; and (3) commitment of a minimum of five full days for videotape training and practice, with an additional day for a refresher workshop prior to each round of data collection. The long-range goal was to maintain a core group of approximately fifteen observers, so that we could complete data collection for 30 to 40 teachers in any given two-week period.

Criterion 2b: Teachers Must Be Observed Both Before and After Exposure To Training

Once a group of trained observers was available, actual observation of teachers presented no more than a tricky scheduling problem. The schedule allowed for two overlapping workshop phases, one with teacher groups trained before the winter holiday season, and one with groups trained during the third quarter of the school year.

Observers were scheduled for back-to-back time periods with pairs of teachers in the same building. Our experience was that two observations at a time left an observer fresh, and permitted other activities to be scheduled before or after the observation period. In contrast, three observations a day approached the limit of concentration for most observers. The observations were spread over a two-week period because of interruptions due to illness, snow, fire alarms, assemblies, and the like.

At the classroom level we experienced little difficulty with observing. Initially curious, students quickly ignored the busy observer. Initially nervous, teachers quickly reduced their anxiety levels. In a few cases, special events had been secretly 'staged' for observation, but these went well or flopped as the teacher's normal verbal habits and classroom procedures permitted. In general, the observation period was a busy, productive time.

Criterion 3: the Capability for Summarizing Data and Creating Teacher Profiles Must Be Developed

When the training programme was begun, no local capability for summarizing data existed. As noted earlier, the process involved optical scanning using large-scale scanners of a type most commonly found in firms specializing in these processes. Similarly, the computer-scoring programmes that Stallings developed for aggregating and summarizing the data operated on equipment of a type not widely available. The most economical approach, then, was to subcontract with SRI. Although there were some anxious moments when all the observation booklets were at SRI and the workshops were fast approaching, a reliable three-week turn-around time was achieved with a total cost (including booklets, marking pens, scanning, pre and post profiles and postage) of $45 per teacher.

While this was satisfactory, the approach did have drawbacks. First, a contract had to be signed each year, which meant additional budget fights and questions over the individualized investments in better teaching. Secondly, the district did not have control over the timeline. Thirdly, the district had limited access to the data-base. If a different format for profiles was desired, if an investigation of new variables was needed, or if there was a need to return to the raw data for evaluation, this was not possible. In recent years Stallings has re-formated the profile and produced a computer-scoring programme available for purchase by districts. It should be more convenient and more economical for large-volume users to achieve local control over the data-summary and teacher-profile process.

Criterion 4a: the Capability for Leading Teacher Training Workshops Must Be Developed

As complicated as the observation system first appears, mastering its intricacies is essentially a technical problem that requires practice and study. Training someone to achieve the desired results from the teacher workshops, on the other hand, requires more sophisticated leadership-development approaches. Here, Stallings's choice of the 'apprenticeship' model was a wise one.

The traditional image of apprenticeship is useful to keep in mind, although clearly a question of degree is involved in a two-week apprenticeship. Stallings had scheduled four teacher groups for workshops in such a way that a workshop session could be observed on one day, and the apprentice could assist in conducting the same workshop content with a different group on the next day. In this way a detailed summary lesson plan that synthesized the two approaches could be developed and then used as the basis for developing one's own plan for a particular district.

To train an apprentice to improve instruction requires creating conditions to which a breakthrough could occur, so that the apprentice can combine past strengths with the technical and attitudinal approaches offered by the master's model. To be convincing, lesson plans for a series of workshops have to be direct extensions of one's own personality, and the apprentice training needs to reinforce and extend those personality elements that contribute to instructional leadership. When the task is as complex as leading experienced teachers to reconsider their habitual teaching practices in light of research evidence, it is crucial that each apprentice be allowed and encouraged to develop an approach that fits his or her own style.

After apprentice training, the next phase was a journeyman's first solo flight — the uneven process fraught with self-doubt and hesitation, as well as moments of glory — of putting what you have learned into practice. To get the programme off the ground, four groups of 4 to 6 teachers were scheduled for 2-hour sessions. Each group met on a different day of the week after normal working hours. Obviously, with this approach it would not be possible for a single trainer to reach many teachers. So as Stallings had done for the second round of workshops, I invited five observers who had shown an unusual interest or aptitude during the initial observer training to participate in workshop leader training. At this point, the dual role of workshop leader and trainer of workshop-leader trainees was assumed.

At the weekly meetings the events of previous sessions were reviewed and parts of the lesson plan for the upcoming session were assigned to the trainees to prepare. Trainees initially opted for the parts of the lesson that permitted them to play either a supportive or an information-giving role, two important hats worn by trainers.

The chief pitfall for a beginning trainer was the desire to be accepted by the group – as a nice person, one of the gang, an ally against the administration or the system. To offset this tendency, ground rules were established to ensure that the primary focus for teacher training was on alterable variables at the instructional level, that is, what each teacher could do in his or her own room to improve.

In summary, our efforts to develop the teacher training capability included, in rapid succession, an apprenticeship period, a journeyman period, and a training period. This progression has been referred to as a pyramid approach, in which small groups of apprentices (at the top of the pyramid) are trained to train observers and teachers, and to select their own apprentices from these groups (to form the next levels).

Criterion 4b: Teacher Training Workshops Must Be Conducted

Teachers met in groups of five to seven, one night per week after school. They reviewed a 15 to 20-page handout to prepare for each session. Each session began with a report from each teacher on his or her success or failure in implementing recommendations from the previous week. Each session ended with participants indicating what idea or strategy they were going to use during the coming days. The rest of the workshop consisted of group discussion of questions related to the day's topic, and of group problem-solving related to specific incidents, individuals or problems raised by teachers. To facilitate this type of group, the workshop leader became both a motivator and a technical consultant – a coach who knew how to play the classroom game, a confidante who could listen to difficulties supportively and non-judgementally, and a standard-setter who would not permit easy evasions of teacher responsibilities.

The internal dynamic of changing teacher practice can be thought of as a process of breaking unproductive habits and building new habits. At least seven features of the ETP programme were important in this process:

(1) a specific, objective mirror or profile of teacher behaviour;
(2) a set of research-based recommendations that are seen as practical;
(3) the establishment of expectations and demands for changed behaviour;
(4) teacher selection of priorities for change;
(5) a small reference group of colleagues before whom one made a commitment to try new behaviour;
(6) accountability; and,
(7) maintenance of changed behaviour through peer support and periodic contact by the trainer.

Criterion 5a: the Capability for Implementing the Training Programme Must Be Extended

A new programme cannot depend for long on the good grace of leaders and supervisors. To extend an innovation that is already underway requires success at the political process of gaining the commitment of personnel and money to a long-range plan of attack. The job of co-ordinating a serious training programme of this type is, at the minimum, a half-time assignment for one person.

Since educators cannot assume resources will expand to permit new functions, and even outside grants have end-points, the real nub of the implementation problem is not so much how to put the innovation into practice, but how to establish priorities to enable the innovation to replace other existing programmes. The complex and difficult choice before top decision-makers, then, is to establish organizational roles that permit a re-ordering of priorities toward (in this case) instructional leadership, by reducing, eliminating, or re-assigning time-consuming responsibilities of less importance.

The programme in Cincinnati faltered in this regard. For the short term, a budget was available through UEPP funds. However, the Planning and Development branch failed to generate an approved long-range plan to which resources could be committed.

At the heart of this breakdown was a disagreement over the relative importance of teacher observation. Several supervisors, concerned with the degree of effort involved, called for the re-packaging of the training programme into a simpler, more transportable form that eliminated (or by-passed) the time-consuming data-collection process and ran the workshops without individual profiles based on third-party observation. The alternative to observation proposed was a self-diagnostic questionnaire, programmed for a micro-computer, that would produce a version of the profile based on the teacher's self-report. This alternative was never employed.

Criterion 5b: a Maintenance Strategy Must Be Implemented

The most rewarding outcome of the workshops was the improvement in supportive relationships among the teachers involved. With a common vocabulary, a common perspective, and a greater awareness of each other's professional strengths and weaknesses, the stage was set for ongoing collaboration. Teachers usually work in isolation — celebrating inwardly their successes and suffering silently their setbacks. One major, yet simple, reason that the training programme was effective was that it created an opportunity for one teacher to talk to other teachers about teaching. This opportunity was extended through a follow-up workshop scheduled approximately eight weeks after training, when a second profile based on additional observations was shared.

Table 10.4 summarizes key practical concerns for decision-makers considering the ETP programme. For reference purposes Cincinnati followed the 'full-cost' approach for criteria 1a, 2b, 3a and 4a. For the remaining criteria we resorted to the 'shoe-string' approach, with the 'middle path' as the goal toward which we were striving.

First Year Results

For our purposes, the success of implementation was to be judged primarily in terms of the degree of change in observed teacher behaviour after training (see also Ghory and Cash, 1981). To select the teacher behaviours of priority interest, two steps were followed. First, a survey containing twenty classroom variables identified by research to be significantly correlated with basic skills achievement was sent to 70 educators in the Cincinnati schools. Returns from 35 respondents indicated that five educational priorities were rated as the most important outcomes of in-service training:

(1) an increase in the amount of supportive corrective feedback intended to motivate students struggling to learn (corrective feedback);
(2) an increase in student learning time devoted to recommended instructional activities (instructional time-on-task);
(3) a decrease in teacher/student interactions related to discipline or misbehaviour (discipline);
(4) a decrease in instructional time spent by teachers and students on classroom management tasks or school-related clerical work (classroom management);

Table 10.4: Approaches to Implementing the Stallings Effective Teaching Practices (ETP) Programme

Implementation criteria System level	'Full-cost' approach	'Shoe-string' approach	'Middle path' approach
1. Commitment to programme as priority school-improvement strategy must be built	Bring in California team to conduct 2-day workshop with top-level leaders and Board representative	Local enthusiast tries to drum up support using reading materials and position power	Bring in person from nearby site to conduct 3 to 6-hour workshop for key people
2. A capability for observing teachers must be developed	Send apprentice to California; periodically train more observers	Have trainer come to district to train observers (one-time groups)	Send apprentice to California or nearby site, then get assistance in training observers
3. A capability for summarizing data and creating profiles must be developed	Acquire or develop necessary computer hardware and software	Send to Minnesota for scanning and California for profiles; or only use snapshot	Modify instruments so can be scored locally
4. A capability for leading workshops must be developed	Send apprentice to California; train pyramid of trainers	Study videotapes and talk on phone; train pyramid of trainers	Send person to California or nearby site and train pyramid of trainers
5. A capability for implementing programme must be extended	Full-time assignment for one person	Extra assignment for person already with full-time assignment	Half-time assignment for one person

Table 10.4 cont'd.

Implementation criteria School level	'Full-cost' approach	'Shoe-string' approach	'Middle path' approach
6. A commitment to programme by the principal and recruited teachers must be built	Part of school-wide plan, 3 years, all staff involved	One-on-one recruitment; one-shot commitment; no school-wide context	School-wide planning; 2-year plan; focus on subgroup of teachers (basic skills, new teachers, etc.)
7. Teachers must be observed	Observation completed in one week; two teachers per observer	2-week observation; two-three teachers per observer	2-week observation period; one teacher per observer
8. Teacher training workshops must be conducted	1 workshop/week/trainer; autumn only; principals and supervisors as trainers	2-3 workshops per week; autumn and spring; one central-office trainer	1-2 workshops per week; autumn only; assistant principals and dept. head with central office support
9. A maintenance strategy must be implemented	Quality circles, semi-annual observations	Follow-up workshop, informal check-ups	Follow-up workshop; District-wide awareness programme; target schools

(5) an increase in the amount of instruction given to small groups, large groups or the total class (group and class instruction).

Secondly, specific variables reported on the profiles were selected to specify each educational priority. Table 10.5 reports the 31 classroom variables that were used to assess teacher change after training. The 31 variables are clustered under the five educational priorities mentioned above.

Two evaluation objectives were set: (1) to determine the degree of improvement in selected teacher practices after training, and (2) to investigate the post-training performance of teachers who showed the greatest need for improvement on the selected variables. The second objective was set to ensure that the programme was effective with its target group: urban teachers experiencing difficulty.

For the two objectives, a paired t-test was used to estimate the direction and strength of teacher change on the 31 variables. Based on correlational evidence, it was clear that teachers should either increase or reduce their behaviour for each of these variables. As a consequence, a one-tailed test of significance was used. Thus, for the first objective the average change in the recommended direction across all teachers was examined on all variables.

The second objective examined the performance of teachers with the greatest need for improvement on each variable. A cut-off point of more than one-half of a standard deviation away from SRI's recommended level for each variable was used to identify these teachers. For example, if research recommended that a teacher be above the mean in performance on a specific variable, all teachers who were at least one-half of standard deviation or more *below* the mean were identified as having the greatest need for improvement on that variable. In this way, cut-off points were selected to eliminate with confidence those adequately performing on the variable.

The following generalizations typify the results obtained from the evaluation of the first year of the project. As a total group, project teachers improved in the recommended direction on 25 of the 31 variables. Similarly, the degree of teacher improvement was estimated to be statistically significant in the recommended direction of 9 on 31 variables. These improvements represent a general increase in interactive on-task learning activities, and decrease in off-task social interaction among students.

Those teachers identified as having the greatest need to improve had an average improvement in the recommended direction on each of the

Table 10.5: Five Educational Priorities and Related Classroom Variables

Corrective feedback	Instructional time-on-task	Discipline	Classroom management	Group and class instruction
Acknowledgement of correct answers	Student reading aloud	Time on social interaction	Time on class management	Adult to group, total
Praise and support	Time reading aloud	Student uninvolved	Time on assignments	Adult to class, total
Probing questions	Time on instruction	All interactions, behaviour	Class management, interactions	Group instruction (subject)
Providing hints	Subject matter instruction	Negative interactions	Teacher-controlled interactions	Class instruction (subject)
All corrective feedback	All interactions, subject	Social comments	Student remarks, assignment	
Positive interactions	Written assignments	Teacher monitoring movement		
Student doesn't know, adult probes	Practice drill			
	Test taking			

28 variables (on 3 variables there were two or fewer teachers who were beyond the cut-off point). Furthermore, statistically significant improvement was shown on 18 of the 28 variables. In addition to the improvements shown across all teachers, the changes of these teachers included improved classroom management, increased corrective feedback, and increased use of quizzes and practice drill.

Table 10.5 presents the major findings in a summary form.

Table 10.6: SRI Effective Teaching Practices In-service Training Summary of Teacher Improvement

Educational priority and variables	Group 1: all teachers		Group 2: teachers in need	
	Direction	Significance	Direction	Significance
Corrective feedback				
Acknowledgement of correct answers	+		+	
Praise and support of student responses	+		+	*
Probing questions	+		+	*
Providing hints	−		+	
All corrective feedback	+		+	**
Positive feedback	+	**	+	**
Student doesn't know, adult probes	+	**	+	**
Instruction				
Student reading aloud	+	*	+	*
Time reading aloud	+		+	
Time on instruction	+		+	*
Instruction, subject	+		NA	NA
All interactions, subject	+	*	+	**
Written assignments	+		+	
Practice drill	+		+	**
Test-taking	+		+	**
Discipline				
Time on social interaction	+	*	+	**
Student uninvolved	+		+	
All interactions, behaviour	+		+	
Negative interactions	−		+	

Table 10.6 cont'd

Educational priority and variables	Group 1: all teachers		Group 2: teachers in need	
	Direction	Significance	Direction	Significance
Social comments	−	**	NA	NA
Teacher monitoring movement	+	**	+	**
Classroom management				
Time on classroom management	+		+	**
Time on assignments	−		+	*
All interactions, assignments	+		+	
Classroom manage-ments, interactions	+		+	*
Teacher-controlled interactions	+		+	**
Student remarks	−	**	NA	NA
Group and class instruction				
Adult to group, total interactions	+		+	
Adult to total class, total interactions	−		+	
Group instruction	+	**	++	**
Total class instruction	+	**	+	**

Key: + = mean improvement in recommended direction
    − = mean group change opposite recommended direction

 * = p $<$ 0.05
** = p $<$ 0.01
NA = not applicabe, n $<$ 1

Conclusion

The case study described in this chapter indicates how a nationally respected teacher training programme contributed to improved teacher performance in urban classrooms. The evaluation of teacher improvement was particularly promising because the training programme was found to be of greatest help to urban teachers who had been experiencing the most difficulty with classroom management and basic-skills instruction. After training, these teachers were able to translate into improved classroom performance the research findings they had studied about the effective use of time in school. Nevertheless, despite continuing success, by the end of the second year of implementation, the training programme ground to a halt.

When the United States government funded development efforts in a major way the primary view of implementation held that a truly 'model' programme if 'proven' successful in representative circumstances, should be capable of producing similar results in related situations. Since the model was developed by expert researchers searching for a preferred approach or a comprehensive implementation pattern, the assumption was made that programme success was due to the operation of variables present in most school situations that were interrelated in a lawful way. Successful implementation became a question of combining those same variables in the same fashion in a related situation.

Implementation difficulties have forced a re-thinking of these assumptions. This implementation case study was part of the search for more realistic implementation strategies. In it, 'implementation' – the attempt to put into practice an idea, programme or set of activities that is new to the individuals using it (Rubin and Stuck, 1982) – was seen as mandating a translation from the theoretical to the practical (Schubert, 1980), a re-organization of a previously defined model so it could make meaningful contributions within an existing context. The concern in this project was to adapt a model programme, not to replicate it exactly in new surroundings (as if it were a wonder drug which if ingested whole would cure a school problem through the predictable influence of scientific laws).

In retrospect, it is clear that an adaptation of the innovative programme to the setting was only half the solution. We did not do enough to *adapt the setting to the programme* by re-defining existing roles and responsibilities so that key implementors could continue with programme implementation.

References

Ghory, W.J. (1980) 'Model Building in Urban Education: The Cincinnati Urban
    Education Pilot Project'. Paper presented at the Annual Meeting of the
    American Educational Research Association, Boston
—— and Cash, K. (1981) 'Improving Teaching in Urban Classrooms: Applying
    More Precise and Demanding Standards'. Paper presented at the Annual
    Meeting of the American Educational Research Association, Los Angeles
Meeham, M.L. and Sullivan, D.K. (1982) 'Implementing the Stallings Staff-
    development Model in a Rural School District: an Evaluation'. Paper present-
    ed at the Annual Meeting of the American Educational Research Association,
    New York
Rubin, R. and Stuck, G. (1982) 'A Method for Enhancing Training and
    Monitoring of Program Adaptations and Adoptions in New Situations'. Paper
    presented at the Annual Meeting of the American Educational Research
    Association, New York
Schubert, W.H. (1980) 'Recalibrating Educational Research: Toward a Focus on
    Practice', *Educational Researcher, 11*(1), 17-24
Stallings, J. (1977) *Learning to Look: a Handbook on Classroom Observation
    and Teaching Models*, Belmont, Ca.: Wadsworth
—— (1980) 'Allocated Academic Learning Time Revisited, or Beyond Time-on-
    Task', *Educational Researcher, 11*(9), 11-16

NOTES ON CONTRIBUTORS

Lorin Anderson is Professor of Educational Research at the University of South Carolina. He currently is a member of the steering committee for the Classroom Environment Study, a study involving eight countries conducted under the auspices of the International Association for the Evaluation of Educational Achievement (IEA). His primary research interests lie in the area of classroom instruction and school learning.

Robert Burns is Assistant Professor of Educational Research at the University of South Carolina. His main research interests are in the general area of learning, instruction, and individual differences with particular emphasis on mastery-based instructional strategies and teacher effectiveness.

Janet Caldwell is Mathematics Education Specialist with Research for Better Schools, Inc., in Philadelphia, Pennsylvania. Her work includes synthesising and applying research findings on effective classrooms and schools, particularly as they apply to teacher behaviours. She has also been involved in the development and testing of training materials for administrators and teachers.

John Carroll is Professor of Psychology Emeritus at the University of North Carolina at Chapel Hill. He spent major portions of his career at the Graduate School of Education, Harvard University, and at Educational Testing Service in Princeton. He has specialized in psychometrics, the psychology of language, and related aspects of educational psychology. A selection of his writings is published in *Perspectives on School Learning*, Lawrence Erlbaum Associates, 1984.

Ward Ghory, one of the original apprentices trained in the Stallings Effective Teaching Practices staff development model, is currently Assistant Principal for Curriculum and Instruction at Walnut|Hills High School in the Cincinnati Public Schools. His research interests include learners on the margins of classrooms and schools, and underachievement among gifted youth.

William Huitt is Instructor in Psychology and Education and Co-ordinator of Academic Advising at Navajo Community College in Tsaile,

Arizona. He was formerly a Research/Evaluation Specialist with Research for Better Schools, Inc., where much of the work for his chapter in this volume was completed. He is co-author with David Squires and John Segars of *Effective Classrooms and Schools: Research-based Directions for Improvement*. His current work focuses on improving the educational experience for students in multicultural, multiethnic settings.

Rhonda Ross is a doctoral candidate in the Department of Human Development and Psychology at the University of Kansas. Using the theory and methods of ecological psychology, she has conducted research on a variety of educational issues. Primarily interested in how teachers organise their environment, she has examined the ways in which teachers arrange both the physical environment of the classroom and how they organise and manage the many activities that occur during the typical day. Currently, she is studying the ways that elementary school teachers are using microcomputers in the classroom.

John Smyth is Senior Lecturer in Educational Administration and Classroom Processes at Deakin University, Australia. He undertook graduate work at the University of New England, Australia and at the University of Alberta, Canada, and is currently editor of *The Australian Administrator*. He also is the author of several books and numerous papers in journals and professional publications, with current research interests in the area of instructional supervision.

Margaret Wang is Associate Professor of Educational Psychology at the University of Pittsburgh and Senior Scientist at the University's Learning Research and Development Center. Her primary research interests and publications are in the design and study of adaptive school learning environments, effective classroom instruction and management practices, evaluation methodology, and student motivation. She is co-editor of *Teacher and Student Perceptions: Implications for Learning*.

INDEX

ability to understand instruction
17, 31
Achievement Directed Leadership
programme (ADL) 204-25
materials and procedures 208-12;
Allocated Time Log 209;
Engagement Rate Form
209-11; for collecting data
208; for comparing data to
research 212-17; for
identifying and selecting
improvement strategies
217-20; for implementing
and recycling 220-2; Observation Record 221-2; reference
graphs 213-17
outcomes of 222-5
Achtenhagen, F. 18, 37
activities 64, 69, 96-9, 103-5
and teacher planning 97
instructional 96, 98
sequencing of 79-80
activity flow 92, 120-3
pacing and 103, 113-15, 123, 147
activity format 103-4, 109-11, 115
activity movement 97
activity segment 6, 71, 97, 100-1,
109
effects on behavior 73-7
features of 71-2
number and duration of 78-84
overlapping 80-1
simultaneous 80-1
activity structure 97-8, 100
Adams, A. 179, 199
adaptive instruction 169-70
Adaptive Learning Environments
Model (ALEM) 9, 169-97
critical program dimensions 172;
instructional-learning management system 176-8; integrated
diagnostic-prescriptive process
173, 175; school-wide
organizational support system
178-80; wide range of
instructional-learning options
175-6

implementation of 183-91; and
classroom processes 187-91
influence on achievement and
attitudes 195-7
major design features 171;
relationship with allocation
and use of time 174
Airasian, P. 23, 32
Allen, V. 178, 199
alterable variables 27
Anderson, L. 26, 29, 32, 38, 132,
140, 148-9, 158, 161, 168, 199,
219, 226
Anderson, R. 178, 199
Applegate, J. 75
aptitude 2, 5, 16-17, 19-20, 24,
28-32, 35
Arehart, J. 30, 38
Arikado, M. 179, 199
Arlin, M. 26-7, 38, 122, 124, 148-9,
161
Atkinson, J. 28, 38
attention 5, 46-7, 66, 132, 138
and absorption 50-1, 57
and genius 50-1
and interest 50-1
and learning 49-51, 55-6,
58-60
and motivation 50-1
and teaching 51-8, 60-2
selective 49, 51-2
sustained 49, 51-2, 54
attentional processes 48, 63, 65
alertness 58, 60
concentration 58, 60-1
filtering 59-60
pigeonholing 59-60
selectivity 58, 60-1
automaticity 59-60

Bandura, A. 175, 199
Barker, R. 70, 72, 85
Barr, R. 123-4
Beginning Teacher Evaluation Study
(BTES) 3, 22, 24, 27, 29-30, 37,
62, 64-5, 105, 107, 133-4, 150
behaviour settings 145-7

255

256 *Index*